HE STILL
heals those who need
HEALING
LUKE 9:11

STEVE PIDD

About the Author

Steve has been involved internationally in healing and freedom ministries since 1997. His main ministry since around 2004 has involved training Pastors and leaders across the world in various healing models. Along with his wife Em he spent many years as a lead Pastor, and has dedicated his life to finding God's provisions for healing and freedom for those in the Church and beyond. Steve has written a number of books and training manuals on healing which are now available in different languages, and are in use around the globe.

Contents

I Introduction

Wherever we go around the world we observe many church people who have not received the healing and freedom that God desires for them. Sometimes this is because healing isn't a part of their church environment and experience. Other times we've found that people have been exposed to a particular healing model, and because they weren't healed in this way, they've concluded that God didn't want to heal them for some reason, and have given up.

My purpose and goal in writing this book is to help you under-stand how God may heal you, and that He is absolutely committed to your freedom. Healing is His idea. He's already paid for it through the sacrifice of Jesus His son on the cross. So, we don't have to talk Him into it. It's a matter of finding how you specifically can receive.

In the modern church we have different kinds of healing ministries that are having some measure of success. Each may believe that their model is the way, perhaps because this is how they've seen God work. Or maybe because this is what they know how to do, having been trained that way themselves. In reality, how God ministers can be quite diverse and tailored to the individual.

On one end of the scale, we see ministries focused on the presence of God, where 'God does everything.' Your faith is ignited and you are simply healed by the presence of God in your seat. We've personally seen God being able to minister like this to those people who are able to accept and receive their healing in this way.

On the other end of the scale, we see ministries who believe that repentance is the key. This is basically a set yourself free model, where 'you do everything,' and you walk away from anything that is causing your illness, in particular negative emotions. Again, they also have a percentage of people who receive healing in this way.

In between these two extremes we have ways that God heals by the Holy Spirit working through people, such as through the laying on of hands, exercising the gifts of the Spirit, emotional healing and/or deliverance.

In this publication we'll be seeking to explain and explore these models. We'll share our experience from decades of working in the healing and freedom ministry, so that you personally can accept and receive the promises and provisions of God. These various healing ministries are all doing a great job of delivering the good news and demonstrating the will of God for mankind. As we progress through Part 1, we'll examine how these ministry streams together flow into the healing river of God.

Part 1

HEALING 101 BASIC PRINCIPLES AND FOUNDATIONS FOR HEALING

- He Still Heals Those Who Need Healing -

The God Dimension
Is God able?

As we work through Part 1 of this book, we're going to explore the basics of Christian healing. I think that before anything else we first need to examine and understand the <u>super</u>natural nature of God. Super as a prefix means; over or above, or even beyond. So, as we contemplate the healing picture, we have to see God as someone who by nature operates in and from a realm or dimension that is over, and above the natural realm. God can do things that are not limited to the dynamics that we are subject to as we live on earth. They simply do not apply to Him.

Things like time, gravity, buoyancy, or even spiritual influences are not relevant to Him, as His abilities are over all of them. In the New Testament we see Jesus walking on water, which to our minds that have been trained in what is naturally possible, is a ridiculous happening. The world has rules and principles that we accept, and consequently submit to, expecting them to govern all matters. Although the following passage is referring largely to rules of behaviour, it still stands as a general concept for believers to not accept, or be limited by, what the world accepts, now that you have through Christ stepped into God's superior, limitless realm.

Colossians 2:6-10
⁶ So then, just as you received Christ Jesus as Lord, con-
tinue to live in him, ⁷ rooted and built up in him, <u>strength-</u>
<u>ened in the faith</u> as you were taught, and overflowing
with thankfulness. ⁸ See to it that no one takes you
captive through hollow and deceptive philosophy, which
depends on human tradition and <u>the basic principles of</u>
<u>this world</u> rather than on Christ. ⁹ For in Christ all the
fullness of the Deity lives in bodily form, ¹⁰ and you have
been given fullness in Christ, who is the head <u>over</u> every
power and authority.   NIV (emphasis mine)

As I write, I've recently returned from a trip through a number of nations located on different continents. I saw a great many people healed through the laying on of hands, most instant or within a minute of prayer. Deaf ears, eyes, knees, conditions, lumps going down etc. How does that happen? I don't know. It doesn't fit with this dimension, or what is possible according to the basic principles of this world.

I don't know how my smart phone, which is limited to the basic principles of the world works either, but I know that if you do this, it will do that. I have a friend who talks to his phone, and it responds to his requests. In this case in the name of his google account. In our case the response that we receive is authorised in the name of Jesus, who told us in Johns Gospel chapter 16 and verse 23 that the Father will give us whatever we ask in His name.

How then should we regard God?

The Bible instructs us to repent. In Acts chapter 3 the tense of the word translated repent is *'metanoeo'*. Which means change your thinking, or think differently and reconsider your ways. So, if we've been limiting God, not thinking correctly about His abilities and His dimension, which is His Kingdom, then we need to examine the Bible to get a true perspective of who He is, in order to change or thinking. In particular, in relation to what He wants to do for and through us.

Think about it...In the Old Testament when we read stories about what God does, we will find events that simply are not remotely possible from a human standpoint. We see stories like Moses, an old man, with what I imagine as a wiggly stick that he found in the desert to use as a shepherd's staff. And with this wiggly stick he delivers a nation from captivity, with the final impossible act being the parting of the Red Sea. Was it Moses, or the stick? No, it was his obedience to the word of God that brought God's dimension into a desperate situation.

Everywhere you look in the Old Testament you see God doing things that simply do not fit into the natural realm. As we reframe how we perceive God in this regard, and encourage you to see Him as He is, let me just mention a few events to stimulate our meditation on this aspect of God.

In Numbers chapter 22 we see the LORD opening the mouth of a man called Balaam's donkey so that it could speak to Balaam. Respectfully, I can imagine that God may have been amused doing such a thing. To our natural minds, ridiculous. In God's realm, no big deal. In 2 Kings chapter 6 we see a man drop an iron axe head that he'd borrowed into the Jordan river. Elisha the prophet was with him and he threw a stick into the water where it had sunk, causing it to float! That's crazy and against all basic principles in this natural dimension.

We see in Daniel chapter 3 men thrown into a fire so hot that it killed those who threw them in, and they themselves come out completely unharmed. Their hair and clothes were not even singed. That is God's ability. For Him it's simple. The problem is our thinking that limits what He can do in our situation. God has limited Himself to faith, and faith is based on truth, which in turn produces a correct picture of who He really is.

The Old Testament is littered with stories of God intervening in the affairs of those relating with Him, and doing miraculous, impossible things as far as the natural order goes. Some were nation saving such as walls of cities coming down, or God personally defeating armies. Others were stories of Him becoming involved in the situations of individuals. For example, Elijah in 1 Kings chapter 17 was sent by the LORD to help a widow from Zarephath. She generously shared what was to be the final meal of her and her son. Elijah prophesied the word that the LORD God had given him, that her flour jar would never run out, and that her jug of oil would not run dry until rain came and ended the famine. Impossible! But this is God's normal dimension, and we need to understand that it's so, to be positioned to accept and receive His abundant provisions.

Shifting Dimensions

Positioning our thinking

In the New Testament we see the Son of Man, Son of God, Jesus, as He appears to introduce the Kingdom of God. We can observe a progression where Luke chapter 4 begins with Him being filled with the Spirit, and then He's led into the desert where He defeats the devil, and consequently returns in the power of the Spirit. Then in Luke 4:18 His mission and the reason that the Spirit of God is on Him is revealed. Clearly this 'job description' reveals that He's been sent to meet the needs of the people and deliver the promises and provisions of God. A key part of the passage proposes that He will be healing the broken hearted and setting the captives free.

In Parts 2 and 3 of this publication, we'll explain how this means to bring wholeness, and to resolve the root cause of spiritual, mental, emotional, physical, and relational problems. The other reference to His mission under the anointing and power of the Holy Spirit is found in Acts 10:38, where we see Him doing good, and healing those who were oppressed under the deceptive power of the devil.

This introduction of God's dimension and the work of the Holy Spirit was not merely to be through Jesus, and for that time alone. So, immediately after the announcement of His mission in Luke 4:18, it appears that He went looking for His church. We assume that His intention was to train them in His ministry focus which we've just detailed, and to fulfill God's purpose to continue to have the Holy Spirit work through believers after His return to heaven.

John 20:21-22
²¹ Again Jesus said, "Peace be with you! As the Father has sent me, I am sending you." ²² And with that he breathed on them and said, "Receive the Holy Spirit". NIV

We see this time of Jesus with His followers, and those He taught, as a time where He consistently tried to move their thinking and expectations from the limitations of the natural world, to the supernatural dimension of the Kingdom of God. S.D. Gordon in his book '*The Healing Christ*' pointed out that 'Supernatural power is what makes Christianity distinctive.'

For example, we see in Matthew chapter 14 Jesus feed five thousand men plus women and children, multiplying 5 loaves of bread and 2 fish. The leftovers were 12 baskets full. That should've gotten the disciples thinking about what's possible for God. Every translation that I've read then says that Jesus 'made' them get into the boat to cross the lake. No doubt they may well have been confused by this, and wondered how he would get across the waters. In any case what happened next must've further challenged their thinking in regards to God's dimension.

There they were far from the shore, trying to deal with the waves that they were encountering, and Jesus arrives walking on the water around 3am. Needless to say they freaked out, because it was so impossible, thinking that it must be a ghost! Jesus reassured them that it was He, and not to be afraid. The point is, what was He doing? It was yet another deliberate example of exposing them to God's realm, and displaying the operation of the Kingdom of God beyond what appeared to be naturally able to occur.

His purpose was to challenge their thinking. Peter glimpsed the possibilities of God's dimension again. He trusted Jesus enough to be prepared to attempt the supernatural if Jesus gave him the word. He did. Peter stepped out of the boat, in a sense into God's realm, based on the word only. He did it! He walked on water for a time. And then he became aware of the natural circumstances and possibilities and began to sink. We say that doubt makes you sink and be subject to your natural situation. It puts you under the power of the basic principles of this world. But faith makes you float. It puts you over or above your natural situation.

This is important for healing and freedom. We need to change our thinking by some means to access the provisions of God. We have to base everything that we accept as outcomes in our lives on the word of God, which reveal His promises. We need to imbibe and meditate on the limitless possibilities for our lives in the Kingdom of God. All things are possible.

I'm encouraged that later on Jesus fed four thousand plus women and children. Soon after, when a practical issue of supply came up, we find Him describing them as; *"you of little faith."* And commenting; *"do you still not understand?"* And He, referring to the five thousand, and then the four thousand, I imagine was amazed that they still didn't comprehend that there are no limits in the Kingdom of God. Only in our thinking. If it was a journey to be made for them to move dimensions, then we have to accept that it may take time for some of us as well.

Our thinking and understanding is the only limit on what God can do

I have a minister friend in Africa who was once running an outreach meeting in another nation. As he was speaking, he noticed them bring a man in on a stretcher and place him near the platform. Later when my friend began to pray for the sick, he remembered the man and went down to pray for him. He prayed a simple prayer commanding him to be healed in the name of Jesus. As he walked away the crowd erupted. He looked around and saw that the man was now sitting up. He still didn't understand what all of the commotion was about. Somebody explained to him that the man wasn't sick, he was dead.

Do you think it makes any difference to God whether you have a slight headache, cancer, or are dead? Nothing is impossible, or even remotely difficult for Him. The only limitations are your own thinking, based on what you believe. God mercifully grows our faith as we seek to understand and pursue His Kingdom provisions. We go from faith to faith. (Romans 1:17)

God does not expect us to believe without exposure to, or experience of, what He is wanting to do for us. I love the story in John Chapter 11 of Jesus raising up the now dead Lazarus from the grave.

Again, purposefully exposing them to God's limitless dimension. His statement to them in verse 15 was that this whole event was; *"so that you may believe."*

I was ministering in a regional city in Australia recently, and I taught on God's dimension. We were to be there for several weeks, and this locality had not had much exposure to God's various means of bringing healing and freedom. So, my intention was to get them thinking about the potential of what God can do to get them thinking. The following week I was going to preach a healing message. But when I finished speaking, people flooded to the front for prayer. I recall in particular one man who reported the next week that he was instantly healed of prostate cancer. Another man prayed for who also had prostate cancer wrote me a letter some weeks or months later, reporting that he also was now healed, but that it happened over time.

Summary

What God is easily able to do may seem ridiculous to us, but we need to accept it to access His provisions and promises. Just as little children accept what they're told without questioning their parents. What we think and believe must be challenged, and considered or meditated on, so that we can decide whether we accept the word of God as truth and thus access the realm of God, or remain limited to the basic principles of this world.

I love the story in Matthew 17:24-27 of Jesus and Peter needing money to pay the temple tax. Jesus instructed Peter, who was a very experienced fisherman, to put his line in, and that the first fish that he caught would have the money they needed in its mouth. Can you imagine needing money to buy lunch for your friends, and being told to put your line in, and that the first fish that you caught would have a Ziplock bag with $40 in it? The truth is that God can do immeasurably more than you could ask, think or imagine. (Ephesians 3:20)

To round out the chapter let me say this. You could get healed today, depending on how you see God, or perhaps more impor-tantly, how you think He sees you. We thank God for the ministries that He's graciously given us in the Church to help bridge the gap.

3

Vision That Releases Potential

Seeing the possibilities

God's provisions

I've noted that many people feel as though they need to talk God into healing, or do something to earn or be worthy of this grace that He freely offers. In the book of Hosea, we see a statement that reveals the foundation of the problem.

> *Hosea 4:6*
> *My people are destroyed for lack of knowledge. NKJV*

This isn't general knowledge, which is plenteous in our times. It's specifically our knowledge of God, His ways, His promises, His provisions, and His committed will to minister to people. In fact, the New Living Translation very aptly renders this verse as;

> *Hosea 4:6*
> *My people are being destroyed because they don't know me. NLT*

That is, they don't really know about me. We had a young man, a new believer, come into a healing service that we were running at our church. When he heard about what God was wanting to do, and saw others being healed he came to the front for prayer. He had a back injury and would lay in bed for hours each morning in pain. He was instantly healed through his simple faith and new knowledge about God's provisions. I saw him a few weeks later, and he reported that he had clocked more hours at the gym than anyone else in the town. He excitedly told me that he wanted to become mister Australia so that he could tell everyone about Jesus!

A number of years ago I heard a story about some men who were in a lifeboat off the coast of South America. They were out of sight of land, and had run out of food and water. When a ship passed by, they waved and shouted. *"Give us some water, we have no water!"* The men on the ship yelled back; *"dip your bucket in, you're in fresh water, you're in the mouth of the Amazon River!"* I've since researched it and found that 20% of the worlds fresh water comes from the Amazon River, and where it spills into the sea the plume is 400 kilometres long, and 200 kilometres wide. The point is, there was far more than they could ever need all around them all of the time, but they were perishing due to a lack of knowledge.

Going to the source

Through our ministry years we've often dealt with people who've had prayer from some kind of model, and not been healed. Most of them have been receptive to other pathways and are able to be set free when what's causing the problem has been dealt with. But, many times, people are stuck thinking that they know best for themselves, or insist on following their favourite ministry or author.

I recall a story of a biologist who was fascinated with processional caterpillars. These caterpillars follow each other in a line up your front path or driveway. The man wondered what would happen if he put them end to end around the rim of a large pot plant. Reportedly they went around and around following each other until they all died from starvation or exhaustion. And yet the food was right there in the pot all of the time. I would liken this to following others in a healing model to the exclusion of all else. We need to interact with God who is the source of the healing. He is our supply. He deals with us as individuals, case by case, not merely as a mass mechanical model.

'God so loved the world' – this is non-specific and doesn't make exceptions. Clearly the problem is that not everyone loves Him, and consequently doesn't seek Him for that which He's more than willing to give.

Vision

We understand vision to be in its most basic form 'seeing.' We need to see, or have vision of the possibilities for us to pursue healing, physical, mental or emotional. Vision releases potential, because once we see what can be, we go after that which we have seen.

As previously mentioned, in the early chapters of Luke, we see Jesus filled with the Spirit, stay in ascendency over the devil in the desert, and then announce the mission and ministry that God the Father had for Him on Earth. We've described how it appears that the next thing that He did was to go looking for His church to train. We see Him dealing with Peter who had been fishing all night and caught nothing.

I spent some of my young life growing up in a fishing village. There were two old fishermen there, and if they went to their boats and went out to sea all of the other fishermen followed them, and got as close to where they were fishing as possible. What I'm saying is that professional fishermen don't just drop a line in and hope that they catch something. They have knowledge and skill, looking at the wind, the tides, the seasons, what the birds are doing and so on.

So, when the son of a carpenter told Peter to put the nets back in, you can see why Peter may have been hesitant. Perhaps he was thinking; '*your dad made our table and chairs!*' When he, out of obedience said; "*nevertheless, at your word,*" it was no small thing. We know that as the story goes the nets were filled to breaking point. Peter was now ruined for anything other than God's plan for him. He had 'seen' the power of God. Now when Jesus told him to follow because he would become a 'fisher of men', he had 'seen' how it could be so. Beginning with vision it now became a pursuit of the realisation of potential.

We have a man in Australia who was diagnosed with liver cancer. He told the doctor that God would heal him. He went to the healing meetings of a friend of mine pursuing what he believed. The first meeting nothing, second, nothing, and so on until as I recall the fifth meeting, where reportedly he felt a little tickle in the liver area. "That's it" he said. He went back to the doctor who confirmed that he was correct, that God had healed him because it could not have happened any other way.

It's so important that we get a clear vision of what God wants to do for us.

Vision and potential

Even in the secular world it is the people who 'see' the possibilities that shape the environment. I read about the famous American Inventor Thomas Edison whose teachers had said that he was too stupid to learn anything. He was fired by his first two employers for being unproductive. Edison saw the potential of electricity and eventually pursued making the light globe. He saw the power, and wanted to be able to access it in a practical way. He made 1,000 unsuccessful attempts at producing the light globe, finally succeeding to harness the potential he'd seen. I've read that when a reporter asked, "*how did it feel to fail 1,000 times?*" Edison replied, "*I didn't fail 1,000 times. The light bulb was an invention with 1,000 steps.*" What kept him pursuing success? He 'saw' the potential!

Our lack of knowledge, and not seeing the limitless potential of God's abilities stops us from relentlessly pursuing what is rightfully ours. We need to see, understand, and access God's dimension.

In Exodus we see a man called Moses who'd long ago given up on his sense of purpose. In Chapter 3 we see the Angel of the Lord appear to him in a burning bush. God was introducing Himself from another dimension. Now it was time to fulfill that which he'd hoped for, and seeing the display of God's power in his life, he simply could not walk away from that which God desired and purposed for him.

Lois Pasteur is famous for his work exposing the unseen world of microbiology and germs. As a student he was considered to be mediocre, ranking 15 out of 22 students in his chemistry class. It was written by a notable professor at the time that "*Lois Pasteur's theory of germs is ridiculous fiction!*" and "*that you're more likely to find bird droppings in a cuckoo clock!*" However, as we know Pasteur pursued and accessed what he believed about this dimension, and the result is countless millions of lives saved.

Christian history is full of countless stories of those who pursued a healing God because of what they believed about Him. They saw the potential of what He says in His word, experienced or observed His provisions through other ministries, or were inspired by the testimonies of others. Once they had vision of what God wanted to do, and saw the potential of reaching a broken World, they could not walk away from sharing God's desires and abilities to help the sick, hurting and broken.

4

The Character of God
Is God willing?

The famous healing Apostle Smith Wigglesworth pointed out that God is more willing to heal than we are to ask. Very often we get our 'God picture' and perception of who He is from his earthly representatives. Our parents. And mostly from our fathers. So, if growing up our father was absent, dismissive, not valuing, harsh, critical, always too busy for us, treating us as unimportant and so on, we'll tend to see God the same way.

We then interpret how God is revealed in the Bible through our expectation of what we think He's like. Many people begin reading the Bible in the Old Testament and think that God is harsh because of how He had to deal with some of the peoples of the time. The truth is that He was protecting His people from lawless, immoral nations, who were wanting to hurt them. There have to be consequences for actions, and people without God need to be restrained so that they don't harm others. So, their activities came under judgement. We need to remind ourselves that these people sacrificed their own children to demonic entities, were violent, practiced sexual immorality and the like. In order to accept our healing we need to be settled about the true nature and character of God, as a good, caring, loving being. God IS love.

1 John 4:8,16
⁸ But anyone who does not love does not know God--for
God is love.
¹⁶ We know how much God loves us, and we have put our
trust in him. God is love, and all who live in love live in
God, and God lives in them. NLT

The gospel of Dennis the Menace

I remember hearing a preacher many years ago talking about an American T.V. series that used to be aired. It was about a little boy, Dennis the menace, who was always getting into trouble and mischief. As the story goes Dennis and one of his friends were invited over for milk and cake by the neighbour's nice wife. Dennis' friend was looking very pleased with himself for being given this treat. Dennis pointed out, *"it's because she's good, not because we're good."*

This is very true of God. He heals because He's good, not because we're good, or can earn healing. In fact, over the years, I've seen God consistently heal people in spite of their wayward behaviour. Even in my own ministry I've seen thousands of healing moments where God has healed spiritually, physically, mentally and emo-tionally, even when the person receiving was often still struggling with sin and ungodly attitudes and practices. When I see God set people free from issues that they've often carried all of their lives I'm touched. Inside I'm saying, *'wow God, you're so good to do that for them.'* You become very sure of who He is, and when for exam-ple, you lay on hands, you know that He always wants to heal. And you know that this is based on His goodness, not our own.

I had some friends who were Pastors in a small Australian city. One day they were having a big argument. You could say that they were not being led by the Spirit of God at that time. There was a knock at the door and a member of their congregation was there. The person announced that they'd come from the hospital after being diagnosed with terminal cancer. The were requesting healing prayer. Although my friends hardly felt holy in that moment, they prayed for the person, who consequently was healed. It's not the minister, or their holiness or 'anointing,' it's the will of God and His love, grace, and goodness that matters. He'll use whoever He can find who are prepared to help those who are in need.

In Acts 10:38 we see how God anointed Jesus of Nazareth with the Holy Spirit and power to do His will. He went around doing good, and healing all who were under the power of the devil, because God was with Him. In the Psalm of David 103:3 we see that God forgives ALL our sins, and heals ALL our diseases. It says forgives, which is ongoing as we acknowledge and confess our condition. Not forgave. Which leaves Him free to minister His love and goodness, and in verse 10 we see that He is gracious, and does not treat us as our sins deserve. Verse 4 says that He redeems us from destruction with lovingkindness and tender mercies.

> *Psalm 103:2 -3,4*
> *Praise the LORD, O my soul, and forget not all his benefits-- ³ who forgives all your sins and heals all your diseases. NIV*
> *⁴ Who redeems your life from destruction, Who crowns you with lovingkindness and tender mercies. NKJV*

Grace unlimited

Healing is not dependent on what we can do, or where we are at in our journey with God, but rather it is solely dispensed because of God's superabundant loving and gracious character. As a result, anything is possible with anyone at any time if they can receive the Father's goodness.

I was ministering in a church a number of years ago, and God gave me a word of knowledge that there was a lady present who had suffered with headaches since she was a small child. A woman in her early 50's responded who had suffered with migraines all her life. I prayed a simple prayer for her, and nothing obvious happened. But after a few weeks she realised that she'd not had any of the regular migraines that would normally have occurred. Four years later it was revealed that she was in an adulterous relationship. Would you have healed her knowing that? God did! He's good and His redemptive nature is unchanging regardless of our condition.

Later, once the affair was discovered she received ministry and was set free from the rejection that had driven her into the relationship. Does God condone sin? Never! But He knows why we sin, and wants to help us get free. Perhaps like Zacchaeus in Luke chapter 19, where Jesus knew how Zacchaeus was going to respond to relationship and acceptance with repentance, God met her where she was. He does not change His nature. His good, is far greater than our bad.

God is always willing to heal

My wife and I have ministered to many young people who have mental and emotional problems. God never fails to heal them, even though at the time of their coming sometimes they're still doing drugs, getting drunk, sleeping around and so on. They then meet Him and are exposed to His loving merciful nature in the ministry room. It's His kindness that leads us to repentance, not His harshness. He chose us, and loved us first. Just as with salvation itself, He saves us in spite of our many sins, and healing is the same. It's Him graciously revealing Himself.

The great healing apostle Smith Wigglesworth once commented that if God marked our sins against us who could stand? I personally believe that a part of the secret to His own faith was His understanding that when he prayed for the sick that He was firmly in the will of God for mankind. I doubt that he had faith or reliance on his personal standing with God, and from what I've read he had a good understanding of his own human frailty.

> Psalm 130:3
> LORD, if you kept a record of our sins, who, O Lord, could ever survive? NLT

I was attending a healing meeting being run by a friend at one time. A lady came out who had a hip problem and God healed her. My friend then interviewed her asking her if her husband was present. She replied that she wasn't married but had a partner. In the break a Pastor friend of mine asked me if it were me, would I get alongside her and tell her that she was in sin living with that man. I replied, *"no, I would probably have a coffee with her and talk about how wonderful God is!"* As she comes into a loving church environment there'll be time to learn of a better way to live. But for the moment building the new relationship with God is what's important. As it happened, her partner was healed of something in the evening meeting as well!

God, it seems, is always prepared to heal and forgive regardless of where a person is in their journey. It's His nature. We see examples in scripture such as the woman caught in adultery. Jesus forgave her on the spot, but lovingly instructed her to sin no more, knowing that living out of God's order would result in more anguish and pain. We see something similar when He healed the man at the pool of Siloam. Instructing him to sin no more or something worse could happen. Implying, that the man could continue with whatever attitudes or behaviour that made him sick, but if he chose to, he may well develop another illness even worse.

In Parts 2 and 3 we'll explain the origins, basis and sources of most diseases. It may well have been one of the problems that we'll describe that the man needed to deal with. So, we can see from this example that just because you're healed it doesn't mean that you're right with God. It means that you've experienced His mercy and grace and been exposed to who He is. Jesus wasn't assuming that they/he wouldn't go back to sin, so He affirmed the possible outcome of such a choice in no uncertain terms. You could sin more if you choose and stay out of relationship with God, ignoring His ways, but the result may be more or even worse sickness.

chapter

5

Healing is a Part of the Package

Do I qualify?

In the previous chapter we've discussed why God heals, and who God will heal. Many people don't understand redemption – which means paying the price and clearing the debt over something in order to regain possession of it. We were all going to have to pay the price for our sin. We often see sin and sickness linked in the scriptures. As we have covered from Psalm 103:3 God forgives our sins, and heals our diseases. When Jesus paid for our lives to be restored back to relationship with God, it included the removing of our sin, opening the way to immortality and eternal life, along with freedom from bondage and sickness.

His part in removing the debt on the cross, dying in our place, is a completed work. What He paid for and made us entitled to is available to every human being, and is accessed by faith, and then facilitated through the work of the Holy Spirit. So, it's very important that we understand what is in the redemption package.

There's the story of the paralysed man in Luke chapter 5 where some men with faith brought him to Jesus. They were so convinced that Jesus could help him that they took tiles off the roof and lowered him into the house so that he would be able to receive from the ministry of Jesus. When Jesus saw that they met the faith component for healing, He said, "*Man your sins are forgiven.*" In a sense He was saying, "*because your sins are forgiven, you can now receive your healing.*" His actual comment in the text was; Is it easier to say, '*Your sins are forgiven,*' or to say, '*Get up and walk.*' What He is implying is that it is the same thing, as far as meeting the requirements of God.

Understanding redemption

This chapter is an important basis for understanding that you're qualified for healing and freedom, so I'll include scriptures to undergird the fact that in Christ we are redeemed and entitled to all of the promises of God. Isaiah 44:22 explains the effects of redemption in this way:

> "*I have swept away your sins like the morning mists. I have scattered your offenses like the clouds. Oh, return to me, for I have paid the price to set you free.*" NLT

This prophetic book is speaking of what Jesus has done for us if we choose to accept His gift, and encourages us to return to relationship with God. In Isaiah 53:5-6 the mechanism of this being accomplished is explained:

> *⁵ But he was wounded and crushed <u>for our sins</u>. He was beaten that we might have peace. He was whipped, and <u>we were healed</u>! ⁶ All of us have strayed away like sheep. We have left God's paths to follow our own. Yet the LORD laid on him the guilt and sins of us all.* NLT (emphasis mine)

And then in verse 11 we see us as now positioned as righteous through Christ, with Him having dealt with ALL of our sins. So, qualifying for healing is not the result of self-effort. It's the result of understanding, believing, and accepting what has been done for us.

[11] When he sees all that is accomplished by his anguish, he will be satisfied. And because of what he has experienced, my righteous servant will make it possible for many to be counted righteous, for he will bear all their sins. NLT

Why does God do this for us?

God is fair and just. Whenever I'm explaining redemption, I love to tell the story of Fiorello LaGuardia, a former New York Mayor. His 3-term service was during the 1930s and 40s. He reportedly was not happy about people who exploited the poor. One bitterly cold night the mayor decided to preside over night court.

An old woman was brought in charged with stealing a loaf of bread. She explained that her family was starving. LaGuardia's response was, "*I've got to punish you. The law makes no exception. I must fine you ten dollars.*" (In those days in the U.S. the average wage was around 22 cents per hour. So, $10 would have been nearly a week's wages). Having said that he reached into his own pocket and paid the fine for her trespass, placing the $10 into his own hat. He then declared, "*I'm going to fine everybody in this courtroom fifty cents for living in a town where a person has to steal bread in order to eat!*" [1]

As the story goes, the incredulous old woman left the courtroom with a new light in her eyes and $47.50 in her pocket to buy groceries. This could be as much as several thousand dollars today; a lot of groceries indeed. It is a great picture of the Gospel. The law demanded that she be punished, but grace insisted on blessing. Indeed, the price for her trespass must be paid. But the person presiding over the law paid the price himself. The law held her accountable, but justice and righteousness held her environment and circumstances accountable.

*Psalm 89:14 As it is written, "**Righteousness and justice** are the foundation of Your throne; Mercy and truth go before Your face." NKJV (emphasis mine)*

1   *God's Little Devotional Bible, HB HONOR Books, Page 33*

What did she do to earn the great blessing and forgiveness that she left with? Nothing at all, she surely had sinned. We come to God with our sin, and we walk away with so many blessings; it's amazing. Fiorello LaGuardia was looking past the sin, to why she sinned. God in His mercy and justice does not hold us accountable for the circumstances and environment that we were born into. We did not choose it, so it would not be fair. After we've received His grace, healing and freedom, we need to be careful not to return to our old ways.

All have sinned but God was looking at *why* we sin. As we have just seen in Psalm 89, the very foundation of God's throne is justice. He would be denying His very nature to not extend grace and help in freeing and healing a fallen and suffering humanity. Jesus paid the penalty demanded by the law, and then sent the Holy Spirit to ensure that the provisions of God are available to be received, and to resolve the reasons for the offense to begin with.

God IS willing

Many people who are sick feel that they are not worthy to be healed. This can be because they simply don't understand what has been done for them. Or it can be an unconscious inner belief in regards to how they see themselves. We'll explain how to resolve these types of blockages in Part 2 and 3 of this publication. But the fact remains, that from God's perspective healing is ours. We see this highlighted in Romans 3:22 and the second part of verse 25.

> [22] *We are made right in God's sight when we trust in Jesus Christ to take away our sins. And we all can be saved in this same way, no matter who we are or what we have done.*
>
> [25b] *We are made right with God when we believe that Jesus shed his blood, sacrificing his life for us. NLT*

6

Healing Streams
Understanding the ways God heals

There are many ways that God heals. In Exodus 15:26 we see God announcing; ".....for I am the LORD who heals you. Over the next few chapters, we'll be looking at some of the different streams, or ways of healing and freedom that feed into God's healing river.

> *Psalm 46:4*
> *"There is a river whose streams make glad the city of God, the holy place where the Most High dwells." NIV*

Stream 1:
Healing through faith

Faith has been called the currency of heaven. In other words, every provision and promise of God is accessed through faith. Clearly then, faith is a necessary component of every kind or form of healing. You don't need much faith for God to move in your situation. So, these streams are fundamentally different mechanisms that God has provided for you to be able to receive what you need. The first, simplest, and most obvious of these is faith itself.

But what is faith? Out of the word translated as faith we find other words such as trust, assurance, belief. When we are talking about faith, we are talking about a belief in Him that gives us assurance that His word is true. It's a belief that trusts that He's able to provide to us His promises. True faith then is not a tool for manipulating God to do what we want. True faith is based on an accurate picture of God's character and goodness that causes us to trust him.

In Hebrews 11:6 we see the statement that *'without faith it's impossible to please God.'* Some people take this to mean that God isn't happy with you if you don't have great faith, and consequently do great things. In fact, what it really means is that God 'is pleased' when we believe in Him, because it means that we have an accurate and true picture of who He really is. As a result, we trust Him to do what He says He will do. In Romans 4:21 we see that Abraham was absolutely convinced, or fully persuaded that God was able to do anything that He had promised. This trust in God released God to be supernaturally involved in Abraham's situation, and able to proceed to fulfill His word to Him.

The late Apostle of faith Smith Wigglesworth once said; *'it pleases God when we ask for much.'* Why is this? Because clearly when we ask God for a lot, it's because we have a correct picture of the fact that He's good, and willing to do immeasurably more than we could ask or imagine.

> *Ephesians 3:20*
> *Now to him who is able to do immeasurably more than all we ask or imagine, according to his power that is at work within us. NIV*

Faith is contagious

We need to expose ourselves to people of faith, and purposefully put ourselves in faith environments. It's important to avoid the influences of unbelief even from unbelieving 'believers.' A number of years ago someone who was close to my wife developed cancer. The lady attended a church that was not focussed on the healing element of the gospel. My wife was encouraging her that from our experience God could do anything. But those around her were accepting the proposed outcome for her illness. My wife began getting calls from people in that church, telling her to not be unrealistic, and to accept the situation.

Knowing what God is able to do, one day when she was receiving one of these discouraging calls, I recall saying something like; *"here give me the phone."* And I remember asking the person on the other end of the line; *"don't you people have bibles in your church?"* And went on to preach at them for some time. In the end I remember that it was if they were waking up from a sleep, and in the end, they commented; *"yes we used to believe that too."* The person that I was talking to did look again into God's healing provisions, and eventually became involved in healing and freedom ministries themselves. Both faith and unbelief are environmental, and propagated by word, and at times testimony.

We ran one of our healing schools for Pastors in a city in Africa. At the end of the school the Pastors took me to the home of a lady unable to walk who had not been able to attend. As it happened a group of Christians from another town were visiting at the same time, so the house was full of people. I began sharing stories of recent healings to help her see what God could, and wanted to do.

As I was sharing, a local lady came bouncing forward and exclaimed; *"that's right! This man and his wife were here last year and I was healed of arthritis."* I looked at the woman, who was in here mid 50's, and realised that even though she'd been at the school all week I'd not recognised her. The year before she'd been all hunched over, and could hardly walk, and now she was upright and moving like a young woman, God had healed her. Her faith was contagious, and her testimony was such that all of a sudden everyone wanted prayer for their illnesses. Her faith and testimony infected the room.

The faith dynamic

Once faith is activated anything can happen. It may begin with gifts operating in a meeting, or power manifest, but like the raising of Lazarus, once people see what God can do, and others being healed faith rises. It's then not uncommon to see people 'expect' healing, and receive in their seats. I recall visiting a strong faith filled church where a friend of mine was ministering. People began to be healed in their seats as they saw others receiving.

One man came out and testified that he didn't want to come to the meeting because he'd had so much of his bowel removed that he could only go very short times without needing to visit the toilet. So much so that the local council had given him keys to all of the toilets around the district. He sat for hours in the meeting with no issues, and the next day spent the whole day on an outing with his family with no problem. Clearly God had replaced some bowel!

We were ministering in Pacific nations a number of years ago, and I recall them carrying in a woman on a stretcher who had terminal cancer. The church was charged with faith, and after we prayed for her, she walked out by herself, and was released from the hospital a few days later. When we returned to that church, as a result of her testimony, there were other cancer patients also wanting prayer. Faith produces the expectation of God doing something. It is highly contagious, and once people are exposed to God working, hear testimonies, they realise that God is no respecter of persons. What He'll do for others, He will do for you.

Dealing with unbelief

In 2 Corinthians 10:5 we read that we're to demolish, or cast down arguments and pretensions that contradict the knowledge of God. What we know of God is revealed in His word, and confirmed through experience. And then we're to take every thought captive, and make it obedient to Christ, who is incidentally the word made flesh. Our thoughts are the product of what we've chosen to believe either voluntarily or involuntarily.

The word translated as 'arguments' in this passage is '*Logismos*', which means computation or reasoning. In other words, if we begin to reason out; '*perhaps God heals people overseas, but not here. Or maybe He will heal that person, but not me. Or, I believe God used to heal, but not today.*' Then, we've entered into Logismos, which is doubt. Jesus said if we do not have doubt then we can receive. Again, our stellar example of a man full of faith, Smith Wigglesworth, used to say; "*carnal (worldly, natural) reasoning will always land us in the bog of unbelief!*" His own position, was; "*God said it, I believe it, that settles it!*"

In other words, there's nothing to work out. The question then becomes how does God propose to do it? Very often I find that the problem isn't that people don't have faith, it's that it's mixed with doubt and unbelief. Which as we see from the passage that I've just quoted, is something that can be dealt with, and it's our responsibility to exercise our free will and choose what we allow to accept as true and allow to happen in our thinking.

We can, by what we choose to believe, put our healing on standby, or pause. Or even cancel whatever has been happening. When faith stops, we take God out of the picture....and it generally stops or is blocked because of doubt and unbelief. At times people receive their healing over weeks or months when they continue in faith. If they don't unbelieve, they often discover their healing, and realise that they can now do what they couldn't before. We cannot have more faith than we have in the moment, but we can refuse doubt and unbelief. This then means that our mustard seed is enough, and it releases God to do for us that which He promised.

Simple faith

We need to become like little children, with a simple faith. This is appropriate, because we really don't know as much as we think we do. And there's certainly much about the Kingdom of God and the workings of God that are beyond our understanding.

I was recently in a South Asian nation where we ran healing meetings and healing and freedom training schools for Pastors. Many people received healing instantly. I recall an elderly lady with a simple faith. She had a lump on her leg which went down after prayer over a period of a few days. She could have seen that it didn't happen instantly and thought; '*Oh well, it didn't work*', and have stopped expecting God to meet her need. But rather than trying to work it out she left the outcome to God. According to her faith God was able to continue to work, and now after that healing, with elevated expectations she'd returned for prayer for something else.

Another lady at the same event who had not been able to come up to the meeting had a deaf ear. But hearing of what God had been doing she approached us in the foyer, and after a brief prayer her hearing was restored.

The faith of others

A number of years ago in a south east Asian nation we ran one of our schools. It had been very hot so by the end of the week I was quite tired. On the way back to the hotel the host Pastors took us to the home of an old lady who wanted prayer for an unspecified ailment. I laid my hands on her and prayed a tired prayer. She responded by getting very angry and pointing at her eyes, implying that I'd prayed for the wrong thing. I realised that she was blind, so I put my hand across her eyes and prayed another simple, tired prayer. The next thing she was counting across the table the fingers held up by the Pastors who had taken us to her.

I looked at them, and realised that through the week they'd been seeing people healed, and although I had no problem that God could do anything, regardless of my near exhaustion, that it very probably was their expectation that released the provision of God into her situation. Faith is released through exposure to people of faith who speak faith filled words, along with environments where

God is moving. Places where people's faith is greater than the unbelief of those around them.

Occasionally I deal with people who have a diagnosis of this or that, and encourage them to attend a healing meeting. Amazingly, many of them simply aren't interested even though they're professing Christians. We really do need to seek God, and invest into giving Him opportunities to touch us. Even if each meeting is simply a progression in building faith.

Positioning ourselves in faith

In Daniel chapter 3 we see Shadrach, Meshach, and Abednego threatened with being thrown into the fiery furnace if they didn't bow down and worship the king. They made a faith statement, placing themselves <u>under</u> God's power and provision, allowing Him to supernaturally come into their circumstances and save them. *"If we're thrown into the fiery furnace, the God we serve is able to deliver us from it, and He will deliver us from your Majesty's hand."* As the story goes, they were completely unharmed, but as we described in an earlier chapter, those who threw them in the fire were killed by the extreme heat.

A faith statement or declaration of what you believe and are prepared to accept can be a good beginning to taking every thought captive, and to not receiving any other outcome other than that which God Himself has decided. They refused to come <u>under</u> and submit to doubt and unbelief, choosing instead to position themselves <u>under</u> God's provisions in faith. The principle is that whatever you choose to submit to and come <u>under</u> has power and authority into your life and outcomes.

7

Stream 2
Healing Using the Gifts
God through us

Our 2nd healing stream is through the gifts of the Holy Spirit. God uses these to stimulate faith and position people in a place where they're able to receive. In order to properly understand the gifts of the Spirit, you need to understand the ministry of the Spirit. This sevenfold ministry of the Spirit was given to Jesus to facilitate the will of God through His ministry, and they also operate through believers, in order to minister God's provisions to those in need.

In the book of Isaiah 11:2 we see a prophetic statement made in regard to what are known as the 7 Spirits, or seven functions of the Holy Spirit that will rest on Jesus to accomplish His ministry to the people. We do not see Him ministering before He came of age and was filled with the Spirit. These manifestations of the Spirit include the Spirit of the LORD, which in the New Testament we would understand to be, perhaps the mind of Christ, or knowing what God was thinking, doing or saying. The gift of prophecy would come under this heading.

Isaiah 11:2
The Spirit of the LORD will rest on him-- the Spirit of
wisdom and of understanding, the Spirit of counsel and
of power, the Spirit of knowledge and of the fear of the
LORD. NIV

Then we see the Spirit of wisdom, and of understanding. Then
the Spirit of counsel and of might or power. And finally, the Spirit
of knowledge and the fear of the LORD. You know whether or not
you have fear of the LORD if in your processes you consider how
God sees your decisions before you make them. If you examine
the gifts of the Spirit given to minister to the needs of mankind
in 1 Corinthians 12, you'll see that the function of the Holy Spirit
through believers is a good match with what Isaiah presented.

For example; prophecy, word of 'wisdom,' word of 'knowledge,'
working of miracles, (Greek = miraculous 'power'), and discern-
ment is 'understanding' what you're looking at.

An illustration of this working practically can be found in Mark
chapter 6, verse 2. We see that the people attributed Jesus' ability
to bring supernatural outcomes to wisdom. The New King James
version renders this; *"Where did this man get these things? And what
wisdom is given to Him, that such mighty works are performed by His
hands!"* So, they were acknowledging that He had wisdom to know
what to do, and might or power to facilitate it. In this case utilising
two of the seven Spirits or functions of the Holy Spirit operating
through Him to minister to the people.

The working of various gifts

One of the most common gifts that operate to initiate healing in
meetings, where there may otherwise be little or no faith or expectation, is the word of knowledge. This is where the Holy Spirit puts
a condition, or situation, into the mind of a minister or believer as
they reach out wanting to help see people receive their healing.
I've observed that most people who respond to these words are
healed.

These words very often relate to issues such as mechanical damage such as knees, backs, function of organs such as eyes, ears, livers, kidneys and so on. They can also relate to Him ministering to diseases or syndromes. At times, God is wanting to deal with these disease problems in more depth, ministering to why they're there to begin with. This is because the root causes have implications for other parts of the person's life and wholeness. We'll cover this later in Part 3.

I'm certainly not proposing that I'm the greatest example of this gift, and am personally impressed that the Holy Spirit can use my ordinary mind. We have however seen amazing breakthroughs that have sparked off a wave of healing in meetings, towns and cities, or even regions. A word of knowledge demonstrates that God is personally aware of a person's condition, and intends not just for people to know about what besets the one in need, but plans to heal them.

I could tell many stories to illustrate the operation of this aspect of knowledge coming supernaturally from God. Perhaps just a couple. I flew into a regional city in an African nation to introduce healing and freedom ministries. When I arrived, I was waiting at the airport to be picked up and taken to speak at a Sunday service. I decided to use the time to wait on the Lord for some words of knowledge to help anyone who may be attending who was sick.

One of these that God put into my mind was in regards to a man who'd had a particular accident, and had a chronic back problem as a result. I remember that when I called out the man and gave him details of his problem that he, not used to words of knowledge, was confused as to how I could know about his situation. Later I heard that he'd been healed. And that previously for some time he'd been everywhere, and tried everything to resolve his problem. Would he have been healed if God had not awakened his faith through the gift of the Spirit?

A couple of years later I was told that as a result of his and other healings that happened on that trip that Pastors in the region began to believe that God would heal, and they began seeing people set free through their own ministries. Gifts raise faith, and faith releases the works of God. There have been, and are, many great ministers who are very gifted in this area who have impacted many lives. My personal position is one of being very ordinary, and so my belief is that if I can do it, anyone can if they genuinely want to help. Many places we've been we've seen God 'break the ground' with words of knowledge, which has led to results that we otherwise wouldn't have experienced.

Very recently we were in a city in another nation, and in one evening meeting I had a particular condition impressed on my mind. The lady who responded told me that she had expressed to God that if He really wanted to heal her that He would have to call her out to confirm it. She proved that she had faith to even put that request to God, and He responded meeting her need. If we really believe that God wants to touch us, it's wise to reach out, and put ourselves in environments where He's moving by His Spirit.

Knowledge, understanding and counsel

The majority of our ministry over the years, when not involved on the mission overseas, has been in a Pastoral setting. Another application of the gifts of the Spirit can be found here, in ministering healing to mental, emotional, and the resultant physical and relational issues. We'll take this up in later chapters in more detail, and discuss the origins, or foundations of disease. But we see knowledge and understanding of the problem, along with wisdom and counsel on how to minister operating in this kind of work. Without God's dimension and abilities working here through the ministry of the Holy Spirit, we would never have experienced the consistent breakthroughs that we have seen.

Being able to impart knowledge about the problem opens the person to understanding what's happening with them. They now have faith to receive, and we can counsel them about how God will resolve their issue. Then we have to have knowledge of what to do and how to minister to create the opportunity for the Holy Spirit to facilitate healing and freedom.

God is faithful, if you will step out

I've found over the years that God will never let you down. I was in a large city where I'd not worked before doing our healing training school. (SOHAF – School of Healing and Freedom) There were several hundred Pastors gathered and I began the event with a few of words of knowledge. The first one was a description of a particular Pastor that I felt that God had put in my mind who had a liver problem. When I called it out there was no response, just a sea of Pastors looking at me with blank expressions. An uncomfortable beginning to the meetings!

I called out the next word which was a young lady with a knee complaint who couldn't walk from the back to the front of the church. I thank God that she was healed, and walked, as I recall, 14 miles to the meetings the next day! With my reputation a little more intact, we proceeded with the teaching. The next morning before we began the sessions there was a commotion down at the back of the building. I was told that it was the Pastor with the liver problem. He'd wanted to come to the meetings, but because of his liver was in hospital. When I called out the word of knowledge he was healed, and had come along for day two.

This raised considerable faith and expectation in the meetings, as well as confirming to me yet again that God can be trusted. In summary, God uses gifts to break things open, and help people receive their healing. If you need to be set free it's worth finding places or ministries where gifts operate. If you're a believer who wants to minister healing, I encourage you to seek to help by letting the Holy Spirit work through you with gifts. I've seen many people who I believe would have not received their healing without the operation of the word of knowledge to ignite their faith.

As I've already described there are many people more gifted in words of knowledge than I am, and yet even with my limited God-given abilities the gift is still powerful enough to open up healing moves of God. Many times, this has been in environments where healing has not been previously present. The Holy Spirit has still been able to work through my limitations because He's been given a platform and opportunity to minister God's promises to the people. In amongst our training, we often activate or guide people into beginning in this gift.

It can create a great deal of excitement when people from in their own church or area are seen operating in this gift that the Holy Spirit works through us. Often these people are clearly much more gifted than I am, and I love hearing stories of what has happened through them after we've left.

8

Stream 3
Under the Anointing
Power

We've already cited from Isaiah 11:2 the seven Spirits, or sevenfold manifestations of the work of the Holy Spirit firstly through Jesus, and now through His disciples. One of these is the Spirit of might or power. In 1 Corinthians 12 it talks about being given the power to work miracles. The word used here in the Greek is *'dunamis,'* which literally means miraculous power. We see this in the ministry of Jesus where in Luke 5:17 He was teaching, and the power of the Lord was present to heal. This power can generally be felt or sensed as it's ministered by the Holy Spirit through a believer, or is strong through corporate faith in a meeting.

In Mark chapter 5 we see the story of Jesus walking through a crowd, and a woman who had suffered with an issue of blood, possibly something like endometriosis, for 12 years. Such was her faith and consequent expectation; she believed that if she could even touch His garment she would be healed. We know that when she did the bleeding stopped. Jesus felt the healing power go out of Him, as this woman's faith drew the Spirit of power through Him. Let me point out here that on His part it was not a mental exercise. He did not pray about this or that condition. Probably nobody other than the woman and Jesus Himself even knew about the transference of the healing power.

At times on trips I've had the privilege to minister to hundreds of people as they've come forward for healing. Between there often being a language barrier, the noise in the meetings, or some other reason, I have no idea what I'm ministering to in that setting. But as people come in faith the Spirit of power comes through me, and meets the needs that they have. Many times, I hear the testimonies of what God has done later. Most people feel or sense this work of the Holy Spirit as warmth, electricity, tingling or being touched emotionally. It seems to vary in intensity, which could be to do with some kind of resistance in the person, or even their personality.

Some people who are very sensitive to the Spirit may fall down, others don't feel anything at all, and either just know they're healed, or discover it over the following hours, days or weeks. Once again, there are many people who have stronger manifes-tations of the power of God than I do. But the fact remains that through whoever has made themselves available, people are touched and healed under the anointing of God.

Impartation through the Laying on of hands

In an environment where there's a culture of healing, or faith and expectation in what God is going to do, you can sense the power of God present to heal. Other times where this is new to people, or perhaps everything/anything to do with the Holy Spirit is a new concept, there may be no sense of the presence of God at all. In these instances, the only avenue for God to work is often through the laying on of hands, or through gifts. We see this in the ministry of Jesus where He could not do any miracles in His hometown because of their lack of expectation resulting from their unbelief.

Even though there was no corporate faith, He could, however, still impart healing power through the laying on of hands. This is the most common means of ministering this working of the Holy Spirit. In Mark 16:18 Jesus said that believers would lay hands on the sick, and they will recover and be healed.

Many years ago, we were standing in a group praying in our first church, with our hands on each other's shoulders. I could feel the power of God on the hand of the man standing to one side of me. I encouraged him that he could lay hands on the sick and expect to see God heal. He was a godly man, with fear of the Lord evident. Sadly, he had very low self-image that he was not prepared to receive ministry for. Consequently, he never tried, and missed the joy of seeing God working through him.

The working of the anointing

Some people have sensation and feel this Spirit of power working through them, and others don't. It doesn't really matter. My wife doesn't feel anything, and yet people are touched and healed just the same as if she did. So don't worry, whether you're the one praying, or the one receiving, whether you feel anything or not, you're in the will of God for you, so God will be doing something.

When you're giving the Holy Spirit the opportunity to release power through you this way you don't necessarily know what He's doing. For me it feels the same in a prayer line as the power of God is ministered. Sometimes the result is healing, other times it could be deliverance or someone being filled with the Spirit. As I've pointed out, it's not a mental exercise on my part. I prayed for a woman once who wanted prayer that her cancer operation was complete, and God healed her back as well. I personally didn't even know that she had a back problem.

I was ministering in a city in Africa years ago, and the Pastors and leaders in the conference were not familiar with the work of the Spirit of Christ, so there was no expectation. As I went along the prayer line not a lot seemed to be going on other than a few people being touched, or wobbling around. So, internally in my mind I said to God, *"I'm doing the pouring, but nothing much appears to be happening!"* The next person I prayed for fell out in deliverance, and then the next, and so on to the end of the line. The point is that we're not in control of what God is going to do through the Spirit of Power, it's not an effort of our will, or thinking.

Cautions

People with unresolved identity issues often gravitate towards this gift of the Spirit. It's easy to get swollen up in pride if you have too much success too quickly. In seeking power and manifestations for the wrong reasons, you may also open yourself up to the working of other spirits and dynamics. If your intention is to fulfill God's purposes in helping His people, you can expect Him to empower your efforts.

But if your motivation is to be somebody important to meet some inner need, I'd encourage you to resolve these identity issues first. Jesus spoke in Matthew chapter 7 of people who did mighty miracles in His name for their own purposes. His statement is that He never knew them. They were serving and motivated by the wrong spirit, seeking power for personal gain.

Another caution, is don't get locked into methods. The Spirit of power under the anointing is just one way that God heals. Often in combination with other methods. For example, gifts may release faith, and then faith in turn releases power. We've been in meetings where there's such a strong presence of God that you become very bold, feeling that anything is possible.

Needing a sign

In John Chapter 4 we see Jesus approached by a government official whose son was very sick. The man begged Jesus to go with him to heal his son who was about to die. Jesus' response was; *"Unless you people see signs and wonders, you will never believe."* In other words, He was saying to them that they shouldn't be looking for manifestations in order to be able to receive healing.

It becomes a block if you believe that you have to see something, otherwise you won't be healed. With the majority of the people that we see healed, you don't see anything, even though they may or may not feel something. One moment they have the problem, and the next moment its changed!

Then Jesus told him, "*Go, your son will live.*" And the man believed the word that was spoken to him, and went his way. While he was still on his way home his servants met him and told him that his son was alive and well. On enquiry the man realised that the healing happened at the moment that Jesus spoke. Simple faith in the word of God brought about this miracle. So, although we note that we don't need, or need to seek for miraculous signs, nonetheless, the spirit of power under the anointing of God is one of the ways that God heals.

If you need healing, I would encourage you to seek out meetings where God's power can be found operating. History is littered with people who moved in the power of God, and there are many great ministries in the body of Christ today. Not everyone is healed this way, but many are. Some simply struggle to believe for some reason, and these blockages need to be dealt with before they can accept God's grace and goodness. We've personally ministered to people where the power of God is on people so heavily that they need to be held up, and they still cannot receive.

9

Stream 4
Healing Through Mental and Emotional Release
Wholeness that produces healing

The scientists tell us that as many as 90% of diseases have a component of negative emotions. Quite possibly the other 10% comes to us through efforts to comfort ourselves because of the emotional damage that we carry. This could be through drugs, alcohol, too much food, and at times even prescription medications, which at times can create their own problems.

We have spent much of our ministry life working with people who are struggling with mental and emotional problems. We've seen healing of the body take place many times as a result of hormonal and other chemical factors coming back into balance as these issues are resolved. As a doctor friend once said, in terms of your physical body operating and being healthy; *hormones make your world go around.* We see this eluded to in 3 John 1:2 where John says; *"I pray that you may prosper in all things and be in health, just as your soul prospers".*

Mental/emotional/physical wholeness and health are intertwined, and we'll discuss how to resolve these problems in more detail in Parts 2 and 3. Your soul is generally accepted to refer to your mind, will and emotions. And as you study scripture you find that the central point, or the main place of influence on the soul is the heart. It's very important to understand what the 'heart' is from a biblical standpoint if you want to see wholeness in mind, emotions and body.

What then is the 'heart?'

In the NKJV of the bible we see that the 'heart' is translated 833 times, whereas the mind is only translated 90 times. The importance, and pre-eminence of the 'heart' from a biblical perspective is significant. So much so that we find in Proverbs 4:23 in the NLT version, that we should '*above all else,*' in other words it's the most important thing that we need to do, '*guard our heart, for it affects everything that you do.*' As we go through the Bible, we find that our 'heart' has its own thoughts that are separate and distinct from those of the mind. For example, in Proverbs 4:12, we find that the Word of God judges or discerns the 'thoughts' and attitudes or intents of the 'heart,' not the mind.

Strongs Concordance renders the 'heart' as the thoughts or feelings coming from your middle or centre. We see this concept of thoughts from a source additional to your conscious mind confirmed throughout scripture. For example, in the NKJV or the KJV the Hebrew text in Proverbs 23:7 is accurately rendered; '*For as he thinks in his heart so is he.*' In other words, his state of being, and consequent attitudes proceed from this internal central thinking.

In Psalm 51 we see King David taking responsibility for his behaviour, and accepting that there was something going on inside him that had influenced him in what he'd done. In trying to understand why he had gone down this path he concluded in verse 6 that God desires truth in the 'inward parts.' And in verse 10 he asks God to create in him a clean, or pure heart. In other words, deal with his inner 'thoughts and feelings.' Those coming from his centre or middle that are affecting his choices, actions and behaviour.

Without healing inside we often tend to justify these influences that can cause us to act out, possibly as sin responses and be-haviours such as bitterness, anger, envy and so on. These compen-sating behaviours are many times our own solutions for negative emotions coming from what we believe. We've found that the *'heart beliefs'* that cause us the most problems are related to things that we've learnt about our identity growing up. We then set about solving these, usually not consciously known self-beliefs, by making various choices in order to make ourselves feel better about ourselves. As well as sinful reactions towards others these solutions could include immorality or addictions of some kind.

In the book of Jeremiah 17:9 we see the statement that; *'the heart is deceitful above all things.'* In other words, we can justify our be-haviour to ourselves as King David initially did, denying what we're doing, in an attempt to make ourselves feel better about how we're acting. Often, we project the blame onto others, and convince ourselves that we have every right to be angry, resentful or rejec-tive for example. Most times we need truth in the inner parts from the damage of previous offences that have crushed our identities, and produced consequent negative reactions and choices that can impact our health.

Why is this important for healing?

A number of years ago I was ministering at a large church in a regional city. Over 2 weeks many people made appointments and came in for help with mental and emotional issues. One lady in her mid-50's had suffered significant sexual abuses as a child. We worked through the negative beliefs in her heart that she now had coming from the situations she had been through, and most importantly that she subsequently held about her identity. With these resolved she left for home.

A few weeks later I received a letter from her thanking me, and explaining how she no longer needed weekly visits to the hospital because her liver and kidneys were healed. I did not even know that she had these physical problems. The point is, once she began liking and accepting and herself and others, now at peace in her heart and thinking, her body came back into order and her illnesses resolved.

I recall another lady from that church who had received ministry bursting into the evening teaching meeting, and announcing excitedly that she'd picked up her cat, and hadn't had an allergic reaction. Without the anxieties caused by her corrupted picture of her 'self,' she was no longer secreting the chemicals that produced her hypersensitivity. We'll cover how to receive this type of ministry in Parts 2 and 3.

We can see why God's number one priority is healing the broken hearted. And why the Spirit of the LORD was on Jesus, and now His church, to preach, declare, and bring the good news that you can have your broken heart healed, and be set free from your captivity. Translated from the Greek, healing a broken heart could just as easily rendered, '*making whole the out of order thinking coming from your centre, or your middle, that imbalances your emotions, and affect your decisions.*'

As we've said, mostly these '*heart beliefs*' relate to identity, however a much smaller percentage relate to beliefs that have been imprinted in other trauma. A young woman came for ministry one day who had been to the doctor and found that she had a thyroid problem. He had explained to her that she would have to be on hormones for the rest of her life. Based on reference books that I'd read which explain the emotional roots of physical problems, I suggested to her that her thyroid disorder most probably related to anxieties.

So, we ministered to her anxieties, some of which related to her identity, and some of which were to do with trauma situations, and were now phobias. After these were resolved she went back to the doctor who retested her, only to find that her thyroid hormone levels were now normal. He reportedly couldn't accept that as being possible, so he tested her again. Still normal! She later explained to me that one of the best things was that she didn't have a panic attack as she usually did when she had the blood test.

Heart to body - how does it work?

In modern psychology some practitioners have come to the conclusion that people have 2 streams of thinking which often are not in harmony or agreement. Some call this cognitive dissonance. For example, this can be where there is conflict between what you know is true, or what you want to believe is true, and what you perceive or feel is really true. For example; it's obvious that you're loved by everyone, and that is what they tell you. So, you know that it's true. But underneath you feel that it's not true, because subconsciously your identity was programmed growing up by events that caused you to believe that you're not loveable. The latter is now your default belief which remains out of agreement with the evidence or what you would like to believe.

This is relatively new thinking for the mental health practitioners, but it has been in the Bible for thousands of years, and clearly evident if you understand the meaning of the 'heart.' In Romans 7:14-25 we see the Apostle Paul working through this situation, trying to understand this other negative influence which is in conflict with how he wants to choose to think and behave. He sees something other than his conscious mind at play, causing him to, at times, default to sinful behaviour. The passage talks about the interplay between the 2 natures now operating in one person.

He speaks of 'I,' who is his mind influence by his born-again human spirit. And 'I', his old sinful nature largely empowered by the programmed beliefs already existing in his 'heart,' or inner members. How do we know that it's beliefs in his 'heart,' or 'inner thoughts and feelings' coming from his centre that are causing him to sin. We know this because Jesus said in Matthew 15:19 that 'out of the 'heart' proceed evil thoughts, murders, adulteries, sexual immorality, theft, false witness, blasphemies.'

The choices, conscious or unconscious, to participate in these behaviours is initiated in the 'heart.' You can make up your own list of sins, you'll find that nearly all of them are sourced directly or indirectly in the influences that come from the 'heart.' So, behaviour that is out of God's order is now the outworking in terms of decisions, behaviour and actions, but it doesn't end there. If negative emotions, reactions, attitudes and responses are involved it most often will have implications for your physical condition. In the book of Proverbs, we can see that having responses and attitudes that are in line with God's instructions will result in health in our bodies.

> Proverbs 4:20-23
> ²⁰ *Pay attention, my child, to what I say. Listen carefully.* ²¹ *Don't lose sight of my words. Let them penetrate deep within your heart,* ²² *for they bring life and radiant health to anyone who discovers their meaning.* ²³ *Above all else, guard your heart, for it affects everything you do.* NLT *(emphasis mine)*

2 streams of thought and disease

What you think and believe in your 'heart' affects what you think in your mind. You have one stream of thought originating mainly in things learnt and believed about yourself in your formative years, or past traumas stored in your heart. And then you have later information learnt not in trauma or formative moments stored in your brain. When they are not in harmony or agreement, your mind, which biblically is your computer, your thinker, your reasoner, tries to work out how to resolve the conflict. Your thinking and mind are now not at peace and problems are unresolved, or not in order, you are mentally disordered.

Your chemical and electrical system plays out your thought life and makes what you're thinking a reality in your body. This includes feeling what we think and believe by what we know as emotions. These are the outworking of thought in a way in which we can feel these emotions elaborated through electrical messages along with hormones and neurotransmitters. It's a thought first, and then comes the matching feeling mediated by electrical and chemical signals.

So, dis-ease in our thoughts caused by conflicted thinking, or dis-ordered mental states coming from the influences of 'heart beliefs,' finish in our bodies chemically as eventual disease or illness. In conclusion, we note this process; the 'heart' influences the mind positively or negatively. The resulting thoughts are elaborated as feelings and emotions, and finish in the body as physical wellbeing or disease. We read passages in the scriptures such as in;

> Proverbs 17:22
> A merry heart does good, like medicine, But a broken
> spirit dries the bones. NKJV

This is a good example of how having a healed heart produces a positive mental, emotional, and finally physical state. But if we're broken through what we believe about ourselves, it will play out as a negative condition. It begins in the 'heart,' but in terms of your personal wellbeing it ends in the body. (In practice these 'heart beliefs' have implications beyond yourself in that they affect and can damage or enhance relationships.)

Negative emotions

We'll visit this in more detail in Parts 2 and 3, but in general it has been catalogued that behind diseases you will typically find, individually or in groups negative emotions, attitudes, reactions or responses such as;

Anger – Self anger

Anxiety – fear/stress/insecurity

Bitterness – unforgiveness/resentment/rebellion
Depression – hopelessness

> *Proverbs 12:25*
> *Anxiety in the heart of man causes depression, But a good*
> *word makes it glad. NKJV (emphasis mine)*

Envy – Jealousy

> *Proverbs 14:30*
> *A heart at peace gives life to the body, but envy rots the*
> *bones. NIV (emphasis mine)*

Guilt – shame (Performance anxiety, drivenness)

Grief – sadness/sorrow

Inferiority – Low self-image/esteem

Rejection – self-rejection – fear of rejection – self-conflict.

10

Stream 5
Healing Through
Deliverance
The Spiritual Component

It's clear from the New Testament, as well as personal experience, that there can at times be an evil spirit, or a demon, as they're also known, behind sickness and disease. Let me say this though; 'the problem is still the problem.' What do I mean by this? The function of demons is to be able to use or influence areas of the personality that are yielded to them. They have normally been able to access these places through openings in the human personality such as; emotional trauma, mental duress, physical weakness, wilful participation, or deception. These areas, or places that they operate from become 'strong holds' that they can work from in the hosts life.

Once they've occupied this ground, or 'topos' as it is in the Greek, you see people locked in to behaviour. This can be evident as 'replay,' where people go over and over the same things, unable to break free. You often see this in problems such as bitterness and unforgiveness. Another function that they have is that they amplify or power up a problem. The evidence is seen as inordinate sized responses. So, there's anger, and then there's explosive, uncontrollable anger that may present as disproportionate to the situation or event that is occurring. As we mentioned in the previous chapter negative emotions are implicated in most diseases, reportedly in as many as 90% of cases.

If then a demon holds the negative emotion, replaying the issues behind it over and over, keeping the person constantly in it, and then amplifies the intensity of the issue, then it makes sense to expect the onset and intensity of disease to be much greater and develop more quickly.

We were involved with a lady who had a spirit of rejection. For her a major response to what she believed as a result of the initial rejection, was resentment and outbursts of anger when those negative beliefs about her identity were triggered by people around her. So, the problem was coming from beliefs imbibed through exposure to rejection in her formative years. And her response was resentment and anger, which were sin, and out of God's order for her. These behaviours were releasing chemicals into her body which were making her sick. At 30 years old she was beginning to grow bone on her fingers as the early stages of the same type of arthritis that her mother suffered terribly from.

If she sat for more than a few minutes, when she rose up to walk, she would hobble around like an old woman for a few minutes until her ankles loosened up. Her father was the same, and his mother as well. A few weeks after she was delivered from the spirit of rejection, a friend observed that when she stood up, she now walked normally. Once the power of the rejection was gone the resentment and anger responses had also lessened, and healing occurred as her hormone balances returned to normal. The question must be asked, was it arthritis that travelled through the family, or resentment? Evidently resentment was in the family line.

I still know this lady, and more than 30 years on she is still healed, and at nearly 70 years old has no arthritis. The bone on her fingers remained just one small spur to remind her of what she'd been set free from. Her mother, who didn't have ministry, has fingers and hands crippled with bone twice the size of what they should be. Later the lady also had ministry to the identity beliefs that were the result of the rejection, and were the true root of the problem. The amplification of the demon was behind the intense emotions that caused the disease in this case. Without dealing with the beliefs as well, she still may have developed the condition later in life.

The spirit of infirmity

Luke 13:11 speaks of a woman was bent over with a spirit of infirmity for eighteen years. Infirmity is translated from the Greek word; 'astheneia,' which means feebleness, weakness, infirmity or disease. We see that this weakness was evidently something to do with her back, as she was unable to raise herself up. Nineteen years ago, apparently, she didn't have the problem. Something had happened that had created the weakness, and it was an entry point for the spirit of infirmity which now held her into the problem.

We were doing one of our healing training schools many years ago, and a Chinese lady came in with her husband. She coughed incessantly throughout the evening session that they attended. The next morning, we had the opportunity to minister to her. It turned out that as a little girl she'd been in an accident where a wall had fallen on her crushing her chest. What had now created a place for the spirit of infirmity was the fear belief that she'd taken in due to the traumatic moment of the event. This belief was that she 'couldn't breathe, and so she was going to die.'

The emotional breach created by what she believed in the event gave place to the spirit. As God released her from the fear belief that she'd imbibed she went into spontaneous deliverance. The truth now in place, the spirit no longer had anything to hold her in bondage to. The result of the spirit being evicted was that she was now healed. That evening she sat quietly in the meeting, and then gave a testimony about her healing. The truth had set her free. The spirit had held a place in her through what she'd believed in the trauma moment, and held her into her physical problem for over 30 years.

Spirits of infirmity, or weakness, as they can also be termed, can attach to any weak area of the body. Once we deal with the problem of why they're there we see people set free from these spirits. At times in a meeting, through the operation of gifts, or under the anointing we see people set free from these spirits and receive their healing. I recall having a word of knowledge for a lady who suffered with migraines. I remember being very tired that morning, and praying a far from powerful prayer commanding the spirit of infirmity causing the problem to leave. She didn't feel anything, I didn't feel anything, but at the time of writing, more than 10 years on, she's never had a migraine again.

Let me note here that we've also seen migraines resolved through emotional healing, without praying against a spirit of infirmity. If they were present, they simply left once they had none of the beliefs that created a weakness, and gave them a place in the person. Sicknesses such as autoimmune diseases, are conditions where the person's body attacks itself. These weak areas of the body exist because of what they believe about themselves, and can be the type of situation where you may find a spirit involved. We'll delve into this in more detail in Parts 2 and 3.

Demons and healing

We see in the scriptures that many came to Jesus for healing, and the report is that demons or evil spirits as they're also known came out of many. We can surmise that often the leaving of the spirits and the healing were connected.

In Matthew chapter 15 we see the story of a woman of Canaan whose daughter had an evil spirit. She kept asking Jesus to cast the demon out of her daughter. Jesus pointed out that the 'bread' or 'provisions' were for the people of Israel. In other words, deliverance from demons is a provision for His people. The New Covenant was to be mediated by receiving from God through faith, which she showed an abundance of. So, Jesus made an exception in her case and freed her daughter. Notably, the problem that she came with was that her daughter was 'severely demon possessed,' and the result of it going was that she was healed.

I'm not suggesting that a demon is implicated in every disease, but it is noteworthy that at times they can possess, influence and exhibit the use of areas of the human personality or body. They then amplify, hold, or replay the issue to promote disease. More information on this can be found in our training manuals, or other of my books that cover this in more detail. [2]

2   SOHAF, School Of Healing And Freedom, Comprehensive or Basic Manuals, or the book, *Healing and Freedom Through Truth Encounters*

11

Stream 6
Healing Through
Knowledge

Mind renewal

In earlier chapters we've discussed God's willingness and ability to heal. Many people do not have knowledge of these elements of God's character. Or perhaps they have no knowledge of healing being paid for, and being a part of the redemption package. They may not understand that God has many ways that He heals. As a result, they don't seek to access God's provisions for their needs.

At times we have to understand the ways of God, and the restoration of His order to have knowledge of the reason for our problem. And then we need knowledge of what kinds of methods God has provided so that we can deal with it. In parts 2 and 3 we're going to cover alternate pathways to healing if you've not been able to receive in any of the other ways that we've described. Proverbs 4:20-22 indicates that alignment with the ways of God will lead to health. Verse 22 in the NLT version says that the result of paying attention to God's words will 'bring life and radiant health to anyone who discovers their meaning.' His word details these pathways to healing if you know where to look.

What is repentance?

In an early chapter we explained that the word translated repent is 'metanoeo.' This word means to change your thinking, or think differently and reconsider your ways. Once you have knowledge of what's out of God's order, we reconsider our ways, and change our thinking about what we're doing. An obvious example would be something such as being in unforgiveness. This is a very common block to healing. Once we have knowledge that if we don't forgive others their sins and weaknesses, then God won't forgive ours, we clear the way to healing by repenting and changing what we're doing.

At times we may need help and ministry to our hurts and offences to be able to effectively do this from the heart. In this, God has provided ministries to help us deal with inner issues that we struggle with.

> 2 Timothy 2:24-26
> [24] And the servant of the Lord must not strive; but be gentle unto all men, apt to teach, patient, [25] In meekness instructing those that <u>oppose</u> <u>themselves</u>; if God perad-venture will give them <u>repentance</u> to the acknowledging of the truth; [26] And that they may recover themselves out of the snare of the devil, who are taken captive by him at his will. KJV (emphasis mine)

This would include dealing with issues such as bitterness, self-rejection, fears and anxiety, ungodly anger, and so on that are considered to be the roots of disease.

There are obvious sin or addictive issues that open, or have opened the way to sickness and disease, such as sexual immorality which can lead to transmitted diseases like HIV aids. Sexual sin may also promote guilt, anxiety and self-rejection which can lead to sickness over time.

Drugs, alcoholism and even abuse of food can lead to illness. We cited earlier the passage from Hosea 4:6 where God reveals that *'my people are destroyed from lack of knowledge.'* Ignorance about the effects of excess sugar, fats, or other materials used in food processing can lead to opening us to disease, or at the very least create an environment for disease to prosper or proliferate. Once we're armed with knowledge we need to exercise a fruit of the Spirit self-control. You'll find reference to this in Galatians 5:23. As somebody aptly put it; self-control begins where self-indulgence stops.

God's order for the body can't be ignored

S.D. Gordon in his book *'The Healing Christ'* [3] told the story of a friend who was suffering severely from a bodily ailment. She had experienced healing supernaturally by God on previous occasions. Now after repeated prayer for her malady she was finding that nothing was happening, even though she couldn't find any hindrance in her spiritual life. Her Christian friends considered that using medical means displayed a lack of faith in Christ.

Finally, through prayer she felt that she should see a doctor. He asked her about her diet, and she explained that she could eat nothing but dry toast, and drink tea. He told her that this was not sufficient nutrition for her body in its present condition. He gave her no medicine, but prescribed a healthy diet. As the story goes, she followed his expert advice, and soon she was well again.

The point is, she didn't need supernatural healing, she needed knowledge that she formerly did not possess, of how to maintain her body according to God's order and design for her health. We often travel and minister in developing nations. For example, in many African nations that we visit there is a high incidence of diabetes. In these countries they fill up on large amounts of grains which are carbohydrate because they are cheap, and make them feel full. Unfortunately, carbohydrate converts to sugar, and in excess creates an overload on the pancreas as they become over-weight, leading eventually to diabetes and other diseases.

[3] *'The Healing Christ', S.D. Gordon, first in print in 1924*

This lack of nutritional knowledge is often behind unnecessary premature death. We are to honour God with our bodies. That is to look after them and maintain them as well as possible for His service. You wouldn't expect to put dirty oil or fuel in your vehicle and have it run well. Many times, people want prayer for these problems, but aren't prepared to discipline themselves with a good controlled diet, exercise, recreation, and sufficient sleep. God still graciously heals, but without changing your thinking and practices once you have knowledge, you may inevitably develop some other problem.

Built in healing

There's an old saying that; *'we can dig our grave with our own teeth.'* In other words, if we eat a poor or unhealthy diet, we can be shortening our lives. I can personally attest to this as being true, finding out the hard way. A few years ago, I developed some symptoms that made me feel quite odd, including beginning to lose my balance at times. I thought that I must have picked up some kind of bug in one of the nations that I'd recently been visiting, so I went to the doctor and he scheduled some tests. When the results came back, he remarked, *"I thought so, you are insulin resistant, or pre-diabetic!"*

This came as a shock to me. But as I thought about it, at the time I did little exercise, sitting ministering to people all day, or on aircraft going here or there. Coupled with this, when I travelled, I paid little attention to what I was eating, just focussing on the task at hand. Let me point out that even though all of this was God's work, it doesn't automatically exonerate you from things that other people, who are not looking after the complex machine that their bodies are, might experience or suffer from.

Getting older, what I could previously get away with was now making me sick. I'm 6'2 (188cm), so the weight that I'd accumulated was not too obvious looking in the mirror face on. But now when I looked in profile it was obvious that I had a large swollen, protuberant belly. I saw a photo of myself speaking at a conference and realised how out of shape I really was. I had to take responsibility for my own illness. I could've asked for prayer, but long term that would not resolve the issue, and I probably would've suffered eventually from something else. Coupled with this, I couldn't recall one single thing that I'd eaten that God had made me eat. I, without knowledge or consideration had done this to myself.

It was time to take responsibility. I did some research and found that the condition was reversible. It was time to un-eat my way out of all that I'd eaten, and get some exercise. I put myself on what I termed a G.O.D. That is, A; 'God Only Diet,' meaning that if God made it, and man hadn't tampered with it then it was good for me. So, for 2 or 3 months I only ate fruit, vegetables, and small portions of unprocessed meat. I went from 104kgs (230 pounds) to 95.8kgs (just under 190 pounds.)

I returned to the doctor who congratulated me, and pronounced me no longer insulin resistant. The point is, that with many complaints, that once we have knowledge, we have a part to play in our own healing and ongoing health. Who knows what kind of other peripheral illnesses may have beset me as time went by. So, in this instance, I'm probably better off in the long run having to exercise self-control, rather than have a miraculous healing. I know that for some people with emotional problems, or stressful situational circumstances, this is very difficult, and they need healing inside and support with their environment before this may be realistically something that they can do.

God wants us in good health, and living an abundant life. In this instance if I'd been supernaturally healed but kept my overweight body, I may have missed the many other benefits that came from disciplining myself. I slept better, had much more energy, and simply could not stay in bed in the morning because I had things that I wanted to get up and do. I felt much, much better, and only God knows how many years have been added to my life. Would instant healing have been the best thing for me? Probably not. Of course, I could have been healed and then gotten into shape, but would I have if I didn't need to?

Many conditions are reversible, as God has placed the ability for the body to heal itself within the workings of this amazing machine that He's given us to dwell in on the earth.

Medical support

Because we know and understand that God wants us healed and healthy, seeking medical help can never be wrong. At times you're not personally in a place or environment where you can receive healing by faith. Or there may be no ministry available in your church or area to deal with the emotional roots and other factors producing disease. In these situations, it's sensible to seek healing through the medical models that are on offer. It may be practical to be receiving this support along with dealing with the spiritual and emotional roots behind your illness.

We would never want to minimise the work of the medical profession and the related science and research. We thank God for these provisions and mercies for suffering humanity. We only need to look at the disparity in life expectancies between the developed and developing worlds. We can be grateful to God for the knowledge, training, treatments, equipment, and medicines available to support us in these times.

Part 2

THE ORIGINS, FOUNDATION, BASIS AND SOURCE OF DISEASE

The Australian Bureau of statistics released a report in December 2023 citing key findings from a survey that they had conducted. The study revealed that eight in ten (81.4%) of people had at least one long term health condition in Australia. One in two (49.9%) of people are suffering from at least one chronic condition. In the U.S. that figure is even higher with 60% of people carrying at least one chronic disease. 4 in 10 adults in the U.S. reportedly have 2 or more chronic diseases. The church certainly has a lot of work to do in these times.

In an earlier chapter we've already cited that scientists consider that as many as 90% of diseases have a component of negative emotions implicated. Quite possibly the other 10% of chronic conditions come through efforts to comfort our ourselves or compensate for the emotional damage that we carry. This could be through drugs, alcohol, too much food, immorality and transmitted diseases, and at times even prescription medications, which can at times create their own problems. In Australia 67% of people are taking prescription medication each year.

In previous chapters we've covered fairly direct, mostly supernatural, intervention into these maladies. If you haven't received your healing through any of these models, then here in Parts 2 and 3 we're going to cover how to receive your healing through processes leading to coming to a place of wholeness. This involves restoring God's order in your life. The most effective way to achieve this is through coming into alignment with the word of God, which generally involves the Holy Spirit doing a deep work in your 'heart.'

> Proverbs 4:20-23
> [20] *Pay attention, my child, to what I say. Listen carefully.*
> [21] *Don't lose sight of my words. Let them penetrate deep within your <u>heart</u>,* [22] *for they <u>bring life and radiant health</u> to anyone who discovers their meaning.* [23] *Above all else, guard your <u>heart</u>, for it affects everything you do.*
> *NLT (emphasis mine)*

Here we'll examine the beginnings of disease for humanity. Initially, for mankind in general, and now affecting us personally. We'll look at how stepping away from God and His plan for us, corrupted our identities, and became a foundation for disease to take hold. In the following passage, and other Proverbs we see a reference to the health of our bones. The white blood cells which are considered crucial for our immune system and health are made in our bone marrow.

> *Proverbs 3:7-8*
> *⁷ Do not be wise in your own eyes; fear the LORD and shun evil. ⁸ This will bring health to your body and nourishment to your bones. NIV*

Most of the words from the Greek language that are translated as heal, or healed embody the idea of restoration to wholeness or being made whole. It's interesting to note that really our bodies and health will not let us be out of order with the ways of God, and how He designed our physical mechanisms to function. We have 12 amazing, and finely tuned systems in our bodies that have to be in balance and harmony for us to be in health. Your body is a reflection of your thought life, and your thought life is a reflection of what we believe. The condition of your body is therefore directly related to what is happening in your soul. That is your mind, will, and emotions. And your 'heart' is the central influence for the condition and function of these elements of your soul.

> *3 John 2*
> *Beloved, I pray that you may prosper in all things and be in health, just as your soul prospers. NKJV*

In recent years we've seen a number of Christian publications proposing the sources and origins of disease. These cause and affect type books cite many being healed of a variety of diseases as the negative emotions and consequent responses are dealt with. I want to acknowledge the great work that these ministers have done in researching the causes of diseases, even though we use a completely different model for dealing with the mental and emotional problems that they have identified.

Although we have not personally ministered to all of the diseases mentioned in these books, we have seen all of the negative emotions and attitudes that they consider to be implicated in producing disease, consistently and predictably resolved, week in week out, for over 25 years. The model that we use will be explained in later chapters of this book. We have found these books an excellent resource to help us to know what we may be dealing with when people come for ministry. So, I applaud all of the hard work of the authors, and thank them for the gift that they've given the church. Hopefully, we can build on it. We'll be at times referencing these publications, and their findings, in chapters towards the end of the book.

Even understanding and having knowledge of the attitudes and responses that produce disease can move our will to disengage practicing them. Our own efforts can have limitations, and it is better to see these negative emotions and consequent behaviours completely resolved through the work of the Holy Spirit.

From scripture, Christians have long known that positive or negative emotions have implications for our physical state of being and health. The Bible has taught us that negative mental and emotional conditions lead to sickness and disease. The secular world, through science, is unveiling these truths as well, even though in some instances these propositions are considered theories or hypothesis, in many Christian ministries these mind body processes are considered proven facts. For example;

Proverbs 17:22
A merry heart does good, like medicine, But a broken
spirit dries the bones. NKJV

In order to see people made whole, we have to see them restored to how God intended them to be when He created them. So, as a foundation, we're going to begin by discussing what happened to move mankind out of God's order and design. How did disease find it's way into humanity, and what are God's plans and intentions to remedy the situation that we now find ourselves in?
Let's begin in these next few chapters by laying a foundation, and coming to an understanding as to why mankind is beset with disease to begin with. Where did these negative emotions, responses and behaviours originate from, and how did they access the human race.

If you're not so interested in how mankind became prone to disease, or how biblical wholeness is the best prevention from these maladies, you can move to **Part 3 - Ministry to emotionally rooted disease**, Chapter 17 - **Glossary of Common Conditions**, where we'll examine what you're likely to find behind specific common illnesses. Later as we continue to work through Part 3 we will begin to explain these negative emotions that are catalogued as being behind disease. And then finally we'll move on to how to see them resolved through the ministry of the Holy Spirit. And how we can be set free by opening ourselves to His work rather than through self-effort.

But if you're continuing here, let's look more deeply into the original source of the problem.

12

Implications of *'the fall'* on Disease

Note: much of the material in the next few chapters is sourced from our SOHAF (School Of Healing And Freedom Manual Unit 1) and slightly modified for use in this publication. [4]

Disease and *'the fall'* of mankind

Firstly, why do we call it the 'fall?' This term is mostly likely used because mankind fell from the high place of being in the likeness and image of God. We were positioned <u>under</u> God's authority, consequently having dominion <u>over</u> the Earth. In accepting and preferring the counsel of Satan as detailed in Genesis chapter 3, Adam and Eve stepped away from God, His perfect order for their lives and His Lordship. Mankind exercised their free will and choice to follow another. In submitting to Satan and coming <u>under</u> him they made him lord.

As representatives for humanity and all who were to come, they chose to no longer follow God's instructions, or to remain in His order, or to be <u>under</u> the protection of His wisdom and ways.

[4] *SOHAF (School of Healing and Freedom) Manual, Unit 1*

Resultantly, we corporately as humanity lost our position by disobedience and choosing to be led by Satan, thereby coming under his power and authority. And by submitting to his suggestions and following him in his rebellion, we were imitating his nature. Remember he was a fallen being himself, not wanting to submit to God and be under His authority, but rather raising himself up in pride and preferring his own way.

What was the reason for his fall? We need to make careful note:

> Ezekiel 28:17
> Your HEART was filled with pride because of all your beauty. You corrupted your wisdom for the sake of your splendor. So I threw you to the earth and exposed you to the curious gaze of kings. NLT (emphasis mine)

The Pride in his **heart** distorted his wisdom. It was his own pride and desire for self-realisation and self-promotion that led him to fall from his privileged place.

The introduction of another nature as a basis for disease

We have a basic understanding that we were created in God's image. This means being spirit, soul and body, 3 parts, just as God is, Father, Son and Holy Spirit. But I believe it means more. (Genesis 1:26-27) Our 'image,' or how we present, appear, and behave, is often a reflection of who we are most influenced by. That is, who we imitate, copy, or follow. Bible commentators appear to confirm my insight in this, suggesting that being in His likeness and image refers more to not only being a material body, but also an immaterial soul and spirit.

It means that we have inherited worth and dignity, being distinct and valuable in the kind of creation that we are. Like God we have the ability to reason and make moral choices, and through these decisions to reflect God's character through our actions, attitudes and relationships. In this we're gifted with the innate ability to represent God, relate with Him Spirit to spirit, and bring Him glory. For this reason, in His image and likeness we have been given the capacity to love, have mercy and compassion, and creativity to empower others.

This is far more than looking like Him. In fact, if we move to the New Testament for confirmation of this, we see that as a key part of the restoration from *'the fall'*, we are being conformed to the likeness or image of God's Son Jesus Christ. (Likeness NIV, Image NKJV)

> Romans 8:29
> For those God foreknew he also predestined to be
> conformed to the likeness of his Son, that he might be
> the firstborn among many brothers. NIV

Clearly, this restoration to resemble Jesus is not talking about a physical conforming to His likeness, or image. Jesus being the exact representation of the Father. Otherwise, our physical beings would be changing in how we look, where as in fact in most cases after 30 years old we're deteriorating. It is indicative of a trans-formed spiritual, moral, behavioural, and attitudal state of being.

So, to summarise, we need to make some very relevant and important notes here:

1. We were originally in God's image. In other words, we were in His likeness, or we could say, we were like Him. We were the result of being seeded by His nature. We were His children in this sense as the offspring of His influence and shaping. Prior to being exposed to Satan, as we understand it, mankind had only been in relationship with God, so He alone had been until that time the model for attitudes and behaviour.

2. Our identity, then, came from His identity. We were His children. We were the product of His intentions for us. He who saw us before we were even formed. He already loved us. We had the identity that He intended for us, and we were content

and accepting of who He had made us to be. This is vitally important in light of what we're going to propose in regards to the foundations and entry point of disease.

For Adam and Eve, when they followed the suggestions and temptations of Satan that the forbidden tree was something that they should eat from, the issue was who they were submitting to.... who they were allowing to influence them, to imprint them. The important factor is whose <u>nature</u> they were following, co-operating with, and now being shaped by. This was the original <u>introduction of another nature</u> for mankind, a nature that had already been corrupted, and had fallen from grace and healthy relationship with God.

Outworkings of 'the fall'

The consequence and result of partaking with this <u>fallen nature</u> is the KEY to understanding the beginnings, or genesis, of every problem faced by mankind! Problems such as mental disorder, emotional and relational issues, along with disease and physical conditions are the result of a life out of God's perfect order. When we understand God's loving, gracious, merciful nature, it makes sense that this is not something that God chose, wanted for us, or put on mankind. These troubles are the self-destructive result of choosing to follow the corrupted deceptive beliefs, attitudes, and behaviours produced by Satan's ways.

Through joining in rebellion and disobedience against God's commands, they were imprinted with the of <u>nature</u> of Satan who fell first. His fall was through pride which led to an attitude of.... *"I don't want it to be all about God, I want it to be all about me!"* His pride and wanting to be <u>'above'</u> others, and like or equal with God produced rebellion, an attitude of; *"I will not submit...I want to be in control."* These attitudes now also appear to have become entrenched in the <u>fallen nature</u> of mankind. In a sense we were converted to Satan's image and likeness, or how he appeared, acted, presented, and the attitudes that he held as a result of the internal thinking in his own 'heart.'

Isaiah 14:12-14
*¹² How you have fallen from heaven, O morning star, son of the dawn! You have been cast down to the earth, you who once laid low the nations! ¹³ You said in your **heart**, "I will ascend to heaven; I will raise my throne above the stars of God; I will sit enthroned on the mount of assembly, on the utmost heights of the sacred mountain. ¹⁴ I will ascend above the tops of the clouds; I will make myself like the Most High." NIV (emphasis mine)*

Note: Whether they believe in him or not, unredeemed, unregenerated mankind, are still looking to this fallen being that they chose to follow to meet their needs through the provisions offered through the world system. They still accept his counsel in regards to what is perceived as best for them to have a successful, happy and meaningful life. They still follow his self-centred ways in how to deal with their fellow man. His deceptive counsel about what to choose is still going on today. And rather than bringing wholeness, peace and joy, his ways will always produce brokenness, separation, destruction, disease and death.

The overwhelming evidence is that many Christians have not experienced a complete sanctification from the old nature either, and are largely beset with the same problems as the rest of the world. Even though a fuller restoration is available.

The fallen nature and physical conditions

What does the old fallen nature look like? It looks like it's father, the devil. Jesus described some of the religious people of the time as 'children' of the devil. In other words, in spite of their religious activities, their true motives for what they were doing were being done according to the leading of the old fallen nature. There is evidence in the scriptures that these religious leaders really didn't care about others, or God's desire to help people, but rather they were seeking the praises of men. (Jeremiah 8:11, Ezekiel 34:2-4)

Their religion was SELF centred, all about self-promotion, self-importance, self-realisation, and ungodly control of others. Wanting to have the 'upper hand' and be <u>over</u> or <u>above</u> others. Prioritising worldly pleasures and wanting to please SELF.

The <u>old fallen nature</u> wants to control others in order to be in a place of ascendency or superiority. In other words, it lifts itself up, seeking to have others submit to you, come <u>under</u> you, and do your will. Jesus in contrast came as a servant to help mankind, and He instructed His followers to have the same attitude, walking again in His image and nature. (Mark 9:35, Mark 10:43-45, Romans 15:8)

> John 8:44
> "You are of **_your father_** the devil, and the desires of **_your father_** you want to do. He was a murderer from the beginning, and does not stand in <u>the truth</u>, because there is <u>no truth</u> in him". NKJV (emphasis mine)

Walking in the New nature for abundant life

The Bible describes this fallen nature in the original Greek language as; '*Sarx.*' It is usually translated as the old nature, the sin nature, the flesh, or the adamic nature, depending on the commentary or Bible version that you're using. In essence it is the 'self-life' in a <u>fallen state</u> modelled after Satan's nature.

Jesus alluded to this self-centered nature in Mark's gospel chapter 8. Quoting from the New Living Translation He says in verse 34; *"If any of you wants to be my follower,"* he told them, *"you must put aside your selfish ambition, shoulder your cross, and follow me."*

In other words, your life must go from being all about what you want, to being all about the will of God. In verse 35 He goes on to explain; *"If you try to keep your life for yourself, you will lose it. But if you give up your life for my sake and for the sake of the Good News, you will find true life."*

So, if you walk in the <u>old nature</u> which seeks to be its own god, you will eventually reap the chaos and destruction that comes to those who prioritise self. (Galatians 6:7-8) But if you put off the <u>old fallen self-nature</u> and live in <u>the new redeemed nature</u> that God imputes, then that life that you live for God will be abundant. (John 10:10, Colossians 3:9-10)

> *Ephesians 4:22-24*
> *²² You were taught, with regard to your former way of life, to <u>put off your old self</u>, which is being corrupted by its deceitful desires; ²³ to be made new in the attitude of your minds; ²⁴ and to <u>put on the new self</u>, **created to be like God** in true righteousness and holiness.*
> *NIV (Emphasis mine)*

The apostle Paul summarises this in the letter to the Galatians Chapter 5:16-18. In verse 19 the NIV version it translates this as; *'The works of the flesh are **obvious:'*** (Flesh = Sarx, old fallen nature) He then goes on to list examples of what you may expect to be exhibited through either walking in the nature modelled after Satan at *'the fall'*, (Galatians 5:19-21) or those following the influences of the Spirit back into the image of God. (Galatians 5:22-23)

It's abundantly clear that the fruit of walking in the old nature is all about what you can get for your SELF. Apart from the obvious moral selfishness, you see hatred, discord, jealousy, selfish ambition and so on. Evidence of the wounded self and broken identity needing to be somebody, and compensate for this brokenness by being above others, being the most important, or being right, and so on. The old nature, the fallen self-life, is all about you.

> *Galatians 5:19-21*
> *¹⁹ The acts of the sinful nature are obvious: sexual immorality, impurity and debauchery; ²⁰ idolatry and witchcraft; hatred, discord, jealousy, fits of rage, selfish ambition, dissensions, factions ²¹ and envy; drunkenness, orgies, and the like. I warn you, as I did before, that those who live like this will not inherit the kingdom of God. NIV*

In contrast, the new nature led by your born-again human spirit in submission to the Spirit of God produces fruit that is about others. This fruit is effortless, and comes as a result of healing of the broken identity. This happens largely through the work of the Holy Spirit through the process of healing the broken heart via sanctification.

> Galatians 5:22-25
> [22] But the fruit of the Spirit is love, joy, peace, patience, kindness, goodness, faithfulness, [23] gentleness and self-control. Against such things there is no law. [24] Those who belong to Christ Jesus have crucified the sinful nature with its passions and desires. [25] Since we live by the Spirit, let us keep in step with the Spirit. NIV

An illustration of the re-creation process from nature

As a brief diversion, let's contemplate the re-creation process from being fallen creatures. Under the old nature we had minimal potential for the life of wholeness and abundant possibilities that God promises. By way of example, I would like to present the process that takes place in an earthbound caterpillar, beginning crawling on it's belly like a small serpent. It then transitions to the re-created ascendant beauty of a butterfly, whose world is so much bigger, and full of potential and destiny. The action of this metamorphosis is amazing, and is such a great illustration of a spiritual principle from a natural source. Romans 1:20

Prior to conversion, we are limited earthbound creatures, but through spiritual rebirth we become creatures who can access the higher spiritual dimension. We are now positionally seated in heavenly places in Christ Jesus. (Ephesians 2:6) The imputing of this new nature, re-created human spirit, and pliable heart, places us in a dimension of limitless possibilities. This new nature brings us potential for fullness, wholeness and healing. It is the beginning of the process, but not the end.

The beginning for our caterpillar is entering the chrysalis, (for a moth a cocoon) which is the place where this transformation will take place. For us, with our renewed spirit, we have entered the Kingdom of God. This exposure for us cannot result in anything other than change. In the chrysalis the caterpillar's structure begins to be disintegrated from the inside out. For us, our old nature comes under attack and begins to be challenged from our new spirit, which is situated in Old Testament terminology as in our 'innermost being.' So, again, the change comes from the inside out.

What was once the structure of the caterpillar proceeds to dissolve into soupy goo. This is the time when inactivated cells known as 'imaginal cells' come out of dormancy. As we can see by the name, these cells have instruction inherently placed in them in regard to the potential new re-creation of the life, and already see through the imagination the sense of what can be. In our case it is God's imaginings for us. He knows the good plans and purposes that He has for us. God sets up a 'beachhead' for His Spirit led invasion of our personality in this innermost, or human spirit, part of our being. From there He leads us to possess the land of our personality.

For our caterpillar, in the chrysalis these 'imaginal cells' begin to work on the construction of the re-created ascendant being. They imagine what can potentially become of the creature, and relentlessly work towards that goal. I think any born again person has a sense of possibilities beyond anything that they could have imagined before their spiritual rebirth. So, for the caterpillar, and us, it's messy. As a result of the activation of the 'imaginal cells' the caterpillars immune system produces a response and tries to destroy them. As we have quoted previously, with the imputation of the spirit nature in us, there is now opposition from the old fallen nature, or 'Sarx'. In much the same way as for the caterpillar, these 'imaginal cells' are a threat to the old creatures existence.

Galatians 5:16-17
[16] So I say, live by the Spirit, and you will not gratify the desires of the sinful nature. [17] For the sinful nature desires what is contrary to the Spirit, and the Spirit what is contrary to the sinful nature. They are in conflict with each other, so that you do not do what you want. NIV

As we know, it is necessary for the caterpillar to be deconstructed for these 'imaginal cells' to complete the task of forming the butterfly. It is to be a completely new being, still retaining the life, but taking on a new and beautiful form as a butterfly. The final outcome of the process instigated by these 'imaginal cells' is to create an incredible new being, vastly superior to the old one.

This is the purpose of God. To take our limited fallen self-life, and to re-create and restore us into His image and likeness for a full and abundant life. The promises of God are for those who imagine and pursue this new life, cooperating with Him in the process of taking down the old nature. The caterpillar and the butterfly, amazingly, still have the same DNA. They are the same being, remade. Now with a new future, and a new ability to experience life in a positive way, with completely new potential.

Wholeness and health are sourced here. The new natures fruit leaves no place for sin and sickness to prosper. Old attitudes, reactions, attitudes and responses are done away with. Deception about identity as the basis of the old nature is healed through truth in the process of sanctification by the Spirit of truth. There is no longer a medium for the destructive soul and body negative thoughts and emotions to work through.

John 16: 13
But when he, the Spirit of truth, comes, he will guide you into all truth. NIV

13

Negative Emotions and Disease

Disease comes in with the old fallen nature, and is a bi-product of the negative emotions, attitudes, responses, sinful reactions and behaviour that stem from living in this nature. As we will soon reveal, anxieties along with responses such as bitterness, resentment, ungodly anger, and so on are attached to the attitudes that are prevalent in the old nature. These responses produce much disease along with fear of rejection, self-rejection, anxieties, low self-image etc.

When we have a negative emotion such as bitterness, it generally manifests inwardly towards self, along with outwardly towards others. These kinds of attacks on self, whether consciously or unconsciously, are implicated in many conditions which we will discuss later.

An article posted by the National Center Biotechnology Information (NCBI) and the United States Library of Medicine (NLM) explains the links between negative emotions and disease.

'This review discusses previously available research on relationships between negative emotions and emotion regulation with inflammation

among both physically healthy adults and those with chronic illnesses.
This model emphasises the influence of negative emotions and their
contribution to heightened inflammation.'

This inflammation appears in many diseases, and although difficult
to state an exact figure it is estimated to be implicated in more
than 50% of chronic inflammatory diseases. Reportedly 3 out of
5 people die from chronic inflammatory diseases worldwide. So,
science is confirming that negative emotions leading to inflammation are a curse, not a blessing. It's therefore a major work of the
church, and central to the gospel to resolve these emotions. The
article continues;

'This highlights how negative emotions promote immune system
activation/dysfunction and ultimately increases risks for morbidity and
mortality. This model also highlights the role that emotion regulation
plays in mediating the relationship between negative emotionality
and immune system activation. Within this framework, the process of
regulating one's negative emotions serves an essential function in un-
derstanding negative emotionality's health impact. Within this model,
emotion regulation serves as a moderator in the link between <u>*negative*</u>
<u>*emotionality and inflammation*</u>*.'*

Without a reason to express our emotions correctly, under the
influence of *'the fall'* we outwork and react to our feelings in a way
that we feel justified, and with self as the centre, that we feel is
appropriate, when measuring ourselves against the world system.
So, without seeing a reason, as their 'own god' often people don't
seek to regulate their negative emotions at all. Most times without
healing and freedom through the Holy Spirit, we find it difficult to
overcome these feelings. It's not just the negative emotion, such
as a sense of rejection, or low self-image that is the problem, it's
the sinful response or compensating behaviour that often produces the harmful outcomes.

Some Christians will only believe the Bible if science confirms
what it says. So, I'll include the findings from a secular standpoint

of the following interesting article written by Dr. Megan E Renna, who conducts research at university on the biological implications of psychological distress. Her studies illustrate the progress that science is making in understanding the links between negative emotion and disease. For the sake of space, I'll only quote text that relates directly to what is proposed in these writings. The full excerpt can be found at: www.scientistdirect.com   Many such articles and studies can be accessed on the internet if you search using the appropriate questions. These only serve to strengthen and lend weight to the proven Christian position.

This is an excellent illustrative diagram (illustration replicated below) that she used in her article. Megan theorises on the processes and mechanisms that may be behind why negative emotions promote inflammation and consequent disease.

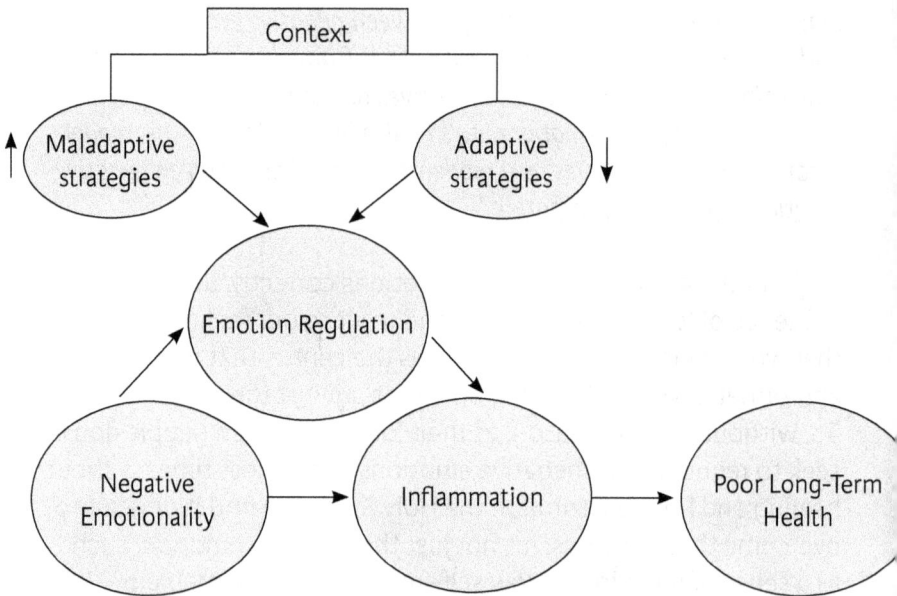

'Researchers from several fields including clinical and health psychology, psychiatry, and psychoneuroimmunology (PNI) have uncovered pathways through which psychological distress influences physical health via inflammation.' [5]

[5] Dr. Megan E Renna, National Institutes of Health (NIH) http://pubmed.ncbi.nih.gov
A review and novel theoretical model of how negative emotions influence inflammation:
The critical role of emotional regulation. ME Renna. Brain Behav Immun Health. 2021

As we've already discussed, inflammation is a feature of the majority of diseases. You can see in the diagram negative emotionality. This could be a sense of rejection, low self-image, anxiety, sorrow and so on. Emotional regulation refers to how we react to, or deal with these negative emotions. Such as responding with anger, bitterness, self-rejection, etc.

'Specifically, this model highlights how negative emotions such as sadness or anxiety enhance immune system dysregulation and contribute to long-term health problems.'

'This increased inflammation resulting from negative emotionality and accompanying maladaptive emotion regulation heightens risk for poor long-term health outcomes.'

'The far-reaching relationships between negative emotionality and inflammation are notable among those with distress disorders such as major depressive disorder, generalised anxiety disorder, or post-traumatic stress disorder.' *(Underlines mine)*

Anxiety disorders are the most common type of mental disorders, and they affect a large percentage of the global populace. There is considered to be a strong association between depression and physical disease such as; cardiovascular disease, type 2 diabetes, high blood pressure, stroke, some types of cancer, Alzheimer's disease, osteoporosis and so on. Research indicates that depression has a link to chronic inflammation which promotes the development of these and other diseases. PTSD is the exposure to some kind of traumatic event.

As we have been proposing, these negative emotions are largely a chemical and electrical elaboration of a thought. And these thoughts are influenced or instigated by beliefs that have been imbibed and concluded in events. We've found over the years that everything starts with a thought, even an unconscious thought. This includes emotion, and physical conditions.

And further:

'Several meta-analyses highlight links between mood disorders and inflammation, reliably demonstrating that people diagnosed with major depression are more likely than their psychologically healthy counterparts to have heightened inflammation both at baseline and in response to stress.'

The article continues:

'Although emotions such as _anger_, sadness, and _anxiety_ are important in the context of health, it remains unclear how specific regulation processes mediate the relationship between negative emotionality and inflammation. _Emotion regulation refers to "the processes by which individuals influence which emotions they have, when they have them, and how they experience and express these emotions"_ (Gross, 1998) (Underline mine)

As we've explained, what is termed emotional regulation in secular circles refers to our responses to stressors. The Bible has much counsel in regards with how to deal with, or regulate our reactions to what we perceive to be offences committed towards us. For example, forgiveness.' Matthew 6:14-15 Make sure that we don't go into bitterness, long term it will not only produce disease in us, it will also draw negative responses and emotions from those around us. Ephesians 4:31, Hebrews 12:15 In your anger do not sin, and deal with it quickly. Long term festering anger will make you sick. Ephesians 4:26-27

> Psalm 4:4
> In your anger do not sin; when you are on your beds,
> search your hearts and be silent. Selah NIV

> Psalm 4:4
> Don't sin by letting anger gain control over you. Think
> about it overnight and remain silent. Interlude NLT

Megan's article continues with an observation in regards to how people may compensate for their negative feelings:

'People who experience negative emotionality may be less likely to engage in a healthy lifestyle due to failures of their emotion regulation systems. Notably, these individuals may be more likely to experience poor sleep hygiene and may utilise alcohol, smoking, food, or drugs in an effort to regulate negative emotions. Collectively, these behaviours subsequently put them at risk for experiencing increased inflammation and poor health outcomes.'

Let me note here that biblically inflammation comes a result of mankind being out of order with God's ways, and continuing to walk after the old nature, and not live in the new.

> Deuteronomy 28: 15 "But it shall come to pass, if you do not obey the voice of the LORD your God, to observe carefully all His commandments and His statutes which I command you today, that all these curses will come upon you and overtake you:
> + 22 "The LORD will strike you with consumption, with fever, with inflammation, with severe burning fever, with the sword, with scorching, and with mildew; they shall pursue you until you perish. NKJV

In the New Testament, or under the new agreement that God has with redeemed mankind, we see that Jesus the Christ has taken the curse on Himself on our behalf. He paid for our freedom, and through faith the Holy Spirit facilitates our healing by some means.

> Galatians 3:11-13
> 11 Consequently, it is clear that no one can ever be right with God by trying to keep the law. For the Scriptures say, "It is through faith that a righteous person has life."
> 12 How different from this way of faith is the way of law, which says, "If you wish to find life by obeying the law, you must obey all of its commands." 13 But Christ has rescued us from the curse pronounced by the law. When he was hung on the cross, he took upon himself the curse for our wrongdoing. For it is written in the Scriptures, "Cursed is everyone who is hung on a tree." NLT (emphasis Mine)

We could rightly say that negative emotions outwork in disease in Christians the same as non-Christians if we have the same unresolved issues. The difference is that as Christians we have the Holy Spirit who can free us of these emotional issues through the model that we'll be presenting in the final chapters of the book. Indeed, in these times very few churches are equipped to offer our blood bought healing. Our freedom is promised and paid for; we just have to access it.

The example of autoimmune disease

Autoimmune disease ranks as the third most common type of disease in the U.S.A. with approximately 1 in 12 people, or more than 8% of the population being affected.

As a reference to the negative emotions that are often found behind various diseases and syndromes, I have utilised a book by Henry W Wright, titled '*A More Excellent Way.*' First published in 1999, over the years I have found it to be a valuable resource with helpful insights. It was the first work of its kind that I'm aware of, going on to be a best seller in the U.S.A. and spawning other ministries that did their own research into the emotional roots of disease.

A number of years ago before his passing I had the privilege of meeting and chatting with Henry. He gave me permission to quote from his book, which I have confirmed with his publisher. I'll lean on his great work and findings as we go forward, his ministry having extensively dealt with many maladies, and citing good results and testimonies.

On the subject of autoimmune disease Henry makes this statement;
When we minister to someone with an autoimmune disease, we find without exception a degree of lacking self-esteem and/or guilt. A person has conflict with himself over his <u>identity</u>*, drivenness, performance, conflict and guilt, at some level causing an autoimmune disease.* [6] *(Underline emphasis mine)*

[6] *Dr. Henry W. Wright, "A More Excellent Way" (New Kensington, PA: Whitaker House, 2009), Pg 286 Used with permission. All rights reserved. www.whitakerhouse.com.*

In another part of his book, he explains what they've found with autoimmune cases that they've ministered to. We'll describe in a later chapter how to minister to these negative emotions and responses, realising that they're invariably stem from corrupted identity and a broken inner sense of self.

Even though the medical community now associates autoimmune diseases with fear, anxiety and stress, I have come to the conclusion that most autoimmune diseases are the result of an unloving spirit producing feelings of not being loved, not being accepted, self-rejection, self-hatred and self-bitterness coupled with guilt. In fact, it could be said that autoimmune diseases are primarily a self-hatred disease with a fear-anxiety-stress rider attached to them. [7]

We'll break these emotions and responses down in a later chapter. Autoimmune diseases will also be explained more fully when we discuss types of diseases, and how to resolve the beliefs that produce the negative emotions, along with the consequent attitudes and negative responses.

Let me note here that there is a great amount of research being done into the effects of negative emotions on your body. In practice you only need to get angry or bitter or sad or anxious to feel the chemical changes in your physiology as the corresponding hormones are released. And in practical terms, even without the research it should be reasonably obvious that if you remain in these states you are going to create weaknesses and a breakdown in the harmony of your physical systems that eventually are going to destroy your health.

Wholeness and healing
In a model that is based on coming to wholeness, disease is therefore largely resolved through the process of sanctification.

[7] Wright, "A More Excellent Way," Pg 210

This process is one of being restored in regards to truth about your identity, who God really is and how He sees you. At times this includes receiving freedom from certain fears and anxieties coming from situations in critical events. For this reason, improvement and healing is at times to the degree that sanctification through receiving truth is ministered to the different problem areas that are implicated.

In an earlier chapter in Part 1 we described how positionally everything has been paid for through the sacrifice of Christ Jesus. So, through redemption we're entitled to healing and freedom. Through this work on the cross God sees us as perfect. He sees us, through Christ, without our sins, bad behaviour and negative attitudes. The Father sees who we 'really are' without our issues. The problem is usually how we see ourselves. In the following passage taken from Hebrews chapter 10 we see both redemption, and sanctification. Redemption and being perfected and made right with the Father is positioned as past tense, but the process of being sanctified is continuing present tense.

> *Hebrews 10:14*
> *For by one offering He has perfected forever those who are being sanctified. NKJV (emphasis mine)*

God sees us in Christ, and through Jesus without our problems. But it's a continuing work of the Holy Spirit through sanctification to restore our identity and self-worth allowing us to see ourselves as our creator does. As a result of 'the fall', we have been deceived about who we really are, sanctification then, is a healing journey into wholeness benefitting our entire person. A large part of this process is coming to see ourselves as God sees us, having His truth about us, as opposed to our own distorted picture. It is a work of the Spirit of truth to facilitate this restoration in our lives.

> *John 16:13*
> *"However, when He, the Spirit of truth, has come, He will guide you into all truth. NKJV*

We observe from scripture that the process of sanctification is mediated by displacing deception with truth. When we receive truth in this journey it will always be aligned with the word of God.

John 17:17
"Sanctify them by Your truth. Your word is truth". NKJV

The benefits of this model are the improvements of the whole person, not just the healing of the body. Relationship with God based on truth is restored. A true knowledge of one's own person and identity replaces striving or some kind of self-effort to create an identity perceived as worthy of self-acceptance. So, spiritually you end up free, mentally you are at peace, emotionally you are happy, and physically you are chemically balanced, and consequently less prone to other illnesses.

14

The Human Identity and Disease

The 'state of being' and <u>characteristics of humanity</u> had now changed as a result of 'the fall'. The fundamental qualities of who mankind were meant to be was <u>altered because their priorities, choices</u> and what they decided that they wanted had now changed.... their priorities and choices were now the lust of the eyes, the lust of the flesh, and the pride of life. Now what they were all about as people became <u>living</u> for these things. Living for SELF, rather than living to be <u>in relationship with God</u>, *pleasing, serving* and obeying Him.... now it was about pleasing SELF. We could say; You align yourself with whatever you decide to follow.

This imprint and influence from the character of Satan distorted the <u>'identity'</u> that God had given them. Your <u>identity</u> is the characteristics that <u>identify</u> you.... particularly in terms of your perception of SELF and self-worth. This relates to who you think you are, and your perceived image of self. In other words, how *'you see you!'* This self-image was now no longer established and certain in God's truth – they had followed deception, and now were deceived, insecure, and uncertain about who they were, and their worthiness.

Now the identity of mankind was corrupted. In a sense who you think you are, as a result of *'the fall'* is no longer accurate. It is tainted, not completely true. But as a result of deceptive influences, it's true to you. The Bible indicates that your image of SELF dictates your state of being! This is powerful in terms of predicting behaviour, attitudes and responses. It appears from the Bible, and our many years of experience ministering to peoples' identities, that these beliefs about SELF are now stored in our 'hearts.'

These inner beliefs have implications for how we live and respond to life. As the old saying goes: *'It's not what you think you are, but what you think, you are!'* It relates to our perceived state of being.

> Proverbs 23:7
> *"For as he thinks in his heart, so is he."* NKJV*

Some Bible versions translate this verse differently for some reason, when this rendering is clearly present in the original Hebrew text.

In an earlier chapter we indicated that the word 'heart' is used in the New King James version 833 times, whereas the 'mind' is only mentioned 90 times. There is good reason for the Bible giving the 'heart' pre-eminence of position because of its influence on the human condition. Above all else, means that it's the most important thing for you to do. Guard your 'heart,' in a large measure means; protect what shapes your perceived conclusions about your characteristics.... what you believe about you, and how you see SELF. This distorted picture of identity is largely the power behind the fallen nature which is causing imbalances in our internal workings, and influencing us to continue to follow what Satan offers. (1 John 5:19)

This is so important, and probably a new concept for many, so let me reiterate, the heart as revealed in scripture according to the very reputable *Strong's Concordance* means:

*2588. kardia; the heart, i.e. (fig.) the **thoughts or feelings** (mind); also (by anal.) **the middle**: --(+ broken-) heart (-ed) (emphasis mine).*

Whether the Old Testament or the New Testament, the 'heart' is considered to be thoughts from your centre or middle which affect your mind, and consequently your feelings and finally your decisions. (Your will.) Very significantly, your 'heart' holds beliefs which produce thoughts that in turn affect your thinking, attitudes and even your motives for what you will to do.

> Hebrews 4:12
> For the word of God is living and active. Sharper than any double-edged sword, it penetrates even to dividing soul and spirit, joints and marrow; it judges <u>the thoughts</u> and <u>attitudes</u> of the heart. NIV (emphasis mine)

> Proverbs 4:23
> Above all else, guard your heart, for it affects everything you do. NLT

Mechanics of disease and identity

I would estimate that probably 90 to 95% of the ministry that we do setting people free relates to beliefs that they hold in their 'hearts' about their identity. The other 5 to 10% is to do with things believed about traumatic, or deeply emotional situations that they've been exposed to. When we talk about mental and emotional disorders, or disease, we consistently find that these upsets begin with conflict about identity, and how we see and perceive ourselves. This sets the scene for how we may negatively respond to others that we consider to be attacking our image of self.

As we've repeatedly highlighted, the experts tell us that behind disease, almost 90% of the time, conflicted mental and emotional states are implicated. All of us were born under the influence of 'the fall', so every person has a tendency to misinterpret their identity. It's worth noting that often pride is the result of us building an image of ourselves that we consider to be more than worthy in comparison to others. So, this element of our fallen nature, which is made in the image of Satan, is usually engineered from a self-perception of inferiority and low self-image. It's our own attempt to deal with the feelings coming from what we really believe about our identities, underneath in our hearts.

So, when people challenge this self-created, supposedly acceptable image, we react with some kind of negative response. Perhaps, anger, resentment, jealousy or rejection of the other person. But remember, they're touching negative beliefs that you already hold about yourself. You may then in turn find yourself being angry, rejective, and resentful of who you truly consider yourself to be.

In much the same way you may exhibit rebellion as a behaviour of the old nature. Generally, it's a response or reaction to perceived unfairness or injustice. For example, as reaction to a common internal 'heart belief' imprinted early in life such as; 'nobody cares about me,' will produce some kind of negative emotion and response. It could be bitterness or anger, along with the rebellion and not wanting to work with others in relationship.

Ungodly control of others is another fruit of the fallen nature. It is usually in place because people are insecure for some reason. Perhaps they never felt loved or cared about. They now make sure that people love and care about them. Or they believe that they won't be provided for because deep inside they believe that they don't really matter, are not significant, valuable or important. So, they make sure that they're provided for, or treated as significant, perhaps by getting people to do things for them.

The fruit belies the real problem. But along with the fruit, there will be anxieties present which will eventually be implicated in physical conditions. These are just a few examples. You can see how we may well feel justified in responding in these ways to our perceptions of how we think people are treating us. Even though they're usually touching into, or triggering beliefs about self that are already programmed into us in early life. We deceive ourselves that it is not sin to hold responses producing attitudes of unforgiveness, bitterness, retaliation, ungodly anger, rejection of others and so on.

> *Jeremiah 17:9-10*
> ⁹ *"The heart is deceitful above all things, And desperately wicked; Who can know it?* ¹⁰ *I, the LORD, search the* <u>*heart*</u>, *I test the mind, Even to give every man according to his ways, According to the fruit of his doings". NKJV (emphasis mine)*

Notably the Hebrew word *'aqob,'* is translated here as deceitful to describe the condition of the heart, also could be rendered polluted. This underlines the message that we're trying to convey about the corrupted beliefs that we hold about ourselves in our middle or centre. This can be found all through the scriptures, and is the basis of the disorder in our humanity corporately and personally that is foundational to our problems.

In the final chapters we will cover how to restore the broken, or out of order inner thinking that proceeds from identity beliefs in the 'heart.' We will learn how to dismantle this deceived nature by establishing God's truth in the new heart that we are given in God's regeneration package, and consequently minister God's restoration into the new nature. (Ezekiel 36:26-27) There are a number of words translated as heal, or healing in the New Testament. A component of most of these words is to bring to wholeness.

In the case of Luke 4:18 and healing the broken hearted, the Greek word used is *'Iaomai.'* So, generally to heal or bring to wholeness the broken heart means to restore the fallen identity through God's truth being received in the 'heart.' This is a work of the Spirit of Truth, communicating to the person. This occurs once what a person believes about their identity is established and identified. This healing cannot normally be achieved by counselling, teaching, preaching, reading the word, deliverance or medication. How this is achieved in practice is covered in these later chapters.

- He Still Heals Those Who Need Healing -

15

How Then Does Disease Result From *'the fall'*?

We now can understand the outcome of *'the fall'* for mankind as being the genesis, or beginning of all kinds of suffering. Once they knew good and evil, they knew that they had done wrong. The negative emotions of guilt, shame and condemnation now entered their lives. Also, what they had done opened the way to conflict within themselves. Knowing that they'd transgressed God's instructions their 'hearts' condemned them. (Romans 8:1 NKJV, 1 John 3:20) Significantly and importantly, this was the origin of mankind many times no longer liking and accepting themselves. It was a beginning point for self-rejection. Although unredeemed humanity is trying to convince themselves that this is not the case, when we do the wrong thing, most people still don't like them-selves for it. This inner rejection of self is the basis of much mental disorder, emotional imbalance, ungodly responses and broken relationships, along with eventual disease and sin.

Let's illustrate how this results in disease with a couple of examples from Henry W. Wright explaining what happens when self-rejection becomes extreme.

The only way to be healed from rheumatoid arthritis and other autoimmune diseases is to accept yourself once and for all and to get the self-hatred, the guilt, the lack of self-esteem and the junk out of your life. [7]

In another place he comments about what they've found behind the common condition of Crohn's disease; (a chronic inflammatory autoimmune disease); [Most autoimmune diseases cause inflammation.]

The root behind Crohn's disease is extreme self-rejection coupled with guilt. Crohn's also has a component of hopelessness because the individual does not know how to solve the problem over which they're tribulating. There is a lot of conflict built into it. Crohn's disease is a disease coming out of massive rejection, abandonment, lack of self-esteem and/or drivenness to meet the expectation of another. In fact, Crohn's disease involves a great degree of codependency and false burden bearing. [8]

It begins in a mind influenced by a corrupted sense of identity. These negative self-beliefs will be found recorded in the 'heart.' In turn this creates a lack of ease or peace in the thinking, which outworks as imbalanced emotions, and finishes in the body as dis-ease. Sin is often mankind's attempt to compensate for, or a solution to, dealing with how he feels about himself underneath.

It's important to reinforce that knowing that they'd done wrong mankind no longer liked they saw themselves, or at least who they now perceived themselves to be. That is, who they thought they were because of what they had done. Humanity now had a distorted, corrupted and polluted self-image. Mankind now didn't see themselves as God saw them. Many times, this is going on unconsciously, and we live behind a mask, acting as if we're doing alright, and trying to convince ourselves and others that we are.

---

[7] Wright, "A More Excellent Way," Page 228
[8] Wright, "A More Excellent Way," Page 225

Compounding this, when we do the wrong thing by following the old nature, we know that something isn't right, and inside we don't like ourselves even more.

We can confirm through many years of ministry that; confusion about identity, along with self-rejection are behind many mental disorders, emotional imbalances, and eventual disease. Your 'heart' beliefs about SELF cause negative thinking. What you think becomes a feeling or emotions which are elaborated or felt in the body by the release of chemicals called hormones and neurotransmitters, along with signals sent by electrical currents. When these are imbalanced, the final outworking is in the body, or outer man. So, a lack of ease in regards to perceived identity or particular situations imprinted in the 'heart,' becomes dis-ease in the physical body.

Rejecting God and disease

Mankind accepted Satan, and in doing so rejected God. Having removed themselves from under God's Lordship they now feared not being accepted by God. The result of this was that underneath mankind often now;

....no longer feels accepted, so rejection entered our lineage. When you don't feel acceptable you fear rejection, and may even reject yourself, which is self-rejection. These anxieties and negative attitudes towards self, produce negative emotions and responses that are behind many diseases and much mental conflict. Fear of rejection of some kind is far and away the most common type of anxiety. You can avoid flying if that is your fear. But if it's fear of rejection from people because of what you believe about yourself, it is a continuous and most times unavoidable condition. Fear and anxiety will be a component of many diseases, contributing with other negative feelings to the onset of specific diseases.

....no longer felt secure in God's love – so we became anxious, fear entered, and unredeemed mankind as a generalisation is now expecting harm of some kind as punishment and judgement. (1 John 4:18)

....is prone to low self-image; because inside we're not liking and accepting who we are, mainly because as a result of 'the fall' we believe that we're less than we should be, having given up our high place of service and relationship with God. We now innately have an inborn sense of inferiority, injustice, insecurity.

These feelings and anxieties leave us vulnerable to continue to accept Satan's deceptive solutions for these issues. We want to raise ourselves up in pride to compensate for our low self-image. We rebel against authority and perceived injustice, preferring to be 'our own god.' We seek to control our environment to make ourselves feel secure. Perhaps we look to sin against our own bodies and self-worth in the form of; devaluing ourselves in immorality, masking our pain with drugs that eventually damage our bodily organs, or excessive alcohol or even overeating. Thus, our distorted sense of identity opens us to continuing in, and perpetuating the old fallen nature.

Let's note here that often people expect punishment because inside they may now believe that they are inherently bad, that they fall short, that they're not doing enough or being enough. This leads to GUILT which can be founding working in with other negative emotions in disease profiles. Under *'the fall'* you have been programmed to believe that there is something about your identity and person that is not right. So now you expect and fear rejection. We have to have God's perspective and love for freedom! (1 John 4:18) This was the entry point for the basic problems that we suffer with as a result: it opened the door to new dynamics and mental, emotional, relational and behavioural issues, along with altered spiritual and physical dynamics.

> *1 John 4:18 Such love has no fear because perfect love expels all fear. If we are afraid, it is for fear of judgment, and this shows that his love has not been perfected in us. NLT*

They were no longer okay with what they believed about themselves, or the situation that they now found themselves in.

Who did this affect? Everybody from *'the fall'* on was born under these influences. Everyone has the tendency to misinterpret their 'identity' and be fearful in emotionally charged situations and circumstances. In part, this is because we have been deceived about God, His goodness, kindness and love. The question in ministry is where did it begin for you as an individual?

The importance of formative years

This means that as people growing up, as a generalisation, every person was prone to misinterpret their identity in a negative way! This is an important key to healing. For example, Gideon. (Judges 6:12-15) In verse 12 the LORD calls him *'a mighty man of valour.'* Remember God is the only one who knows our true identity. Gideon responded in verse 15 with who he believed in his 'heart' that he was. *"I am the least in my father's house."* He'd learnt this from someone. It was the conclusion that he'd come to through how he was dealt with, regarded, and possibly spoken to growing up. He had to hear truth from God about who he really was in order to be whole, free, and reach his potential. This is how identity healing, and freedom comes for us all.

We now see how these negative emotions and responses found their way into the lives of mankind. It was never what God wanted or intended for us. He did not put disease on mankind, we opened the way for it ourselves by coming out from under His protective covering. In the next chapter we'll look at God's plan for how the restoration and revival of humanity, spirit, soul and body is to take place. It includes our healing and freedom, but is far greater in scope than those alone. His plan includes a full relationship with Him, along with wholeness and health in our own person.

Following is a list of the emotions and reactions to our environ-ment that create stressors for our sense of identity and security which, either in isolation, or identifiable in groups, have been documented as being behind diseases.

Anger – Self anger
Anxiety – fear/stress/insecurity
Bitterness – Resentment/rebellion
Depression – hopelessness
Envy – Jealousy
Guilt – shame (Performance anxiety, drivenness)
Grief – sadness/sorrow
Inferiority – Low self-image/esteem
Rejection – self-rejection – fear of rejection – self-conflict

If these are the problems behind our conditions, then we need to ask questions to find out why they're present in us such as:

What do you reject/hate about yourself?

What are you anxious/stressed/fearful or insecure about?

Why do you feel guilty? What about?

What is making you angry, resentful, bitter or conflicted?

Why do you feel inferior, or have low self-image – what do you believe is wrong with you?

16

God's Plan of Restoration and Wholeness

Because in scripture sin and sickness are linked, the best means of achieving and promoting health, and preventing and defending against disease, is establishing the Kingdom of God within us through the process of restoration.
Psalm 103:2, Mark 2:3-11

> *Psalm 103:2-4*
> *² Praise the LORD, O my soul, and forget not all his benefits- ³ who forgives all your sins and heals all your diseases, ⁴ who redeems your life from the pit and crowns you with love and compassion. NIV*

Recap and review

As I have previously explained, in the New Testament the word in the Greek usually translated as the 'flesh,' or 'sinful nature,' is '*Sarx*' which = the Satan <u>influenced and programmed</u> version of you! The old fallen nature, imprinted with his characteristics, attitudes and behaviour. Pride, rebellion, control, SELF seeking. *Sin began with him.* His '<u>heart</u>' was corrupted and it distorted his own created identity.

Mankind was created **originally** in God's image. The **new nature** which God imputes to us at conversion is the <u>beginning</u> of **a restoration** to this image. The new nature <u>looks like God</u>, seeded by Him, birthed by His design, and moves towards fullness once He is submitted to and we accept His Lordship.
Romans 8:29, Ephesians 4:13

Let us now examine couple of things that we need to consider that are the result of the introduction of the fallen nature:

Man was formerly secure in answering the following questions – they were centred in our original identity. Now confused under deception, uncertain.

Who am I?   How does God see me?

Am I acceptable, significant, worthy, valuable, worth something?

What am I here for? (Purpose)   What should I be doing? (Mission)

Where do I belong? (Where do I fit into the Kingdom on Earth - what is our specific 'tribe?' or place of operation.)

When ministering to people you will find over and over that many believe that they're worthless, have no value, no significance, are not cared about, are rejected and so on – all require a restoration of identity from Father God through the work of the Spirit of Truth. What we term 'compensating behaviour' is when, as your 'own god,' and own provision, you now seek to prove that you're worth something, acceptable, valuable. You attempt to convince yourself you're as good or better than others etc. (Or you attempt to mask or deny your issues with lusts, addictions, the pleasures of the world, wealth, success etc.) These 'do it yourself' attempts are the grounds for the old nature to flourish, and they mostly come from beliefs about identity sourced in the 'heart.'

In Johns Gospel we see Jesus make this statement.

> John 14:30
> *"I will no longer talk much with you, for the ruler of this world is coming, and he has <u>nothing in Me</u>. NKJV (emphasis mine)*

Jesus was the 1st person since Adam not born with a fallen nature, so He is stating that Satan has no power over Him to manipulate Him or deceive Him as he does with the rest of humanity. The reason? He has nothing 'in' Me! No deception about His identity. Jesus knew exactly who He was, He'd heard directly that the Father was pleased with Him, and He clearly knew what His mission was. In fact, His purpose in coming to earth was to introducing grace, (which for us means redemption and forgiveness) and truth. (Which is the basis of sanctification, healing and wholeness) John 1:14

> John 1:17
> For the law was given through Moses, but _grace_ and _truth_
> came through Jesus Christ. NKJV (emphasis mine)

For mankind the basis of faith – that is 'trust' in God's person and character was now distorted. As we progress in sanctification and healing, we go from faith to faith. Romans 1:17 NKJV

True faith comes through a true and right picture of God, and this picture was now corrupted through deception by what Satan was implying about Him. Something like;

'God's the bad guy, I'm the good guy....I'd let you eat from the tree.'

Our ability to receive by faith has a lot to do with us having a correct picture of our own identity and what we believe about ourselves. If we judge ourselves as unworthy for some reason, or not good enough, we don't expect God's love, acceptance, approval or supply. So, we could say that we unconsciously tend to incorrectly conclude that God regards us through the deceptive picture of how we now see ourselves. Consequently, beliefs about our unworthiness, fear of rejection, low self-image, guilt, and even our inner self-rejection affect our faith.

We unconsciously expect that God views us as we see ourselves, even though we may be unaware of what we really believe about our identity. We see that King David arrived at this place in the

Old Testament, and sought God's help to understand his internal workings.

> Psalm 139:23-24
> [23] Search me, O God, and know <u>my heart</u>; test me and know <u>my thoughts</u>. [24] Point out anything in me that offends you, and lead me along the path of everlasting life. NLT (emphasis mine)

In the New Testament in we see the Apostle Paul also perplexed about these influences coming from his old fallen nature, and the conflict that this causes with his born again spirit influenced new nature.

> Romans 7: 15
> [15] I do not understand what I do. For what I want to do I do not do, but what I hate I do.[16] And if I do what I do not want to do, I agree that the law is good. [17] As it is, it is no longer I myself who do it, but it <u>is sin</u> living in me.
> [18] I know that nothing good lives in me, that is, in my <u>sinful nature</u>.(Sarx) For I have the desire to do what is good, but I cannot carry it out. NIV (emphasis and Sarx insertion mine)

God's process of restoration and personal revival

It's appropriate to round out our study on the introduction of many physical conditions, via the fallen nature, by including God's plan to return humanity to spiritual connection with Himself. His intentions and priorities are also to make us whole by restoring our identity through receiving His truth. So, now understanding the implications of 'the fall' we can comprehend two important elements that needed to be addressed for the revival of mankind to relationship with God, along with the restoration of our persons to His likeness.

The human spirit had been cut off from direct relationship with God, and needed to be regenerated. And the identity of man was corrupted in our hearts. Consequently, we find these 2 key elements relating to the revival of humanity, and the consequent return to wholeness. The <u>human spirit</u>, and the <u>human heart</u>.

God's plan is all about the revival and restoration of the people that He created -

> Isaiah 57:15
> For thus says the High and Lofty One Who inhabits eternity, whose name is Holy: "I dwell in the high and holy place, With him who has a contrite and humble spirit, To <u>revive</u> **the spirit** of the humble, And to revive **the heart** of the contrite ones. NKJV (emphasis mine)

So, why do we need to be revived, and <u>what from</u>? We need to be revived from spiritual death and the effects and imprint of the old nature on our identity at 'heart' level. The Old Testament word for revive/revival is 'Chayah' which means to <u>make alive</u>, <u>recover</u>, <u>repair</u>, <u>restore</u>, <u>be whole</u>.

God's remedy for 'the fall'

God has promised to reset the lives of those who want to turn away from Satan and back to Himself through faith in Jesus Christ. The process entails being supernaturally given a new human spirit that is reborn, or born again. A human spirit that was not born in the natural way under the influence of the natural fallen world, but rather born of the promise of God. John 3:3-8, Galatians 4:22-26, 28-31

Formerly mankind had rejected God, now the way to return to Him is to accept Him again through His offer to pay for our sin through the sacrifice of Jesus Christ. God's rescue plan is to reintroduce Himself and His nature into our lives. God is a Spirit, and so the first stage of restoration is to have our human spirit reconnected in relationship with Him. We accept Him as Lord, and worship Him as God, which is something that our fallen nature did not want to do. Mankind had initially preferred to follow another spirit, and under that influence we all unwittingly chose to be our own god. Ephesians 2:1-3

John 4:23-24
²³ Yet a time is coming and has now come when the true worshipers will worship the Father in <u>spirit</u> and <u>truth</u>, for they are the kind of worshipers the Father seeks. ²⁴ God is spirit, and his worshipers must <u>worship in spirit</u> and <u>in truth</u>." NIV (emphasis mine)

Because God is Spirit our point of contact and relationship is our human spirit relating to Him as Spirit. We note from John 4:24 that we worship – or lift Him up as God – through our spirit, but also in truth. This truth relates to a knowledge of who He is, but also being made new in the truth of who we really are. I would propose that our human spirit receives this truth at conversion, but our broken hearts require healing, which is the process of sanctification by truth. And our minds need to be renewed in knowledge of God and the ways of His Kingdom.

God's' promised method of restoration

Ezekiel 36:26
*"I will give you **a new heart** and put **a new spirit** within you; I will take the heart of stone out of your flesh and give you a heart of flesh. 27 "I will put **<u>My Spirit</u>** within you and cause you to walk in My statutes, and you will keep My judgments and do them. NKJV (emphasis mine)*

We observe from this passage that God replaces our 'hearts' that were hard towards Him. He gives us a 'new human spirit' which is again connected to Him. And in verse 27 He indicates that He will then put His own Spirit in us.
1 Corinthians 6:17

So now we have a new <u>soft heart</u> that is open to God's workings to bring about change, but we have a problem! The introduction of this new nature doesn't automatically delete the old nature. So, now we have 2 natures in one person. This means conflict. The power of the old nature is largely driven by <u>identity beliefs</u> programmed into the human 'heart.' These need to be sanctified by truth which is an ongoing process. (Hebrews 10:14) But our hearts are now soft and receptive to the work of the Holy Spirit. King David longed for his own heart to be recreated, understanding that it was the root of his issues.

> Psalm 51:5-6,10
> ⁵ Surely I was sinful at birth, sinful from the time my mother conceived me. ⁶ Surely you desire truth in the _inner parts_ ;(sometimes translated heart – certainly referencing the human soul of which the heart is the central point) you teach me wisdom in _the inmost place_. (By implication his human spirit)
> ¹⁰ Create in me a **pure heart**, (see James 4:7)
> O God, and renew a steadfast spirit within me.
> NIV (emphasis and inserted comments mine)

In the book of James, we see the necessity to deal with deliberate deeds and sinful acts, (wash your hands), and to purify your hearts as the means of dealing with your double-mindedness, and unstable mental conditions. The Greek word here translated as purify is; 'hagnizo', which means – sanctify, to make clean, to purify.

> James 4:8
> Come near to God and he will come near to you. Wash your hands, you sinners, and _purify_ your hearts, you double-minded. NIV (emphasis mine)

Permit me to reiterate. Once God reintroduces relationship with His nature to revive mankind, and begins the process of returning us to wholeness, we have conflict! Now we have 2 competing natures imposing themselves on our freewill and choice. 2 natures seeking to have a manifestation through us to represent their respective kingdoms in the earth.

> Galatians 5:17
> The _sinful nature_ wants to do evil, which is just the opposite of _what the Spirit wants_. And the Spirit gives us desires that are the opposite of what the sinful nature desires. _These two forces are constantly fighting each other,_

so that you are not free to carry out your good intentions.
NLT (emphasis mine)

Summary

The process of sanctification is a journey into wholeness, and restoration back into the likeness and image of God. (Romans 8:29, Ephesians 4:12) The new nature is imputed through regeneration and having our human spirit reborn. We receive a new soft heart that is open to the healing influences of the Spirit of truth. How we may choose to behave is transformed by knowing God's ways through the renewal of our minds. Romans 12:2

We continue to work with the Holy Spirit, personally on Sanctification, and corporately on the priorities and Mission of the gospel, qualified for this on the basis of redemption. Ephesians 2:10, Isaiah 58:6-9

The Condition and Universal Church Focus

A LOT of ministry to this area (Evangelism etc.)

A LOT of ministry to this area

BORN AGAIN
(A new human spirit)

MIND RENEWAL
Teaching / Preaching

SPIRIT FILLED
Ezekiel 36:26-27

TRAINING
Resources

PHYSICAL HEALING

HEALING THE BROKEN-HEARTED

GIFTS OF THE SPIRIT

SETTING THE CAPTIVES FREE

A LOT of ministry to this area

ALMOST NO ministry to this area (Neglected)*

THE MAIN MINISTRY OF JESUS WAS TO HEAL THE
BROKEN-HEARTED AND TO SET THE CAPTIVES FREE!
*HEART = THOUGHTS & FEELINGS COMING FROM YOUR CENTRE

Part **3**

MINISTRY
TO EMOTIONALLY
ROOTED DIESASE

As we progress through Part 3, we will examine common diseases that are typically associated with, and rooted in negative emotions and responses. This will be in the form of; if you have this disease, you can expect that your inner beliefs have produced emotional profiles such as this or that. As we examine these illnesses in isolation we'll be leaning heavily on the excellent work of Dr. Henry W. Wright.

We know from many years of experience referencing his work, that his conclusions are usually fairly accurate. This has been confirmed to us over and over in the ministry room working through peoples' issues and the resulting conditions that they suffer with. Further confirmations and reinforcing of his experience, insights and research have come in prayer lines, where someone tells us of the particular disease that they suffer from. I then proceed to explain the negative emotions that they likely struggle with that will need to be dealt with. They often look at me amazed thinking that I'm having a word of knowledge, when in fact I'm bringing a word 'from' knowledge.

In these instances, not having the opportunity to work through healing of these emotional problems, we still pray for, and expect healing of their condition/s. We do encourage them to seek help to resolve these emotional issues and their corresponding reactions, in order to prevent them either having a relapse of their problem, or developing something else.

Next, having seen the need to understand the negative emotions commonly cited as being behind diseases, I want to spend several chapters working through, and explaining the mechanics and foundations of these emotions.

And finally, in the last chapters we will share how to completely resolve and be free from these negative emotions and responses. This comes about through the ministry of the Holy Spirit and not your own human effort. Our part in the process is accepting what we hold as being true about ourselves, and then co-operating with Him in being open to receive His truth.

As we've already cited, 60% of adults in the U.S. have at least 1 Chronic condition, and 4 in 10 adults reportedly have 2 or more chronic diseases. Very often these conditions are sourced in the same negative emotional states along with the predictable consequent negative attitudes and responses behind them. I recall one lady that we ministered to who had a variety of emotional issues. Mostly these came from self-beliefs that she held about herself as the result of rejection. She suffered from arthritis, asthma, cancer, chronic fatigue syndrome, thyroid problems, migraines, and had developed a large tumour.

She now has none of these diseases and is quite healthy. We did not pray for, and she had no prayer from anyone else for any of the conditions mentioned. These illnesses simply resolved after ministry into the 'heart beliefs' that she held. These self-beliefs almost exclusively related to her identity, and the resultant emotional healing proceeded from a re-ordered inner thought life.

In the next portion of this book, we're going to examine what are considered to be the emotional pathways to various common physical conditions. You will note that these will relate to negative emotions and their corresponding responses and attitudes.

In order to understand how to resolves these problems you will need to visit the ministry model chapters in the later part of the book. You will then need to begin to work through the origins of these imbalances.

We've already noted that we have not personally ministered to every condition that is going to be listed. We have however successfully ministered directly to every emotion, attitude and reaction listed, week in week out for decades. And we've consistently seen them resolved by the work of the Holy Spirit.

At times we've used the knowledge about the root causes that we have to target and undermine the sickness. At other times people have presented with mental or emotional problems and not even mentioned that they also have had a physical condition. Later we've heard that they've had a physical healing of some kind as a result of dealing with the issues that they've presented with.

So, in this final section we'll be leaning on the experience, re-search, and ministries of others who have been doing great work in this area. We greatly appreciate and acknowledge the insights and knowledge that they've collated as a result of their personal experience in ministry. I thoroughly recommend the excellent materials and resources that we'll be referencing for further study.

Along with these there may be medical or scientific articles that we'll be referring to. We thank God for this work of the doctors and researchers that has helped many, and helps us understand what needs to be ministered to for health and healing. I read a comment from a high-profile doctor recently about his frustration with the medical community. He was troubled because the medical world is largely fragmented into specialty areas, and doctors often have limited knowledge beyond their own area of training. This relates to Christian ministry as well, to be successful we certainly need to piece together the whole picture.

One of the main purposes that I have in writing this book is to build on the work of others by introducing the very effective ministry model that we'll present in final chapters. It is the most effective and complete way that we've found to resolve the docu-mented negative emotions and responses that are considered to be behind disease.

It differs from other ministries that we know of, in that it does not involve self-effort, only cooperation with the Holy Spirit who brings complete healing, freedom and wholeness, fulfilling the promises and delivering the provisions of God. We want to share it so that many more can be helped in their journey to accept and receive the help that God has intended for them.

It can be distressing to see people encouraged to 'free themselves.' When in fact in most of these cases complete freedom can 'only' come through the work of the Holy Spirit, most often through trained ministries. Romans chapter 6:11 says that we should consider ourselves dead to acting out in sin. So, our part is to want to stop any sinful emotional expressions and responses. But it doesn't say consider yourself dead to mental or emotional problems, because many times you don't know where they're coming from. As if you could fix them yourself without God. We've found that we are healed by His abilities, and it's our cooperation with Him and the commitment of our will to His processes that brings healing.

Unfortunately, we've seen far too many Christian people unnecessarily get disease because they didn't believe in the origins and pathways of these conditions, or didn't seek ministry for their emotional states because of ignorance, or because the church they attend is untrained, or some other reason. You cannot afford to deceive yourself that you can continue with your issues, and somehow, they won't play out in your body.

Finally, we don't have the space to tell stories about every illness that we're about to discuss. I will mention a few here and there to help the reader to get the general idea of how negative emotions play out in disease profiles.

Note 1: Terms that I use throughout this publication such as; 'heart beliefs,' 'self-beliefs,' 'identity-beliefs,' 'inner beliefs,' or even, 'unconscious thoughts,' are interchangeable. I use them in order to not be too repetitive. They all refer to beliefs that are learnt in the formative time beginning from prenatal times in the womb, through to around 10 years of age.

It is in this period that beliefs about identity, and at times conclusions in regard to emotionally charged or traumatic situations become a fixed part of our operating system, and our default beliefs. After this we tend to interpret life and respond to our environments through these beliefs. These, often unconscious negative 'heart beliefs' then influence our thinking, which mediates our emotions, and finally ends in our bodies as disease.

Note 2: Our earthly identity, or how we identify ourselves, is largely formed by God's 'father image representatives' on earth – our fathers. They are to cover us and represent God to us. Unlike God, because they themselves may still be functioning in the old nature, they may be; selfish, absent, busy, critical, abusive, unfair, ignoring etc. We generally have a God picture that is based on how our earthly fathers, and to a lesser degree our mothers or other authority figures dealt with us. Typically, fathers impute identity, whereas mothers provide nurture. Together they're intended to supply an accurate picture of the nature of God.

17

Glossary of Common Conditions

Most often we are safe to make the statement that in regard to physical and mental conditions that everything starts with a thought. That is, a thought that is shaped and influenced by a negative belief held about self and identity in your heart.

So, what you're looking for in order to dismantle what is behind your condition, is what you have believed about yourself that has made you; angry, bitter, reject yourself, anxious, fearful and so on. Deliberately changing your attitudes once you understand the root of the problem can help. For example, stop rejecting yourself, or being resentful. And it should be a normal part of the Christian life to repent (which mean's to: 'change your thinking, reconsider your ways') and align yourself with the nature of God.

However, the most complete, maintenance free, and effective way to deal with it is to deal with the root behind the problem, and be set free from the effects of the belief that produces the emotional issue to begin with.

By way of illustration, I knew a man who would get very angry with certain people. I cautioned him to curb his anger or he was a candidate for a stroke. Eventually he did have a small stroke which frightened him enough that he didn't let himself get too angry anymore. The point is, they still triggered him, and he still got angry. So, it wasn't resolved, just controlled and minimalised. And whilst there was a behaviour change, he's not healed. It requires his continuous efforts to not let the anger become too much. This is 2nd best to resolving the anger completely.

So, as we begin to examine the sources of disease, be aware that self-effort and behaviour modification have limitations. But when Following are the sources, or Etiology, of diseases as accepted and observed by various credible Christian commentators and ministries.

(Etiology = the cause, set of causes, or manner of causation of a disease or condition)

ORIGINS OF COMMON DISEASES AND CONDITIONS

Allergies

It is considered that your immune system becomes compromised when your system is stressed by fears and anxieties over a protracted period of time. Allergic reactions are cited as causing inflammatory responses throughout your body. This inflammation is described as an exaggerated or hypersensitive response to substances called allergens. Why does one person have a response to certain things, and the person beside them does not. Because the other person does not have the hypersensitivity that proceeds from the anxieties, fears, and stresses that the allergic person carries.

I ministered to a man recently who had anxiety that was related to a belief that he held as a result of a rejective event in childhood. He didn't mention allergies as a problem when he came for ministry, so that was not his presenting issue. After ministry, when he went home, he mowed his lawn, and was amazed that he didn't have a response to what ended up in the air when he cut his grass.

A lady that I ministered to for anxiety a number of years ago went home and picked up her cat whom she loved. To her amazement she didn't break out.

Another lady that I ministered to at the same training seminar kept getting every bug that was going around. She'd just get over one, and a few days later had another. As I recall, her anxiety was related to guilt about doing enough. Once it was resolved her immune system picked up and she no longer succumbed to everything that was going around.

The question is, 'what is making you anxious or fearful and keeping you stressed? Where did it begin?' These ministry examples of 'bi-product healing' were all coming from just one belief that they held. At times there may be several.

> Note: You can be healed of allergies in a prayer line through faith as well, or perhaps deliverance of something that is amplifying an anxiety.

Henry W Wright makes these comments regarding his findings in relation to allergies;

...the more we increase in fear and anxiety, the more the immune system is destroyed. The more the immune system is destroyed, the more we have an increase of allergies.
Wright, "A More Excellent Way," Pg 189.

Alzheimer's disease

Alzheimer's disease is considered to be a specific form of dementia characterised by memory loss and cognitive decline. Sufferers may become confused in regards to times and places. For example, where they are and how they got there. It is commonly found co-occurring with other conditions and disorders that share common root causes, such as; anxiety disorders, PTSD, depressive disorders, insomnia, delusional paranoia, emotional incontinence, and so on.

In addition, the sufferer may believe that people don't really care about them, are unfair, out to get them, and consequently become fearful and anxious in relationships. It appears that as the brain cells progressively deteriorate that the mental and emotional ability to hold in behaviours, attitudes, anxieties and beliefs imbibed in childhood becomes. This can result in the manifestation of childlike behaviour, (which is where the beliefs that are held were initially formed) such as; tantrums, mood changes, problems with vocabulary, and poor concentration or the ability to stay focussed on tasks. These are the kinds of behaviours that you would expect to see in young children.

At the time of writing, we've just heard a testimony of the healing of an elderly man that we know who was suffering with this disease. He was prayed for by member of a church that we're connected to, and following the prayer, his brain was scanned and found to be clear. Formerly the same type of scan had revealed structural changes in the brain which are now absent.

At this time my wife is also ministering to an elderly woman with the complaint. She has gone from extremely anxious, distressed, and full of negativity, to peaceful, calm and content with her situation. We're waiting to see if there are improvements in her working day to day memory.

I'm adding this disease profile to our study realising that along with disease in general, most times prevention is better than cure, and perhaps even more so in this instance. So, I'd like to encourage people to deal with the likely roots to the problem before the disease has taken hold.

I offer this next part in the hope that it helps in understanding the beginnings of this malady. My own observations of the people that I've been exposed to who have deteriorated with this disease, (who did not want ministry earlier – although it was offered), was a lot of self-rejection, anxiety and guilt, generally about not doing enough, or being enough to be worthy of acceptance. This suggests possibly a loveless childhood where the person did not receive validation. At times this could lead to an identity based around being what everyone else wants them to be.

Even later in life their personality presentation could be observed changing with environments, to being what they felt they needed to be for people to like them in those situations. But always unconsciously unsure of who they should be, and how they should be. The guilt component has seemingly come from beliefs that they're not doing enough, or being enough to receive love and acceptance. The anxiety will generally relate to being worried about how people regard you, and you'll be fearful of them accepting who you are. Along with rejecting yourself you may well resent others who don't seem to care about you – confirming your self-beliefs in regards to your worth, value, and significance.

So, if you find yourself excessively thinking or planning how you should present yourself or appear in certain environments, then chances are that you didn't grow up in an environment where you're your identity was established to be confident in who you believe that you are, and that it's okay to accept yourself. Seek ministry, and receive your freedom as early as possible.

Suggested roots of this disease by our experienced Christian commentator:
Self-hatred, guilt
Wright, "A More Excellent Way," Pg 260.

Other ministries also suggest that a loss of identity may be present. This would certainly tie in with at least a part of the anxiety and possible depression commonly associated with this disease. Reportedly, there's a growing body of research indicating a link between chronic stress, including anxiety, and increased levels of beta-amyloid, a protein that forms plaques in the brains of those with Alzheimer's disease.

Note: Alzheimer's disease is a specific type of dementia that causes a progressive cognitive decline in cognitive abilities, particularly memory. It is considered to be the most common cause of dementia, accounting for 60 – 70% of dementia cases.

Arthritis

Once again let me reiterate that God can heal in many ways. In our own ministry we've seen crippling arthritis healed by the power of God in a prayer line. We've also witnessed it being dealt with by ministering to distorted inner self-beliefs relating to peoples' identities. This is a process that the bible terms healing the broken hearted.

There are different kinds or categories of arthritis. Simple or basic arthritis is considered to stem from resentment and bitterness towards others. The most common forms of this disease are Osteoarthritis and Rheumatoid arthritis which is an autoimmune disease. Both of these versions of the disease share the negative attitude of self-rejection, even to the point of being bitter towards yourself, or even hating who you perceive that you are. You do not forgive yourself for the shortcomings that you have been programmed to believe that you have. The result is that you are angry with yourself for being, or not being who or what you think that you should be.

With people that we've ministered to, we've also observed that guilt usually will be present. This could be because you believe that you're not enough, or don't do enough. Or because you think that you've done something that you cannot be forgiven for. A person with this profile may well be full of self-conflict in regards to who or how they think that they should be to be acceptable. This is where fear and anxiety are involved in the profile, because many times sufferers are worried underneath that people will discover who they really are, and not accept them.

We have had cases where those afflicted create a persona, or a way that they want to appear to be acceptable to others. But this is in conflict with who they really perceive that they are. In these cases, there are often other co-existing physical conditions that appear.

We've already cited a case history where the daughter was set free of this self-anger and resentment, and had total healing of arthritis. This was now over 30 years ago with no recurrence. But the mother didn't seek healing for her inner beliefs and is now badly crippled with the malady.

As we've previously established, there will be anger and resentment towards self, but there will also be anger and resentment towards others who may be stirring up or triggering their damaged self-image in some way.

In ministry, you're looking for what it is that they believe about their identity inside, their belief about self, that they now reject. These 'heart beliefs' will be found being formed almost exclusively in rejection events beginning from as early as in the womb, and right up until around 10 years old.

Dr Wright considers that the causation behind Basic simple Arthritis involves *bitterness against others.* * Whereas he considers that; *Osteoarthritis is the result of self-bitterness and not forgiving one's self.* * As we'll explain in a later chapter where there is self-rejection of some kind you will usually find co-occurring emotions such as anger towards self and others. Fear and anxiety will usually also be present in the form of fear of rejection. This is as a result of what is believed about yourself that you expect others might reject you for. And this same self-perception is what causes you to reject yourself to the point of self-bitterness.

Rheumatoid arthritis is the autoimmune version of arthritis, which differs from the other forms of arthritis, in that it includes inflammation. This is mediated by both T and B immune cells which are white corpuscles that attack your own body and produce inflammation. You can still expect to find the same negative emotions operating such as; self-rejection, self-hatred, self-bitterness, anger, guilt, anxiety and fear. We'll explain the mechanisms of how these come about and usually co-exist in the chapters following the glossary of common conditions. We'll also examine autoimmune disease after we cover the foundations and Etiology of asthma. *Wright, "A More Excellent Way," Pg 240.*

Asthma

As with many diseases we've seen Asthma healed through simple prayer. With one particular case that I can think of the subject now has over 35 years of being completely free, and counting. Probably more often we've seen asthma dealt with through emotional heal-ing. One person who came for ministry for fear found that their asthma disappeared after the anxiety was resolved. In this case the lady in question had been knocked off a monkey bar as a child and was rendered unconscious. She was taken to hospital, but her parents weren't notified.

In her fearful state, when she regained consciousness, in the emotionally charged moment she believed that; 'there was no-one there who should be there to protect her, and so she could die.' This belief remained embedded in her heart subconsciously, and continued running in the background producing anxiety, and anxiety attacks, until it was identified and the Spirit of Truth set her free.

This case fits with the normally accepted root of 'fear of aban-donment,' that is the considered the most common specific fear that has been recorded as being the genesis of asthma. It is cited as being one of the fastest growing diseases in children. With the breakdown of the family unit, or trouble in the home, it is easy for children to feel rejected, not cared about or wanted. This type of rejection leads to a child not feeling secure that the people who should be there for them will be. Or to put that another way, fearing being abandoned when they need to be protected or provided for.

Another lady that we ministered to at one time had been put into a van with other children. The vehicle had exhaust fumes leaking into it, but none of the adults involved cared. This rejection and failure to care or protect, led to her believing that there was no help, she was abandoned to not being able to breath. The Church that she attended had gas heaters, and even the idea of the fumes would trigger an asthmatic episode in her. I say the 'idea' of the fumes, because one day when she attended church there were so many people in the building that she couldn't see the heaters were actually running all night. She had not received ministry for the problem at this point.

Towards the end of the evening someone commented to her how well she was going considering the gas was on. She immediately had an asthma attack. So, the thought of choking fumes triggered her pre-existing beliefs, which in turn switched on the mechanisms that produced the hypersensitivity and consequent hardening of the alveoli in the respiratory tract.

For ministry, the source of the fear/anxiety coming from insecurity beliefs, and beginning generally in some kind of event with relational implications needs to be identified and ministered to.

To be abandoned means to not have anyone there for you. Fear of abandonment then, is fearing that there will not be anyone there for you that you need to be. Once it has happened, you now have a fear belief that it could happen again, and you are vigilant, most times more than others, about the possibility of it occurring. Key people may be present, but the fear was locked in as a belief in a traumatic moment, even as early as in the womb. A common prenatal situation could be a biological father abandoning the mother and baby at some point in the pregnancy. Or even an event such as an attempted abortion if the parents really didn't want the child.

Henry W Wright writes; *Nothing that you breathe causes an asthmatic attack. It can be inherited, but it is coming out of deep-rooted fear, anxiety and fear.*
Wright, "A More Excellent Way," Pg 209.

Autoimmune Disease

In the U.S.A. reportedly 8% of the population, or approximately 1 in 12 people are affected by autoimmune disease. There are more than 100 diseases that come under this category, making it the third most common type of disease. Notably an article posted on WebMD proposed that 78% of people with autoimmune disease were women. Perhaps this could relate to women being more wired to be relational and therefore more vulnerable. Often it also appears to have come out of a need of covering and acceptance from a father. It is generally accepted that this is largely the primary source of where we tend to get our identity and decide and conclude identity beliefs in regard to if we are worthy.

Autoimmune diseases usually cause inflammation because they involve the activation of both T and B immune cells which are white corpuscles that dysfunction and attack your own body. Here we'll list the most prevalent and common conditions of this kind:

1. Rheumatoid and reactive arthritis
2. Lupus
3. IBD (Inflammatory bowel disease) Ulcerative colitis.
4. Crohn's disease
5. Celiac disease
6. Multiple sclerosis
7. Type 1 diabetes
8. Psoriasis
9. Graves' disease
10. Hashimoto's thyroiditis
11. Myasthenia Gravis
12. Scleroderma
13. Sjogren's syndrome
14. Addisons disease

Henry W. Wright in his bestselling book, A More Excellent Way, cites good results and has numerous testimonies of dealing with autoimmune diseases. In his publication he makes this statement;

When we minister to someone with an autoimmune disease, we find without exception a degree of lacking self-esteem and/or guilt. A person has conflict with himself over his identity, drivenness, performance, conflict and guilt, at some level causing an autoimmune disease. *
Wright, "A More Excellent Way," Pg 286

We cover and reinforce these themes repetitively throughout this publication. Whatever your inner thoughts are about your identity, it inevitably plays out in your body. Your immune system is designed to attack and destroy your enemies, normally things like allergens, germs and microbes, viruses, even cancer cells. But, if in your thought life you don't like yourself you have become your own enemy, your immune system responds to your distorted and disordered thought life, and misfires attacking your own body. This is why having more than one autoimmune disorder is not uncommon, because they have their origins in the same beliefs about self.

In general, these disorders appear to attack the most vulnerable or weakened areas. For example, if you have autoimmune thyroid conditions such as Graves' disease or Hashimoto's thyroiditis, the attack could have gravitated here because the person is also suffering with significant anxieties and fears that have overloaded the stress system. Perhaps this is why Hashimoto's is associated with Addisons disease (Adrenal glands) and even Diabetes (Pancreas) which both have components of anxiety.

We have seen thyroid anti bodies reduce after ministry, and hormone levels return to the normal range once the self-rejection and anxieties are resolved.

We were running a Conference on healing at a church recently, and after I'd proposed the link between not liking and accepting yourself, and autoimmune disorders, a young woman came up to me to confirm that it was true. She explained that she'd come to Christ in this very good church, and that the people were so loving, accepting and encouraging, that she'd begun to accept herself more. The result was that her symptoms had reduced. This highlights the importance of environment. She was not healed, but she was improved. Hopefully the ministers used what was taught at the conference to minister to the self-beliefs that she carried in order to bring about full restoration.

Dr Henry W. Wright considers that all autoimmune diseases have a root of self-hatred, self-bitterness and guilt.

Even though the medical community now associates autoimmune diseases (including lupus, Crohn's, diabetes [type 1], rheumatoid arthritis, multiple sclerosis) with fear, anxiety, and stress, I have come to the conclusion that most autoimmune diseases are primarily the result of an unloving spirit producing feelings of not being loved, not being accepted, self-rejection, self-hatred and self-bitterness coupled with guilt. In fact, it could be said that autoimmune diseases are primarily a self-hatred disease with a fear- anxiety-stress rider attached to them.'
Wright, "A More Excellent Way," Pg 210.

Feelings follow beliefs. They are the outworking of inner conclusions about yourself, that have come out of how you have interpreted events in regards to what they mean about your identity. That is, who you perceive that you are. We could summarise this by proposing that autoimmune disorders begin with a rejection event. The resulting beliefs about who you are produce self-rejection and fear of rejection.

Everything is always spiritual because we are spiritual beings, living in a fallen, spiritually manipulated world. Our behaviour is in fact manipulated and influence by spiritual kingdoms. God wants us to love ourselves, and Satan, the opposer, the deceiver, wants to put us against ourselves, breaking down created order, and destroying us and others by our participation with him. The only true freedom can come through displacing this deception about self, by receiving God's truth at every level.

Pastor Wright concludes: *The only way to be healed from rheumatoid arthritis and other autoimmune diseases is to accept yourself once and for all and to get the self-hatred, the guilt, the lack of self-esteem and the junk out of your life.*
Wright, "A More Excellent Way," Pg 228

The only truly complete, maintenance free way to achieve this is through ministry by the Holy Spirit, bringing God's truth to your heart about your identity. And when you know His truth, it will set you free and deal with contradictions between what you know is true in your mind, or would like to think is true about being acceptable. And what you really feel is true in the programming of your heart. Hence ending the conflict within yourself. See the ministry process from chapter 22 on.

Cancer

I feel that I need to spend a little more time on a study of cancer, as it's a disease that generates a lot of fear.

Let me begin by saying that cancer can be healed through simple faith in a prayer line. We have seen people healed and delivered of late-stage terminal cancer when we've prayed for them in a faith environment. I recall one lady who was carried into a meeting, and when the power of God came on her, she was powerfully and deeply delivered of a spirit of grief. This was present because of the emotional woundedness that she carried coming from her mother.

She walked out of the meeting on her own, and was discharged from the hospital two days later. In another meeting that I recall there were two men both presenting with prostate cancer. One reported that he was healed immediately after we prayed for him. This was apparently confirmed by a doctors test the following day. The other man contacted me a number of weeks or possibly months later, explaining that he'd also received healing, but it happened over a period of time.

So, as with all disease, God is always willing, able, and wanting to heal. But if there's an issue with your environment, and if you don't get healed in a meeting, God hasn't given up on setting you free, and may minister to your illness through the emotional healing process.

Cancer is the second most common cause of death across the globe, and comes through inflammatory processes of some kind. Cancers of various types can be linked to virus, environmental, lifestyle, and other factors. Additionally, there may be the presence of other diseases or conditions that cancer can be connected to. These can create weaknesses in parts of the body. These weakened states can then in turn make those people with an emotional profile that makes them vulnerable to cancer, susceptible to cancer in these specific areas. For example, different autoimmune diseases are linked to an increased risk of certain types of cancer. This is not surprising given the commonality of the negative emotions observed in these disease profiles.

Research indicates that people with autoimmune disease are at increased risk of developing certain cancers, and some cancers are linked to the initiation of autoimmune conditions. Both conditions are generally accepted as being connected with emotional dysregulation and psychological factors.

A probable emotional profile for cancer
Research has exposed factors that can be found causing cancer. Today it's relatively easy to do your own research on the internet. And if you ask the right questions numerous articles will become available for further studies. Here I'll propose the emotional components, and the disease profile, that my own investigation has led to, in regards to the toxic nature of certain specific negative emotions.

Bitterness and resentment, which are an ongoing form of anger, are the leading emotions that produce toxicity and corruption of cells, creating a propensity towards cancerous cells being formed and proliferating. Cancer reportedly occurs when the cellular safeguards fail and cells are damaged. Depression has been linked to certain types of cancers. You can see that if a person in a depressed state gives up on life, the body playing out your thought life could give up on defending your physiology at cellular level. A person who gives up on life is often exposed to failed relationships of some kind.

They may have internalised or externalised anger, resentment, and bitterness towards others, but perhaps more dangerously, towards self. I'll breakdown depression later in the section on the mechanics of emotions behind disease. Brooding, replayed bitterness, in regards to perceived rejection of some kind was once coined relevantly with the old saying; 'it eats them like a cancer.' Where there's been rejection there will invariably be fear of rejection, along with self-rejection.

Let me propose that rejection in the formative stages of life leading to negative self-image is going to be found as a major source existing in most disease. These identity beliefs lead to fear of further rejection, and at times fear of situations where these beliefs have been imbibed. There will be a particular type of responses that people may gravitate to cope or compensate with the possibility of further rejection.

Research indicates that a person who fits a cancer susceptible profile is often a person who is in denial about certain emotional needs and probably represses or supresses their feelings. This can be a protective mechanism to attempt to prevent them from being hurt or rejected again. So, emotionally they just close up shop. Possibly they live behind a persona that they consider is acceptable. This includes internalising the resentment, bitterness, and anger. The depression and hopelessness factor that is often involved comes because they don't see a solutions to their feelings, in terms of the emotion coming from the negative self-image that they carry as a result of the rejection.

As I'll explain in a later chapter, depression comes through anxiety about things perceived about your identity that seem as though they can never be resolved. This creates hopelessness, and then the person becomes overwhelmed, and may despair even of life. In that instance it appears that the immune system, which would normally deal with the damaged cancerous cells stops protecting us, because in our own thought life we've given up.

Issues and areas that a person with cancer susceptibility may struggle with

1. Resentment and bitterness are the result of unforgiveness. So, you can expect that with this profile that people may struggle to forgive others. As with most negative emotions, the reason for this is some kind hurt that has previously produced a negative inner belief. You can expect that these are likely people who once they feel that they have been wronged or let down in some way by others or themselves, continue in resentment, either internalised or externalised. In summary, this resentment could be towards others, or yourself. Most commonly both.

2. As a result of the inner beliefs that produce low self-image, they may gravitate towards depression, feel sorry for themselves for how they feel they've been dealt with, and at times exhibit melancholic self-reflection.

3. They may be people who've become disconnected from their own feelings and emotions. Perhaps learning as a child that emotional expression isn't acceptable. So, they may have a tendency to hold in or suppress and repress their feelings. Another reason for the suppression may be tied to beliefs about worth. For example, believing that you're not acceptable or loveable if you express emotion. It could also originate in parental modelling in regards to how to deal with emotion. As a result, they may internalise these feelings of resentment, anger, bitterness or anxiety.

4. Along with this denial and lack of acceptance of their true inner feelings to themselves, they may well want to appear as if everything is okay to others. They may unconsciously build what they perceive as a suitable image of self that they project towards others. Underneath these undealt with issues could be simmering away. In a Christian context people often feel that they have to meet certain standards of joy, holiness, or success in God. And to appear any other way seems unacceptable, so denial of true feelings may be a preferable way of coping.

5. These people might, when triggered by some emotional stressor, have behind the anger, resentment, and anxiety, feelings of hopelessness, and despair. This is the depression component that may be present in the profile. They feel that they can 'never ever' be what they need to be, and feel powerless to change their situation.

6. You may find that in order to protect the wounded identity, that many times sufferers construct various protective systems to guard themselves from further hurt. In fact, unconsciously, anger and resentment may be at times emotional mechanisms to blame others for how you feel, and can even be a perceived means of keeping them at a distance. Consequently, somebody with a cancer profile may have difficulty developing and continuing relationships with certain people because of a fear of rejection.

7. There is a high probability that many times the likely bitterness, resentment, and unforgiveness is towards yourself. Even though this is often internalised, suppressed and going on underneath. You resent and are angry towards others for hurting you, not valuing you in some way, or seemingly not caring about you or accepting you. That is the outward expression. But you respond to what people make you feel, because at heart level you have already believed something negative about yourself. Otherwise, how they now deal with you wouldn't bother you, or not beyond your ability to forgive and graciously overlook the offence. (Realising that others have their own issues!)

Art Mathias in his book, '*In His Own Image*' made these observations from his own research in regards to a cancer profile:
The association of stress with cancer has led investigators to identify the personality or behavioural profile of the typical individual who is at increased risk for cancer. Now referred to as "type C," such an individual is characterised by denial and suppression of emotions (especially anger), "pathological niceness," avoidance of conflicts, exaggerated social desirability, harmonising behaviour, over-compliance, over-patience, high rationality, and a rigid control of emotional expression.
Art Mathias, In His Own Image, Pg 49

In other words, someone who lives behind a mask or facade, in an effort to be what they feel that they need to be for acceptance. Someone who in their hearts believes that they're not really acceptable or good enough as they are. You harmonise, because of fear of rejection coming from historically rooted beliefs that if you're not what you feel that people want, then they won't accept you.

We're speaking about a person, who because of rejection does not believe that they're enough, and has probably learnt that emotional expression is not ok. They don't deserve to be who they are. They have many times been crushed and oppressed growing up. Remember cancer is in part a breakdown in your immune system protecting you from rogue damaged cells, and your immune system is in your bone marrow. Possibly, growing up you weren't given permission to be happy about yourself or your life.

> Proverbs 17:22
> A cheerful <u>heart</u> is good medicine, but a crushed spirit dries up <u>the bones</u>. NIV (emphasis mine)

> Proverbs 18:14
> A man's spirit sustains him in sickness, but a crushed spirit who can bear? NIV

Henry W Wright made this profound statement in a small book that he wrote on his insights into cancer;

Malignancy at cellular level (which is what cancer is) is despair that has been experienced biologically. It may be seen, then, that none of us just gets cancer. We reach a point at which our deepest need is to withdraw from life, and we therefore choose to develop cancer, although we would aggressively deny that as truth.
Henry W Wright: New Insights Into Cancer Pg 42

We could say, that if you don't like you at some level, and don't see how it can be changed, then you give up on yourself. As with any disease, as a principle, our state of being is conformed to what we think about ourselves at heart level, be it actions, behaviours and attitudes, sense of self, emotional expression and so on.

> Proverbs 23: 7A
> For as he <u>thinks in his heart</u>, so is he. NKJV
> (emphasis mine)

Authors note. Some translations do not render this verse in this way and omit this for some reason. It is clearly present in the Hebrew text. People who are susceptible often replay perceived offences within themselves, which prevents the resentment and bitterness from being resolved. At times they may explode with anger, but research suggests most times it will be held deep inside. The old saying is that you need to *'feel it to heal it.'* This means that you need to accept, embrace, and be real, about what you feel inside so that it can be ministered to.

Fear and anxiety will likely be coexisting with these other negative emotions, because once it has initially happened you will be afraid of being hurt, wronged or let down again. It is considered that the resentment form of anger, along with fear and anxiety that's associated with the offences are the most prevailing factors amongst the different types of cancers.

Ministry involves dealing with *'heart beliefs'* coming from rejective events where you came to conclusions about yourself and your identity. They will be places where you interpreted the events in some negative way that now open you to resentment towards others and yourself. We'll explain how to minister to negative emotions in later chapters.

Examples and illustrations of how this may play out in life

Environmental sources
Clearly, exposure to toxic chemicals, viruses, radiation, and so on can cause damage at cellular level leading to cancer. Additionally, lifestyle factors such as promiscuity, smoking, obesity, drugs,

excessive alcohol consumption, a poor diet, and lack of exercise, are all samples of factors that create physiological environments where cancer can take hold, and then proliferate in those who have a cancer prone disposition.

In terms of cancer coming through lifestyle sources, I read an article recently where a famous male movie star acknowledged that his throat cancer was most likely the result of his promiscuity in the area of oral sex. No doubt his doctors had explained this to him. Statistics report that research has proven that people engaged in oral sex are 58 times more likely to develop throat cancer because of the HPV 16 virus, which is reportedly present on the genital area.

I was recently listening to an old sermon on YouTube by Billy Graham titled; *'Breaking the chains of sexual immorality.'* On the clip he related how young people suffer greatly from guilt when they are promiscuous. Citing the Canadian cancer society, he stated that *'promiscuous sex relations contribute to cancer for women, and that 64% of those who get cancer in that way die.'* What I found interesting was the increased risk of cancer through exposure to various HPVs. But then also because of the strong moral code of the times, the mental and emotional effects on self-esteem and guilt, in my opinion illustrates the possible potential power of negative self-perception in outcomes for disease.

Once these events have taken place the possibilities for self-bitterness, and hopelessness of ever being right again leading to depression are certainly present. Other studies that I have done have revealed a huge increase in mental disorder in young people following the sexual revolution beginning in the late 1960's.

Emotional sources
Although someone in later life may trigger feelings of resentment in you, the beliefs producing offense, resentment and bitterness, as with other negative emotional responses leading to disease, have their source and origin in the formative years of life. The true source of our negative self-beliefs is most often coming from

parents. I saw a picture recently that had the caption; 'when parents criticise their children, the child doesn't stop loving the parent, they stop loving themselves.' All too true.

A number of years ago I knew a couple who were both deeply rejected people. Depressively so. Both carried internalised anger and resentment, very much fitting the characteristics that I've just related. Their relationship, and clinging together carried them through, although the deep rejection from the negative self-image that they both carried was clearly unresolved. The results of deep rejection are often that you don't like you, that is who you perceive your identity to be.

At one time they had an argument about something, and she said something that crushed his hope of her ever prioritising him. Her comment, after all of these years together, shattered him, implying that he was not the most important person to her. You could see that following this rejection he just gave up on life, with his seeming only source of true acceptance gone it was hopeless. Within a short time, he developed cancer and died. Without him as her source of acceptance being present, she soon also developed cancer and died.

I recall many years ago warning a Christian friend who had a great deal of resentment towards her husband that she needed ministry to deal with it. I explained that she was leaving herself open to getting sick. And although I didn't say it, based on my understanding, I was thinking specifically cancer. She left her husband, and later had an affair, in spite of her faith. Underneath she must have been rejecting herself for her behaviour and living with tremendous guilt, even if in denial.

A couple of years later she developed cancer and died relatively young. This was not something that God wanted for her. It's a tragedy when we don't take God's offer and provisions for healing our broken hearts. She had not wanted ministry for her bitterness and resentment. Later, when she developed the cancer, she visited healing meetings hoping to be set free. To no avail. Potentially she could have been healed through these ministries, but most likely the inner beliefs she held about her worthiness and acceptability behind the anger and resentment, and consequent cancer, blocked her from being able to receive by faith.

Another case that I did have the opportunity to work with was a lady who was around 45 years of age who had Leukemia. Once it was discovered she was immediately rushed to hospital where she underwent chemotherapy. Various people had prayed the prayer of faith with her, and between their faith and the expertise of some wonderful doctors she survived the ordeal. We then began to minister to all of the negative, cancer related emotions that were present.

Around 18 years later in a routine examination her local doctor found a large lump under her armpit. Upon investigation it proved to be a huge tumour extending down into her chest cavity. Reportedly it had been there slowly growing over many years, possibly decades. Both she, and we, were very confident that it would not be cancerous, as all of the negative emotions that normally can be found in a cancer profile had been resolved. The surgeons operated and removed the tumour, still not sure if it was cancerous until it had been tested. As we expected, it was benign.

Some Christians would be superstitious about these kinds of statements, and fear that you might be tested on it. These diseases aren't random. They're cause and effect. The devil can't just put things on you. There are reasons in your life that need to be ministered to so that there is no place for the devil. We see even high-profile Christians with thousands praying for them who pass away with these diseases. This because the causes aren't dealt with.

Unfortunately, God then gets a bad name for not healing them, and He looks like a bad angry God, not answering prayer, keeping good things from them. This is what the devil suggested about Him back in the garden of Eden in regards to the tree of the knowledge of good and evil. They perish for lack of knowledge. We need to find what the real cause is, what God wants to do, what He's provided, and how we should go about it.

> *Proverbs 26:2*
> *Like a flitting sparrow, like a flying swallow, So a curse* <u>*without cause*</u> *shall not alight. NKJV (emphasis mine)*

Notably, the sister of the woman whose story I have just related, who had a completely different personality, but the same upbringing and consequent negative emotional profile, also developed cancer in her mid-40's and without receiving ministry died. The third sibling also contracted cancer and after treatment survived. Given the prevalence of cancer in the family, and her own previous blood cancer, it would be reasonable to conclude that if she had not been set free from anger, resentment, anxieties, and other predisposing emotions weren't resolved, that her tumour most likely would have been cancerous. It highlights that these diseases aren't random, and are indeed, cause and effect.

Some examples of specific cancers
Below are a few insights and observations into some common cancers.

Breast Cancer
Breast cancer is coming out of the sins of conflict and bitterness between the female and either her mother and/or her sisters or mother-in-law. (Disclaimer: This profile represents a large percentage of breast cancer cases, but there are many other causes for breast cancer also.)
Wright,
"A More Excellent Way," Pg 235

Hodgkin's disease and Leukaemia
Hodgkin's disease and Leukaemia are very similar. They are similar because the root cause is the same in Hodgkin's (Lymphatic) and Leukaemia (blood). The factors are the same. I've found that many times, Hodgkin's disease and Leukaemia are caused by deep-rooted bitterness coming from unresolved rejection by a father.
Wright, "A More Excellent Way," Pg 236

We have found the same profile in ministry.

Ovarian Cancer
Ovarian cancer comes out of a women's hate for herself and her sexuality.
Wright, "A More Excellent Way," Pg 236

The author goes on to suggest that this can lead her into self-bitterness.

Prostate Cancer
Prostate cancer comes out of anger, guilt, self-hatred and self-bitterness.
Wright, "A More Excellent Way," Pg 236

There are some indications from people that we've dealt with that this anger may often be towards males, suggesting possible father issues in the initial perceived rejection.

Cancer in infants and children
I've heard people say over the years, how can God let children get cancer. Let me propose a possible reason why this can occur. We readily accept the research that teaches us that if a person drinks alcohol while pregnant that it reaches nearly the same concentration in the baby's blood. In turn this can affect the development of organs and body structures along with the brain. In much the same way chemicals imbibed through smoking can disrupt hormone levels leading to a variety of physical and emotional issues.

What we've been revealing through our study on cancer here, is that through long lasting anger mediums such as resentment and bitterness, that the toxic environment created damages cells leading to cancer. Studies indicate that chronic resentment in the parent, just like other negative emotions in pregnancy, can potentially impact a developing baby. Reportedly, persistent negative emotions can be chemically, and hormonally, mimicked by the baby.

What I'm suggesting, is the child possibly having cells compromised and damaged through these toxic conditions created by the parents' emotional state while they are developing? Is this why suddenly, mysteriously a child develops some kind of cancer or other physical issue while still in childhood? We really need to get ministry for our emotional issues. They don't just affect us, they damage our relationships, and very possibly pass to our children. Is this a practical outworking of the consequence of sin extending beyond the individual sinner?

Celiac Disease

In his book '*In His Own Image*' Christian author Art Mathias states that Celiacs disease exists as a result of fear that's been inherited, along with anxiety, self-hatred, and guilt. This is consistent with what we've presented as the general roots of autoimmune problems. In our own ministry we've seen a reduction in symptoms as these issues have been dealt with. Celiac disease is another autoimmune disorder where, in this instance, the inflammatory response creates an allergy to gluten. It's commonly associated with type 1 diabetes, with as many as 10% of sufferers having both illnesses. As we've already described, people who have an autoimmune disorder are vulnerable to developing others.

Art Mathias notes that there can be thyroid related auto antibodies that disappear when people are placed on a gluten free diet. An article by the Australian Thyroid Foundation indicated that as many as 10% of people diagnosed with Celiacs disease also suffered from thyroid autoimmune disease, either Hashimoto's underactive thyroid disease, or Graves' overactive thyroid disease.

Ministry involves resolving self-beliefs relating to autoimmune disease that have been imbibed through whatever source. We explain how these inner beliefs can successfully be resolved later in this book.

Cholesterol

Dr Henry W Wright makes this spiritual diagnosis: *cholesterol is directly related to people who are very, very angry with themselves. There is a high degree of self-depreciation; they are against themselves; always putting themselves down. It is more than merely putting themselves down; they are very hostile with themselves. They are very angry with themselves. He goes on to later state; It all begins with rejection.* *
Wright, "A More Excellent Way," Pg 262

A few years ago, a lady came to see us who suffered from, amongst other things, high cholesterol. Based on Henry's insights my wife ministered to, and resolved the self-beliefs that she held in her heart that caused her to be angry with herself. The result was amazing, her cholesterol levels dropped through the floor, along with some other radically improved test results.

Based on his comments and experience you can expect to find people who are very, very angry with themselves, rejecting themselves by being self-depreciating and putting themselves down. Because of their negative self-image you can expect them to be anxious about how others see them. And most probably they will have guilt present about being enough or doing enough to be acceptable.

Chronic Fatigue Syndrome

In the U.S. it has been estimated that there are around 3.3 million sufferers of CFS/ME. (chronic fatigue syndrome/Myalgic Encephalomyelitis) It is proposed that between 60% to 80% of these cases begin with an infection, and usually a viral infection. The result is that bodily systems shut down like a circuit breaker protecting overloaded systems, closing them down to protect the systems implicated. In the case of chronic fatigue syndrome, these systems don't reboot and the patient remains running on empty without energy. As a result, most sufferers can point to the time of the crash, or the onset of the illness.

Multiple systems are implicated. We know of faith ministries who regularly see CFS/ME healed by simple prayer. There are also a number of other ministries who deal with what they have found to be root issues behind the problem. These also report having significant success. These latter ministries have found common emotional characteristics behind those who develop the syndrome. This makes you wonder if these emotional issues don't affect the immune system in a way that makes those who crash susceptible to the infections to begin with. If this is the case then these factors may also explain the continuance of the problem up until these predisposing factors are dealt with.

One case that we have personally dealt was where both the husband and wife contracted a virus that led to them both succumbing to CFS at the same time. They were both quite different in emotional make-up, with the man reserved, and the wife being quite emotionally available. Both did however have the accepted emotional pathways that would be expected to be behind the syndrome, and after ministry both experienced around 90% improvement. They had suffered with the illness for more than 30 years, and so there was an element of deconditioning that had occurred through a long-term lack of physical activity.

Dr. Jacob Teitelbaum a medical doctor from the U.S., and an expert in CFS includes the need to deal with the mind/body connection in his treatment protocols. He suggests that sufferers may have experienced low self-image as a child. He considers that they may be people who are trying to get approval from someone who is just never going to give it, possibly attempting to please everyone. In later chapters we'll described how we arrive at conclusions about our unacceptability which causes us to have this low image of self.

To compensate for these inner beliefs, we try to meet these perceived expectations and perform to standards that make us acceptable. CFS people have been noted as often being overachievers who burn themselves out. They are often highly achievement orientated, basing their self-esteem and respect from others on being able to meet high standards for acceptance. This can lead to anxiety about their performance, and guilt about not doing or being enough.

One group interviewed made reference to a desire for accomplishment and success, and a need to achieve perfection. Failure to live up to these standards would be indicative of being a failure as a person. This confirms to them that they are not good enough, or at times not as good as others, which is what they learnt experientially in childhood, and now believe is true about their person. If you feel that you can never meet standards and expectations, never measure up, the idea that you will never get there, be what you perceive that you should be, this in itself is overwhelming, exhausting.

For ministry and freedom, the *'heart beliefs'* learnt experientially in childhood, driving you to gain approval and please others need to be exposed. And what you have accepted as 'your truth,' in regards to these matters, need to be displaced with God's truth through the ministry of the Spirit of truth. These beliefs will commonly have been formed through how a person was dealt with by parents.

Guilt is commonly present as a biproduct, as the person feels that they haven't met expectations and done what they should have been able to. Depression has also at times been associated with CFS. This is probably because inside the person feels that it's hopeless, they will 'never, ever, be able to be what they were expected to be.' (It could also exist because they feel that they will 'never, ever, get better.') For Christians, the thoughts and feelings coming from this programming of the heart are readily transposed onto God. What I mean is that they now believe that He also has high expectations for them, when in fact He is looking for how we regard Him, rather than what we're able to do for Him.

Our expert commentator who reports a lot of success ministering to CFS, tells us that behind this syndrome you can expect to find the following issues.

I consider CFS to be a fear and anxiety disorder producing drivenness to meet the expectation of someone in order to "measure up" to receive love.
Wright, "A More Excellent Way," Pg 288

Other Christian ministries have also found there to be guilt, low self-image, and the consequent self-rejection. To resolve all of these negative emotions in a ministry setting, the beliefs that produce these behaviours and responses need to be dealt with.

Crohn's disease

Crohn's disease is a chronic inflammatory autoimmune disease of the gastrointestinal tract. (Most autoimmune diseases cause inflammation.)

Those have had success treating this disease consider that the root behind Crohn's disease is 'extreme self-rejection coupled with guilt.' Reportedly an element of hopelessness is also implicated because the sufferer can't resolve the issue that is causing the self-conflict. Henry W Wright states;

The root behind Crohn's is extreme self-rejection coupled with guilt. Crohn's also has a component of hopelessness because the individual does not know how to solve the problem over which they're tribulating.
*

This self-conflict and hopelessness explain why Crohn's disease is commonly associated with depression. Sufferers of this disease reportedly also suffer from other psychological problems that fit the profile. These include anxiety, worry, shame and frustration.

There is a lot of conflict built into it. Crohn's disease is a disease coming out of massive rejection, abandonment, lack of self-esteem and/or drivenness to meet the expectation of another. In fact, Crohn's disease

involves a great degree of co-dependency and false burden bearing.
Wright, "A More Excellent Way," Pg 225

As with any emotionally rooted disease the source and origin of the self-beliefs producing these feelings and behaviours will be found in formative memories. We'll cover how to successfully resolve these negative feelings in subsequent chapters.

Diabetes type 2

Type 2 diabetes is not considered an autoimmune disorder, but research is indicating potential links to immune cell dysfunction and it is being related to other elements of how the body may attack its own cells and organs. *(Reference: khealth.com - diabetes)* Research suggests that as a result of fears and anxieties there is an over secretion of stress hormones such as cortisol which can inhibit insulin. These negative emotions can also affect the cells in the immune system increasing the release of proinflammatory cytokines.

In practical terms, when you add in the element or condition of being overweight, where you now require insulin to regulate blood sugar levels, then it's logical that the overload will affect an already struggling pancreas. It's noteworthy that obesity is only one risk factor for type 2 diabetes, and that thin people also develop the disease. Clearly losing weight and getting regular exercise will take some of the load off the pancreas, but for a complete resolution the following emotional components will need also to be dealt with.

Dr Wright considers type 2 diabetes to be anxiety disorder and proposes; *Possible spiritual roots are fear of failing others, fear of failure, fear of man, performance and drivenness. There may also be an inability to receive love.... **
Wright, "A More Excellent Way," Pg 213

Note: fear of failure, fear of man, performance and drivenness, are all forms of fear of rejection that produce anxiety. We'll cover these in a later portion of the book. Some consider that often this begins with rejection, in particular from the father, with the consequent additional fruits of rejection; self-rejection and guilt. Depression is also commonly linked to type 2 diabetes. Once again, this is consistent with the emotional profile, and proceeds from the same emotional self-beliefs. This may exacerbate the situation, in that excessive food intake could be utilised to comfort an emotional state precipitated by negative self-beliefs.

Ministry involves identifying and resolving the *'heart beliefs'* imbibed through rejection that have been perceived and received in the formative years. An inability to receive love is present because of what you believe about the worth of your identity and person. This is the self-rejection element. I.E. "I don't love myself because of what I 'subconsciously' believe about myself, so how could I believe that you really love me. What you think about yourself on the inside can become an invisible force field that prevents you from receiving complements, encouragement, love, acceptance, significance, value and so on.

Diverticular disease

Dr. Art Mathias considers that diverticulitis is rooted in the following emotional profile. As with other maladies, the origins will need to be identified and freedom ministered through the ministry of the Spirit of Truth.

*Anxiety, fear and anger ***
Art Mathias, In His Own Image, Pg 145

Endometriosis

Just like many other diseases, we have seen endometriosis healed through the prayer of faith. I know of many other ministries who have had the same experience. To resolve this issue using the emotional healing model, the following Etiology, or set of causes, that successful Christian authors attribute to endometriosis would need to be dealt with to undermine this disease.

If these emotional reactions to identity beliefs are present, they are best dealt with for the peace and wholeness of the sufferer regardless of the disease. Not to mention the likelihood of other potential disease states being realised. Not surprisingly, given the accepted emotional roots, endometriosis is linked to certain cancers, autoimmune diseases, and a significant list of other chronic conditions that also have inflammation as a feature.

One author has observed that the self-rejection/self-hatred involved in this disease, usually is related to not liking being a female for some reason. The conclusion that causes the person to take these positions against themselves is generally found in a negative event of some kind. Again, it's not surprising with these emotional states that research suggests that women who suffer from this condition are more likely to experience anxiety and depression. The type of anxiety that is experienced may relate to insecurity in regards to your perceived sense of identity. Christian authors agree that additionally you can expect to find self-rejection, self-hatred and guilt.

Environmental Illness

EI is a condition where people become hypersensitive or allergic to multiple stressors. Some of the worst cases reportedly have allergic responses to virtually everything. The commentators that I'm citing consider that sufferers have often developed the emotional predisposition for this illness through abusive events. These abuses could be emotional, verbal, physical, sexual or rejective abuses. Any of these abuses deeply devalue a person. The subject consequently feels insecure about being protected and cared about. When these events have been interpreted and negative heart/self-beliefs about identity established, the following emotional condition and responses have been observed by Art Mathias of Wellspring ministries, Alaska.

Fear, anxiety, broken heart, unhealthy introspection, self-hatred, and self-pity. *
Art Mathias, In His Own Image, Pg 150

These issues need to be dealt with through the ministry process that we'll describe in later chapters. As with most diseases with common emotional profiles, EI is linked to a variety of other chronic diseases and conditions.

Erectile Dysfunction

ED can be attributed to a wide range of causes. For example, low testosterone or other hormonal problems could be indicated. Alcohol and drug abuse, even many prescription medications produce ED as a common side effect. Other physical conditions such as diabetes or high blood pressure can also be implicated and may need to be resolved. Stress, anxiety, fear of failure and other negative emotional states can be further pathways to this condition which would require ministry and freedom.

As in most cases where fear of rejection is a part of the profile you can expect self-rejection to also be present. In cases that I've personally worked with guilt, anger and depression were also a factor.

Fibromyalgia

According to one study, Fibromyalgia often co-occurs with chronic fatigue syndrome presenting in around one third of CFS cases. It also commonly co-exists with other conditions such irritable bowel syndrome, migraine or other kinds of headaches, along with various other physical conditions, as well as emotional issues such as anxiety and depression. Women are more likely to develop this condition than men with a prevalence of 80% to 96% of cases being reported by researchers as being female. It is a disorder characterised by fatigue, musculoskeletal pain, (that is muscle, ligament and joint pain) along with issues relating to mood, sleep and memory problems.

As you can see below Henry W Wright considers that the pre-disposing factors for fibromyalgia in females is found *'when they don't feel covered, protected, nurtured, don't feel safe, and are always looking over their shoulder, are driven, anxious, moving pieces of their life around and are insecure.'* * We can confirm that this is certainly an existing profile that we've found in cases of Fibromyalgia that we've ministered to.
Wright, "A More Excellent Way," Pg 269-270

In order to protect themselves these people have often become very controlling of their environments, which in turn can create relational issues which push people further away. This then exacerbates the situation as the person being pushed away is unable to understand and help with the root problem. The sufferer then feels even less cared about, and even less secure in relationships.

The beliefs that produce these feelings are generally found in childhood memories where most times a father has failed to put in value, worth, significance, acceptance and security. They may be absentee, or even present, but because of their own rejection issues, they may be unable to give the necessary attention, along with demonstrative caring, that is necessary for a healthy perspective of identity and self-worth to be established at heart level. So, in this instance they are present, but absent in terms of being considerate of the needs of others. Usually this is because they are consumed with trying to meet the needs of their own wounded self.

Fibromyalgia is frequently linked to other chronic health conditions such as; CFS, IBS, Migraines, and mood disorders such as anxiety and depression. Once again, these and other related conditions are consistent with the shared emotional profile. And this profile proceeds from the same emotional self-beliefs. We'll explain how to be set free further on in the book.

Grave's Disease (Autoimmune Hyperthyroid Disease)

We have already touched on this condition when we were discussing autoimmune diseases. Hyperthyroidism is a condition where your thyroid is overactive and produces too much thyroxine hormone, or T4 as it is known. It is the inactive form of thyroid hormone which converts to T3 (Triiodothyronine) which is the active form of Thyroid hormone. T3 stimulates the cells to regulate your metabolism and has other functions. Stress and anxiety are considered to contribute to the development or deterioration of the condition. Stress and anxiety can also make the symptoms worse.

When the components exist for autoimmune disease, and because the thyroid is under stress and in a vulnerable state because of specific anxiety, it can become a target for autoimmune antibodies to attack your own body's tissues. Ministry involves dealing with the beliefs and circumstances that produce these stresses and anxieties. These could relate to beliefs about identity and situations, as well as present circumstances that trigger these beliefs. As with other autoimmune conditions, the identity beliefs about self will need to be exposed and ministered to. These will include conflicts within the persons acceptance of their identity, low self-esteem, consequent self-rejection, fear of rejection and guilt. Further information see 'autoimmune disease.'

Hashimoto's Disease (Autoimmune Hypothyroidism)

Hashimoto's disease is the autoimmune version of hypothyroidism. In this instance the thyroid gland under produces the hormones needed to regulate your metabolism and other bodily processes and functions. This produces fatigue and a variety of other symptoms. You can see that the causes are considered to be the same as hyperthyroidism, in fact at times a person can swing from over secretion to under secretion. Perhaps this is because the stressed gland is wearing out? We've seen the resolution of anxiety beliefs completely resolve this condition, with the result of hormone levels returning to normal.

Thyroid problems are often linked to adrenal issues, as the systems work together through feedback loops to try to cope with stress. Low hormone production in both of these areas is commonly implicated in multiple other diseases and syndromes.

Heart Diseases

Heart disease is the leading cause of death worldwide. Clearly, there can be environmental, and lifestyle components, along with other co-occurring disease factors that contribute to the likelihood of heart disease. Diabetes, hypertension, arthritis, cancer, COPD, kidney disease, and celiacs disease all often exist along with heart disease. Again, this makes sense given that the same negative disease producing emotional profiles are found behind many conditions.

As you would expect, there appears to be some common threads through what are considered to be the predisposing negative emotional factors behind the different types of heart diseases. For that reason, I will list the most common heart diseases, rather than deal with them individually, and then note the typical negative responses to the identity beliefs that are held by the individual.

Coronary artery disease, Cardiomyopathy, Angina, Congestive heart disease, Heart Arrhythmias, heart valve disease.

As a sample, our credible Christian commentators consider that you will find the following negative emotions behind heart diseases.

Angina – Fear, anxiety, anger, depression, bitterness, and hostility.*
Cardiomyopathy – Fear, anxiety, anger, self-hatred, hostility, depression and addictions. *
Art Mathias, In His Own Image, Pg 162

Congestive heart failure – Fear, anxiety, anger,
self-bitterness, hostility and depression. *
Coronary Artery Disease – Self-anger, anger, rage, anxiety, fear, hostility, type-A behaviour and depression. *
Art Mathias, In His Own Image, Pg 163

Dr Henry W Wright instructs us;
In reviewing case histories of people in ministry, we have discovered those suffering from coronary artery disease are filled with self-rejection, self-bitterness and self-hatred, and they have never overcome it. *
Wright, "A More Excellent Way," Pg 206

Ministry involves finding out what it is that you believe, often unconsciously, about yourself that causes you to reject yourself. Even to the point of being angry with yourself, and hostile towards others if they make you feel what you believe to be true about you. For example, that nobody cares about you. Or they make you feel inferior, or whatever it may be.

We've also found these indications to be accurate with people with heart conditions that we've dealt with. As you would expect with similar negative emotional roots to many other illnesses, consistent with other diseases, heart conditions are linked to a myriad of other chronic conditions.

Mitral valve prolapse is considered to be the result of fear and anxiety.
Wright, "A More Excellent Way," Pg 285

Beginning in Chapter 22 we'll explain how to deal with the self-beliefs that produce these emotional issues.

High Blood Pressure (Hypertension)

Reportedly around 48% of adults in the U.S. suffer from high blood pressure (hypertension.) As is the case with many chronic illnesses, this condition is associated with a considerable number of other diseases including heart disease, stroke, kidney disease and even vascular dementia. Reducing saturated fat, excess sugar, getting regular exercise, losing weight, and eating a healthy diet are all considered to help reduce, or delay risks associated with this condition. Whilst lifestyle is implicated in the worsening or speeding up of onset, the emotional component cannot be overlooked.

Most commentators considered that high blood pressure, along with many heart conditions, exist because a person is wrestling with thoughts that produce fear and anxiety. The physiological response to this is that the persons heart muscles constrict reducing the blood flow through blood vessels. Fear can be a broad term, but in this instance, it appears that dealing with the specific fear of the future is a key to reducing blood pressure. People I've ministered to have had an event in the past that has led to them expecting something bad to happen in the future.

This is consistent with the link that's been found to PTSD. Studies have shown that individuals with PTSD are at an increased risk of developing hypertension. PTSD being sourced in childhood trauma includes: Physical, emotional or sexual abuse, neglect, witnessing abuse or violence, loss of, or separation from a parent or family member if they leave home, or from traumatic situations such as accidents.

The internal beliefs imbibed and encoded in these emotionally charged situations need to be resolved through ministry for complete healing. Once you've received your freedom you can then align with the counsel of Jesus in terms of what to choose as your default position about the future.

> Matthew 6:34
> "Therefore <u>do not worry</u> about tomorrow, for tomorrow

> *will worry about its own things. Sufficient for the day is*
> *its own trouble". NKJV (emphasis mine)*

In Luke's gospel we clearly see the link to fear and heart conditions.

> *Luke 21:26*
> *"men's hearts failing them from fear and the expectation*
> *of those things which are coming on the earth, for the*
> *powers of heaven will be shaken". NKJV (emphasis mine)*

Many times, we have a choice whether or not we worry and get anxious about world events, or even our own daily circumstances. In this case there are a great many scriptures to comfort and encourage us, and if our walk with God is steadfast our trust is automatically in Him, and so choosing faith over fear is relatively easy.

However, as we've just proposed, many times a person's fear and worry come from historical events where something bad has happened. They are now on guard expectantly watching that it doesn't happen again. A common example could be someone who wasn't cared for properly growing up. In the process of that experience, they have imbibed into their heart a belief something such as; 'there's no one there to protect me,' 'nobody is in control,' and so on. These are not conscious beliefs, they're going on underneath and producing fear and anxiety, even though the person tries to stop worrying.

These or other kinds of beliefs from different historical sources will need to be dealt with using the ministry model described in later chapters. We've seen blood pressure go down as the Holy Spirit brings the truth of God's perspective into these areas.

Irritable Bowel Syndrome

Given that we find the same negative emotions implicated in many conditions it's not surprising to find that as many as 6 out of 10 people with IBS also suffer from Fibromyalgia. Chronic Fatigue Syndrome, sleep disturbances and Migraines may also present. 2 out of 3 people have co-occurring rheumatic diseases, and IBS can exist along with various digestive diseases. The medical community notes that it has also been found to coexist with mental disorders such as anxiety, and depression. In fact, clinically anxiety and IBS are considered to be common comorbidities, with increases in anxiety resulting in worsening IBS symptoms.

When a person is stressed by their fears and anxieties nerve receptors called dendrites become inflamed causing the condition. Reportedly in more than half of IBS cases the source of the fear and anxiety beliefs that produce the problem can be found in physical or sexual abuse events. It's not therefore surprising that our Christian commentator includes insecurity and even bitterness as a part of the profile that they've built on case histories.

Ministry involves resolving the inner *'heart beliefs'* producing the fear and anxiety using the model described later in the publication beginning in chapter 22.

IBS comes directly out of anxiety, fear and insecurities. *
Wright, "A More Excellent Way," Pg 289

Lupus

We have already listed Lupus under autoimmune diseases so we won't spend a lot of additional time here. The specific autoimmune action in the case of Lupus is an attack on the body's own tissues, and reportedly it can also affect joints, skin, kidneys, blood cells, heart, brain and lungs. One article that I read cited between 6% and 30% of people with Lupus will have coexisting autoimmune conditions such as rheumatoid arthritis or Sjogren syndrome. And around 1 in 3 people with Lupus will develop Fibromyalgia. They are also susceptible to cardiovascular disease and thyroid disorders. In this publication we're proposing that multiple conditions can often occur together, because there are common negative emotion profiles present.

It's worth repeating Henry W Wrights insight on autoimmune diseases.

*When we minister to someone with an autoimmune disease, we find without exception a degree of lacking self-esteem and/or guilt. A person has conflict with himself over his <u>identity</u>, drivenness, performance, conflict and guilt, at some level causing an autoimmune disease. ***
Wright, "A More Excellent Way," Pg 286

In the case of Lupus Dr. Wright identifies what he has found specifically in people who have been set free through his ministry.

*Lupus is rooted in extreme self-hatred, self-conflict and includes guilt. Performance may also be implicated. ***
Wright, "A More Excellent Way," Pg 227

We will more fully explain emotional components such as guilt, self-conflict, and self-rejection in later chapters. Ministry involves identifying, primarily identity beliefs, and possibly some situation beliefs as well, from the subject's early history that have produced these responses and behaviours towards self. As we've pointed out repetitively, these beliefs and feelings are often going on underneath, although the fruit is evident in compensating behaviour. Only the Holy Spirit can resolve these beliefs once they have been identified.

Malabsorption

Malabsorption is one of a number of gastrointestinal conditions considered to be caused by anxiety, fear and stress. Other illnesses caused by this type of emotional profile include ulcerative colitis, irritable bowel syndrome, and other bowel problems such as constipation and diarrhea. We've found repetitively that most of these anxieties are areas that are stressed in your current circumstances, because of beliefs about yourself, or certain situations, that you've learnt in your historical past.

Ministry involves identifying and resolving these inner beliefs through the work of the Spirit of truth.

Fear, anxiety and stress. *
Wright, "A More Excellent Way," Pg 212

Migraine

As with many conditions Migraine often coexists with other conditions such as depression, anxiety, bi-polar disorder, panic attacks and insomnia. It has also been found to have an association with physical problems such as stroke, heart disease, hypertension, epilepsy, asthma, and gastrointestinal disease. One study concluded that sufferers of migraines are three times more likely to develop Alzheimer's disease. And women are three times more likely to suffer from migraine than men. None of this is surprising, as many of the same emotional problems are common to all of these conditions.

In ministry we've seen people healed or delivered of migraines in the prayer line, as well as through resolving the negative emotions coming from internal *'heart beliefs'* that are held.

In cases that we've dealt with people are usually conflicted about whether or not they are acceptable. This has been learnt in childhood where often they have not been validated, and are consequently not secure in their identity. Many times, they've had to be what others wanted, or do what key figures wanted to get acceptance. They've ended up believing that they're not enough to be loved, accepted, or cared about unless they perform to expectations. They now often have a fear of rejection because of not meeting the standards perceived as necessary for acceptance. Remember these beliefs were learnt in their early history, so the process that produces the negative emotions is most often going on unconsciously.

This leads to a fear of rejection and anxiety that if they are not what others want, or do something that people disapprove of, that they will be rejected again. They commonly present with self-rejection for not being enough, or doing enough. Also guilt that they haven't done what was required, or been what was wanted, triggers the anxious negative emotions coming from the negative 'heart beliefs'/self-beliefs that exist.

Now, in the present, they are conflicted in themselves worrying about whether or not they've done enough, let anybody down, upset anyone, or whether or not they're alright. It's not surprising that the condition is linked to other worry and self-conflict-based conditions such as insomnia, Alzheimer's disease and depression.

In my book titled 'Taking Down Goliath,' which is focussed on resolving mental disorders, I have detailed what we've found to be behind depression. Namely what we call; 'never, ever beliefs.' This is where growing up a person learns something that causes them to believe that they can 'never ever' be what they need to be for some reason. This could begin in a household that demands performance, and they believe that they can 'never ever' be what they need to be for love and acceptance. They conclude that they'll never be enough, and don't know how to repair the problem. They conclude corresponding heart/self-beliefs about their identity, and possibly certain situations, all of which will need to be identified and ministered to.

This conflict could also come through events such as rejection of gender in the womb, where they now believe they can 'never ever' be what was wanted. Or through sexual abuse, where they now believe, for example, that they can 'never ever' be like other people because they are ruined. These kinds of beliefs can also be found behind migraines, and are commonly triggered in relationships.

Some Christian commentators have proposed that liking yourself produces serotonin. Deficiencies in serotonin are implicated in both depression and migraine. It's function as far as blood vessels in your brain go, is to control the diameter of the blood vessels to allow the flow of blood to go where it is needed. When your sero-tonin is low because of your guilt, self-rejection and consequent self-conflict, and your anxiety releases histamines which dilate your blood vessels, you then have pressure against nerve endings which produce the migraine.

Our reputable Christian commentator considers that behind migraines you will find;
*Conflict about self, conflict in life producing guilt in conjunction with fear. All Migraines are rooted in guilt and then fear, in that order. * Wright, "A More Excellent Way," Pg 280*

Multiple Sclerosis

MS sufferers are considered to be prone to developing other au-toimmune diseases such as autoimmune thyroid conditions, type 1 diabetes, psoriasis or inflammatory bowel disease. High blood pressure, depression and anxiety are considered to be comor-bidities. Several years ago, I prayed for a lady in a prayer line who suffered from MS. Much to her surprise her hands became warm for the first time in many years. She was a brand-new believer and was shocked and could not work it out how it happened.

Later, I had the opportunity to investigate her history, and found considerable rejection in her background leading to the self-re-jection and lack of acceptance of self that she was experiencing. She had been a very fit person and was quite lean even with her condition. I made the comment that if she'd been overweight the weakest link in the chain may have been her pancreas, and her body may have attacked itself there. She told me that her sister was overweight and that she had diabetes. They grew up with the same background, and likely ended up holding similar identity be-liefs. Note: In the U.S. both type 1 and type 2 diabetes have around the same rates of obesity implicated.

As with other diseases, ministry involves resolving the beliefs pro-ducing these feelings through identifying what is believed inside about identity, why it is believed, and then receiving truth from the

Holy Spirit. Our expert commentator cites the following emotional issues as being behind MS.

MS is rooted in deep, deep self-hatred and guilt, and spiritually is very close to diabetes (type 1) because it involves a father's rejection. *
Wright, "A More Excellent Way," Pg 227

Osteoporosis

My information search indicated that reportedly 79% of people with osteoporosis have at least one other chronic condition, with the most common other complaints being listed as arthritis, back problems, mental and behavioural conditions.

Additionally, it can coexist with metabolic diseases such as, cardio-vascular diseases, diabetes, obesity and non-alcoholic fatty liver disease. Not surprisingly given the proposed negative emotions behind this complaint, other conditions sharing these emotional roots such as celiac disease, inflammatory bowel problems, kidney or liver disease, and even cancer potentially develop alongside this condition.

Osteoporosis is a bone disease where the bones become weak and brittle, and new bone development fails to keep up with replacing old bone removal. It is a situation where bone mass and bone mineral density decreases, leading to decreased bone strength and consequently the increased possibility of bone fractures.

There are reduced chemical and hormonal values, as well as environmental factors that contribute to the development of the condition. The question remains, why would your body not be able to store these vitamins and minerals, and why are your hormone values lower than other peoples? The Bible offers a practical answer for why the condition exists, pointing again to the 'heart' as being the area that needs ministry, as described in earlier chapters.

Proverbs 14:30
A <u>heart</u> at peace gives life to the body, but envy rots the
bones. NIV (emphasis mine)

Our Christian authors indicate that the following issues will need to be worked through. Henry W Wright shared a case of a 60-year-old woman that he ministered to with MCS/EI along with advanced osteoporosis, whose bones returned to the condition of a 30-year-old woman.

Do you know what the Bible says the spiritual root is for non-meno-
pausal osteoporosis? I'll tell you - envy and jealousy are the cause of
rotting bones.
Wright, "A More Excellent Way," Pg 73

Envy and jealousy are generally produced from low self-esteem. A low image of self and one's worth will make a person jealous and/ or envious of someone who seems more celebrated, provided for, or accepted as person of value or success. So, you can expect, as other commentators suggest, co-occurring negative emotions of anxiety, fear of rejection, self-rejection or self-bitterness, and possibly depression. Researchers have found that depression can affect bone health through various mechanisms, including increased levels of stress hormones, such as cortisol. These fear/ stress/anxiety hormones can decrease bone formation, and possibly result in bone loss.

Parkinson's disease

Parkinson's disease (PD) is a nervous system disorder that gets worse over time. Implicated are low values of the hormone dopamine. This neurotransmitter and hormone has a number of functions in the body. One function is stimulating activity in the motor cortex which helps control movement. Consequently, when it's low in PD the messages controlling body movement are impaired. Dopamine is commonly known as a key hormone that can cause feelings of pleasure, satisfaction, and notably promotes motivation and goal setting. It is typically very high when a person experiences and receives love and acceptance.

[Some people are loved but are unable to receive it because of pre-existing identity beliefs.]

Diseases such as diabetes and cancer have been linked to the development of PD. It follows then that it is often associated with psychiatric disorders such as apathy, depression and anxiety. Around 80% of PD cases eventually develop dementia. Also noteworthy is that approximately 50% suffer from depression and anxiety. As we've stated in an earlier chapter, hopelessness stemming from a belief pertaining to identity, concluded and imbibed in developmental years is generally implicated in depression.

Remember the development and release of hormone in order for you to experience feelings physiologically follows thoughts, not the other way around. So, when you have low hormone values it's indicative of negative thinking that relates to not accepting yourself because of something that you perceive to be true about yourself. Ministry involves resolving these beliefs. Cases that I've worked with have had significant changes in their emotional make-up.

The usual fruits of rejection will be present but some 'disease specific traits' <u>may</u> also be implicated. I.E. The need for achievement and success in order to validate acceptability, and possibly a sense of being worthy of belonging. This plays out as a need for projects that provide potential hope for acknowledgment of worth. But on the <u>inside</u>, you still never really feel like you are good enough, or can perform well enough to be acceptable. This is probably why there is a depletion of dopamine......you never feel that what you do is enough, that you are worthy of the pleasure of reward or a sense of contentment. So, you can never be truly satisfied with who you are and what you have done. You still perceive that you're not loveable, not acceptable.

The depression/hopelessness component is that no matter what you do you will never ever really be acceptable. This can be overwhelming. People will either gravitate towards high achieving or will just roll over and give up, or possibly experience seasons of both. As you would then expect, anxiety and fear of rejection in the form of fear of failure is another common element. Failure may represent the potential for rejection and abandonment. Proverbs offers some insights into how *'heart beliefs'* relating to the hope of ever being enough may be a factor.

> *Proverbs 12:25*
> *Anxiety in the <u>heart</u> of man causes depression, But a good word makes it glad. NKJV (emphasis mine)*

> *Proverbs 13:12*
> *Hope deferred makes the <u>heart</u> sick, but when dreams come true, there is life and joy. NLT (emphasis mine)*

This can also, in some people, relate to a sense of people not receiving you if you fail. The feeling that if you are not what they want you to be, you may be abandoned. This profile can also be behind dementia which as already mentioned is a common peripheral disease that is connected to the progression of Parkinson's disease, developing in as many as 80% of known cases. Ministry using this model involves resolution of rejection issues, hopelessness, and other implicated emotional components. As with any condition, healing can occur in a prayer line as well. Given the other potential ailments that may proceed from these emotional issues, it is certainly worth dealing with the ground as a preventative measure.

Christian author, Henry W. Wright, suggests that the following profile needs to be dealt with:
In the case of Parkinson's, my initial investigation indicates unresolved rejection, massive amounts of abandonment, rejection and hope deferred.
Wright, "A More Excellent Way," Pg 259

Rejection is a fairly generic term. What we've found to be the key here, is what did you believe about yourself as a result of the rejection. These beliefs are the true cause of the problem, and the issues which need to be resolved. We'll cover this in upcoming chapters. If hope is deferred, or not realised, of course this will manifest as hopelessness, which as discussed, is a key component of the depression that is frequently linked to this illness.

Psoriasis

We've previously covered this on our list of autoimmune disorders. The association of Psoriasis notes the clustering of this condition with various other autoimmune conditions such as; Crohn's disease, celiac disease, multiple sclerosis, systemic lupus, and autoimmune thyroid disease. It has also been linked to Rheumatoid arthritis, type 1 diabetes, Sjogren's syndrome and other maladies.

Psoriasis is an autoimmune skin condition where immune T cells attack skin cells. It's not surprising to find it coexisting with other diseases given the existence of the same emotional profile. You can expect to find people with this complaint holding inner beliefs leading to perceptions that they are not loved or loveable, and/or not acceptable for some reason. The resultant self-conflict in regards to their worth and value, in turn leads to negative self-attitudes, for example; rejecting and being bitter towards themselves, and probable guilt about not doing enough, or being enough to be loved and accepted.

As with other conditions, ministry will involve identifying these beliefs, and sourcing the original memories where they began for context. Then receiving truth through the Spirit of truth about your true identity. Our Christian author Henry W Wright considers the following as the areas that need to be resolved.

Psoriasis is rooted in self-hatred, lack of self-esteem and conflict with identity. *
Wright, "A More Excellent Way," Pg 265

Shingles and Hives

Henry W Wright proposes in his book that; Behind all skin eruptions, which would include many rashes, humps and bumps, hives and shingles, you are going to find an over secretion of histamine and, in conjunction with it, a congregating and a proliferating of white corpuscles. Shingles is an anxiety and fear disease coupled with an autoimmune component involving self-rejection. Hives are a direct manifestation of fear and anxiety. *
Wright, "A More Excellent Way," Pg 263

We were ministering to a young lady one evening, and as we were identifying and focussing on the event where she imbibed beliefs producing anxiety, she suddenly broke out in hives all over. Many years on we still know her, and she's never reported having hives again after ministry. We've found over the years that Henry's position and research in regards to skin issues and anxiety are a helpful insight for those ministering. We've found all kinds of skin eruptions including problems such as pimples have some kind of fear implicated, at times a specific anxiety, producing a particular issue.

For example, in persons suffering from shingles we have noted that there is self-rejection present along with fear of rejection. Negative emotions requiring ministry that you can expect to find behind shingles are as follows.

Anxiety and fear, coupled with an autoimmune component involving self-rejection and self-hatred. *
Wright, "A More Excellent Way," Pg 263

Sjogren's Syndrome

Listed in our family of common autoimmune diseases Sjogren's syndrome can occur as an isolated condition, or be associated with a long list of other diseases. For example; it often exists with Rheumatoid arthritis, systemic lupus, systemic sclerosis, celiac disease, and a variety of other complaints. Around 20% of people also suffer from the autoimmune disease scleroderma, which is a similar disease to lupus. The most common additional autoimmune disease is autoimmune thyroid disease.

Ministry will involve identifying the events and consequent self-beliefs that lead to the negative responses listed by our Christian commentator. And then resolving these beliefs through the ministry of the Holy Spirit, via the simple process described in later chapters.

*Sjogren's shares certain autoimmune features with scleroderma. I am familiar with scleroderma. If Sjogren's is related to scleroderma, we have very obvious extreme self-rejection and self-hatred coupled with much guilt. The autoimmune component gives us the key. The inflammation indicated there is a proliferation of white corpuscles, so we know we are dealing with a person in conflict with self. *
Wright, "A More Excellent Way," Pg 289*

Stroke

Globally stroke is the second leading cause of death, and the third leading cause of death and disability combined. In western nations it is generally listed as the third leading cause of death behind heart disease and cancer. Other related conditions include; heart disease, high blood pressure, diabetes, (which doubles the possibility of having a stroke) and people who suffer migraines have a higher risk of stroke, with migraines bearing similar symptoms. Both involve restriction of blood vessels in the brain.

There are numerous medical and scientific articles that implicate anger, even rage, as a primary cause of stroke. *'Anger and other negative emotions may be triggers for ischemic stroke, according to a study published in the December 14 issue of Neurology, the scientific journal of the American Academy of Neurology.'* The study found that people who had strokes were more likely to have experienced anger or negative emotions in the two hours prior to the stroke than at the same time the day before the stroke. As a part of this particular study, they had participants rate their anger as; "very angry," "furious," or "enraged."

So, we're talking about significant anger of some kind, not just anger that may be expressing general displeasure that may be appropriate. If you're angry to this degree you may see generalised aggressive behaviour and unforgiveness towards others, and most importantly also towards yourself. This can be noted in the form of strong self-rejection.

We'll discuss anger in a later chapter where we'll examine negative emotions that lead to disease and their causes. If you feel that people are, for example; being unfair, don't care about you, treat you as unimportant and so on you will generally find an anger response. These feelings are rooted in beliefs about your worth that you've already interpreted in early life. In present life you are triggered by your perceptions of how you think that people see you, or are dealing with you. These perceptions touch into what you already believe about yourself inside. You respond in anger. Anger is the fruit of self-beliefs concluded, interpreted and im-bibed, in rejective events. These 'heart beliefs' that you now hold because of the rejective events is the real issue.

So, even though you're angry with others for making you feel what you already believe about yourself, you're now also angry with yourself for not being worth treating as important, valuable, acceptable, significant, worth caring about, and so on. Ministry involves visiting the memories where you learnt what you now believe about yourself, and possibly certain situations, which make you reject yourself.

Many times, we've seen anger resolved quickly by the Spirit of truth as He brings God's perspective to our distorted areas of personal perception. I recall one man being sent to me who had an explosive anger problem. He'd been told to learn every scripture in the Bible about anger. So, now he was an expert on scriptural positions in regards to anger, but this 'head knowledge' didn't change a thing. We did a short session finding the root of his anger in a rejective childhood event. God communicated truth to him and dealt with the deceptive 'heart knowledge' about his identity that he held, and his anger issue was completely resolved.

Examples of triggers that we've observed is when a person feels that they're not being listened to, heard, or they are not being valued or cared about. This taps into their low self-image and produces a strong reaction. Art Mathias notes that *'Alzheimer's and other dementia patients may also display worsening anger, as they lose the ability to control their emotions. The anger has always been there, but as they lose control it manifests. Scientists call this "emotional incontinence.'* * He proposes that behind strokes you can expect to find *spiritual/ emotional strongholds of anger, rage, and self-bitterness.* *
Art Mathias, "In His Own Image", Pg 198 – 199

Dr. Henry W Wright states:
It has been my observation that individuals who have strokes also have self-rejection, self- bitterness and self- hatred. I suppose that you could say that when you do not like yourself, clogging of your arteries is the immediate fruit physiologically. I guess it might be a good idea to not kill ourselves in our self-esteem because our body might conform to that image very quickly. *
Wright, "A More Excellent Way," Pg 206

Indeed, the process of disease is as follows: our corrupted and deceived beliefs about our identity stored in our hearts influences our mind and thinking negatively. In turn this produces negative emotions and responses that disrupt the balance of finely tuned bodily systems, finishing in the body as disease.

Ulcers

Fears, anxieties, and stresses can weaken the immune system causing what is known as immunosuppression. This condition makes it harder for your defensive immune system to be able to fight off infections. Bacterium are considered to be behind ulcers. But then you have to ask the question. Why doesn't everyone have ulcers? Clearly, not everyone is immunosuppressed! Other conditions can lead to immune system problems, along with some medications or recreational drugs.

As with other physical, mental and emotional complaints, ministry involves identifying and processing the inner beliefs that cause the fears and anxieties that stress the body. Christian authors cite that the areas of fear, anxiety, stress, insecurity, and self-rejection need to be dealt with. We have certainly noted that people with Ulcers that we've been exposed to suffer from these emotional states.

Ulcerative Colitis

This autoimmune condition can lead to a number of other maladies, and has been associated with inflammatory autoimmune diseases such as; Hashimoto's thyroiditis and Sjogren's syndrome. Years ago, we ministered to a particular anxiety that was crippling a middle-aged lady's quality of life. At the time we weren't aware, and weren't told of accompanying physical complaints. We heard later that once she was free of the anxiety that she discovered that a physical healing had occurred as a biproduct.

Henry W Wright considered that the particular type of anxiety which could lead to irritation, inflammation and finally ulceration; *However, stress and anxiety, or things bugging you over the long term, lack of trust, even feeling like you don't belong, can cause the dendrites to pulsate.* * (Dendrites are extensions of a neuron or nerve cell that receives signals from other neurons or sensory receptors.) *Ulcerative Colitis is an anxiety disorder, rooted in extreme fear and anxiety and dread....* * Being an autoimmune disease, you can also expect that self-rejection will also be present in the profile.
Wright, "A More Excellent Way," Pg 226

Ministry will involve with dealing with the inner beliefs about identity and situations that produce this extreme fear, anxiety, insecurity and sense of rejection. In ministry we've most often found that feelings that you don't belong begin prenatally in the womb where the parent/s don't want the child for some reason. These feelings are imbibed into the child, and even if the parents later change their minds, the belief and feeling that they aren't wanted, should not be here, and don't belong, remain. Freedom comes through God's truth from the Spirit of truth.

Varicose veins

Reportedly some people with varicose veins may also develop deep vein thrombosis (DVT). This is not surprising considering that our commentators consider that DVT also comes as a result of anger, even to the point of rage. Environmental elements such as standing or sitting for long periods of time can be implicated in creating a situation where blood pools in the leg veins, causing increased pressure. These same factors can promote the possibility of DVT as well.

It's well documented by the medical community that anger, even brief, can impair the ability of blood vessels to expand and contract. It is considered by the medical community that anger and other strong emotions can contribute to varicose veins. Given that these develop over time, it's reasonable to deduce that you're dealing with long term anger. This can be suppressed and internalised in some personality types, possibly because of some belief systems held that expressing emotion is unacceptable. Or it may be expressed explosively through a more volatile, emotionally available type person.

Dr Wright suggests: *Could I say the person is brooding, steaming and deep inside they are filled with anger, rage, and resentment. So whether externalized or internalized, it is still sin and the result is the same.* * Wright, "A More Excellent Way," Pg 207

Ministry will require dealing with the beliefs that produce the anger and resentment. Commonly a person has learnt that they're not cared about or valued by others for some reason. The initial place where they learnt this will need to be identified, and inner beliefs resolved through the ministry of the Holy Spirit as described in the coming chapters.

EMOTIONAL ROOTS OF DISEASE

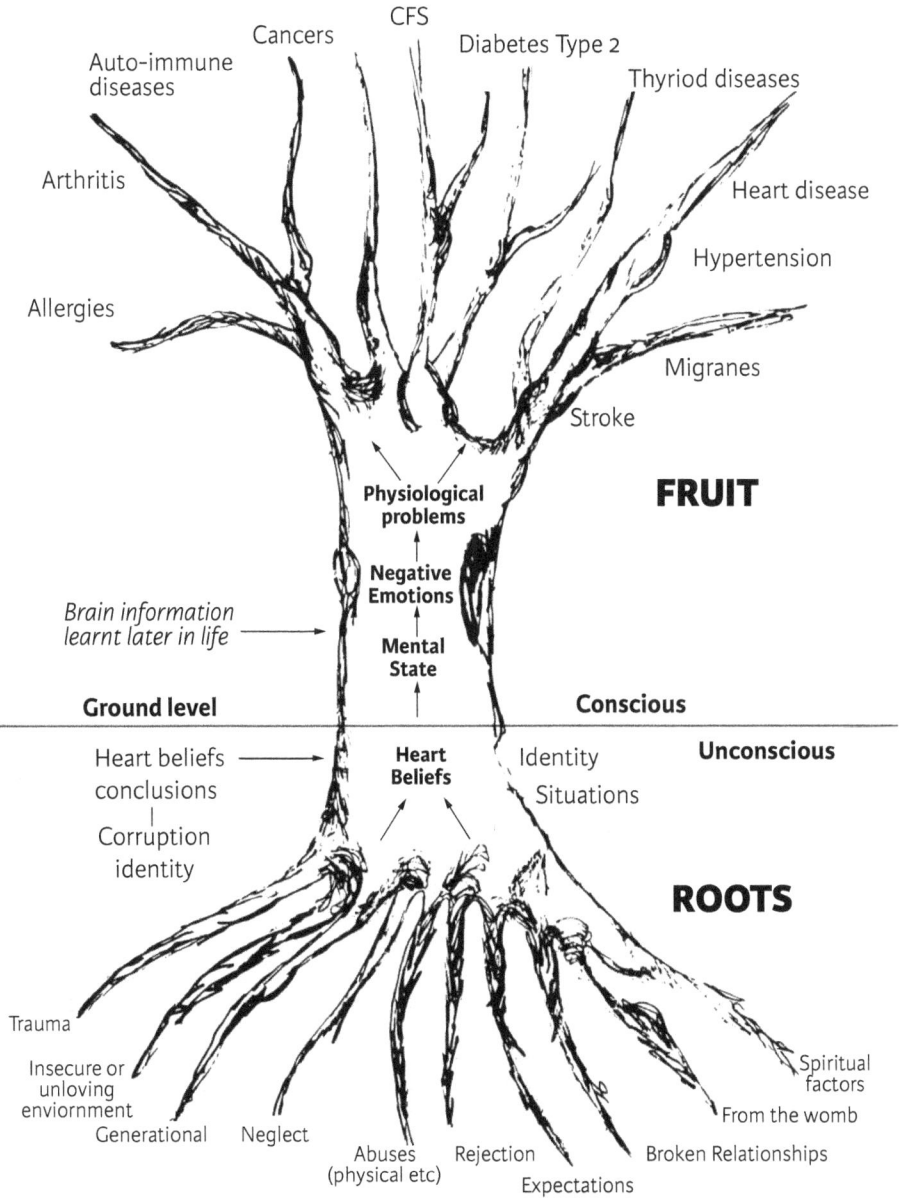

CFS

Cancers

Auto-immune diseases

Diabetes Type 2

Thyriod diseases

Arthritis

Heart disease

Hypertension

Allergies

Migranes

Stroke

Physiological problems

FRUIT

Negative Emotions

Brain information learnt later in life

Mental State

Ground level

Conscious

Heart beliefs conclusions

Heart Beliefs

Identity

Unconscious

Corruption identity

Situations

ROOTS

Trauma

Insecure or unloving enviornment

Spiritual factors

Generational   Neglect

From the womb

Abuses (physical etc)

Rejection

Broken Relationships

Expectations

Final thoughts and summary

There are many other diseases that could be listed here. And you would find that as illustrated with our tree, they all pretty much are sourced in the same types of places, and involve the resultant groups of negative emotions and reactive attitudes. Let me state that many of these issues and beliefs that you hold, you may not be consciously aware of. They're going on underneath, so many people may well deny how they really feel about themselves, and not accept that they suffer with these emotions. With any disease, the emotional healing model of ministry involves resolving the beliefs producing these feelings through finding what is believed inside about identity, and why it is believed.

As with other conditions, ministry then will involve identifying these beliefs, and sourcing the original memories where they began for context in regard to what you believe, and why you have accepted these beliefs as being true about you. And then finally for freedom, receiving truth through the Spirit of truth about your true identity.

Many people believe that they can keep their emotional issues and compensate for them in some way. Perhaps blaming others for how they feel, or masking their turmoil and pain with food, alcohol, drugs or even immoral behaviour. Often people choose to live in denial of their problems. They fail to understand how these negative emotions affect their whole person, leading to sin, spiritual, mental, emotional, relational and finally physical issues. I wouldn't consider these disordered states to be a blessing, but they are certainly a curse.

It's therefore vitally important to deal with them. For yourself, your health and wholeness, and for those around you that your problems impact; such as in particular, your children.

The good news is that Jesus became a curse for us, paying for our freedom. Galatians 3:13. Now paid for, we're entitled by faith to access the provisions of our healing and freedom, which are facilitated and received with the help and work of the Holy Spirit.

Dealing with these areas is vitally important and can't be ignored. There's an imperative to get your whole life and being into God's order. A full relationship with Him through sanctification of our inner self, and through wholeness for the broken disordered thinking coming from our hearts. Sadly, many Christians never take God's offer for help in this area, even though it's available to them. They then end up afflicted with the same conditions as the people in the world.

A biblical picture is God delivering the people from captivity in Egypt. He did everything, and the Israelites did nothing. This is like redemption. We're saved and born again in spirit in a moment of time, with God doing everything through the work of Christ Jesus on the cross, and we do nothing but accept it. But then He had the promised land for them. This was different. This was something that they were to work through with Him. This is a picture of sanctification, where working with God we possess the land of our soul little by little.

Many Christians are wandering around in the wilderness. They were redeemed and born again, but never entered into the process of sanctification. Or they were taught that sanctification is a process that you go through on your own, as your own god, without the work of the Holy Spirit. Redemption is instant and a past tense completed work. Sanctification is an ongoing work. We see it presented in the continuing present tense in the following passage in the book of Hebrews.

> Hebrews 10:14
> For by one offering He has perfected forever those who _are being_ sanctified. NKJV (emphasis mine)

Possibly one of the largest problems that we see, is that people seeking help and support in the sanctification process can't find churches or individuals who are trained and equipped to help them. In short, God is not getting what He wants. His church is largely off mission, and not focussed on what He intended for His people. They are not prioritising healing and freedom as central in confirming the good news of the Kingdom of God coming. We need to be able to not just talk about the good news, but fulfill God's plan and deliver it. As a young minister I personally took the admonition of Ezekiel 34 very seriously.

> *Ezekiel 34:1 -2,4*
> *[1] And the word of the LORD came to me, saying, [2] "Son of man, prophesy against the shepherds of Israel, prophesy and say to them, 'Thus says the Lord GOD to the shepherds: "Woe to the shepherds of Israel who feed themselves! Should not the shepherds feed the flocks?*
> *[4] "The weak you have not strengthened, <u>nor have you healed those who were sick, nor bound up the broken,</u>*
> *NKJV (emphasis mine)*

One result of our own journey into finding God's answers for healing and freedom for His people, is now being able to share what we've learnt. Today we spend most of our Christian ministry training Pastors across the world in these ministries. God willing, we will see an explosion of revival across the churches in these times as we return fully to God's primary intentions for the work of His church.

My prayer is that this publication helps you in your journey, and that you find the peace and wholeness that God intended for you to have in every area of your life. Let's move on to examining the mechanics of these emotions that are the fruit of our disordered inner and outer conditions. And then conclude in the final chapters with a ministry model covering how to be set free.

In Chapter 15 we provided the following as a list of these emotions and reactions to our environment that create stressors to our sense of identity and security which, either in isolation, or identifiable in groups, have been documented as being behind diseases. As a reference I'll repeat them here before we begin to breakdown an understanding of these emotions in the coming chapters.

Anger – Self anger
Anxiety – fear/stress/insecurity
Bitterness – Self bitterness - Resentment/rebellion
Depression – hopelessness
Envy – Jealousy
Guilt – shame (Performance anxiety, drivenness)
Grief – sadness/sorrow
Inferiority – Low self-image/esteem
Rejection – self-rejection – fear of rejection – self-conflict

Over the next few chapters, we want to explain the dynamics and mechanics of how these negative emotions function.

Rejection - a Major Source of Disease

Rejection is a major tap root for problems that lead to disease and health conditions. In fact, you will find it implicated in most chronic illnesses. Often people come for ministry for various issues declaring that their problem is rejection. As we've repetitively described, generally the problem is our corrupted or distorted perception of our identity. Our beliefs about self.

So, the issue is not so much rejection per se, but more importantly what you have ended up believing about self as a result of being rejected. It is these inner *'heart beliefs'* that keep you in a rejected state. And it is these beliefs that produce all of the corresponding negative responses, reactions, and attitudes that are also generally found accompanying physical, emotional, and mental conditions.

Put simply, rejection is a state of not being accepted. Let me present a definition of rejection or non-acceptance in order to clarify attitudes and actions that we could have been exposed to that may have led to our current problem;
- to refuse to acknowledge or accept
- to forsake

- to refuse to have or use
- to cast or throw away as useless, worthless, or unsatisfactory
- to refuse to love
- to discard as unwanted or not filling requirements

Many people hold *'heart beliefs'* that they are not wanted, don't belong, aren't a part of things, or perhaps that they're not loved or loveable. Still others feel inside as though they are worthless, a nothing, useless, in the way, not cared about, will never be good enough, or don't measure up to what is wanted, and so on. They feel that they fall short of the expectations of others. These kinds of beliefs all fall under the category of the results of rejection.

Sources of rejection

God is accepting of us as His created beings. He accepts who we are, although He doesn't accept many of the things that we do as a result of our woundedness or deception. So, in His love, grace and mercy, through Jesus, if we're repentant and accept that our be-haviour is out of His order, He forgives what we do. Jesus Himself bore our rejection, and was Himself rejected on our behalf as He exchanged His righteousness for our sinfulness. In the following passage we can see that Jesus not only took our rejection and paid for our sin so that we could receive healing, but He also carried our weaknesses. He was Himself familiar with emotional pain and sorrow. He bore the weight of our own emotional sorrows so that we could be set free from them and come to a place of peace.

> Isaiah 53:3-6
> ³ He was despised and <u>rejected</u>--a man of <u>sorrows,</u>
> acquainted with bitterest grief. We turned our backs on
> him and looked the other way when he went by. He was
> despised, and we did not care. ⁴ Yet it was <u>our weaknesses</u>
> he carried; it was our sorrows that weighed him down.
> And we thought his troubles were a punishment from
> God for his own sins! ⁵ But he was wounded and crushed
> for our sins. He was beaten that <u>we might have peace</u>.

He was whipped, and <u>we were healed</u>! [6] All of us have strayed away like sheep. We have left God's paths to follow our own. Yet the LORD laid on him the <u>guilt and sins</u> of us all. NLT (emphasis mine)

God's intention for us was always to have acceptance. But as we've previously described we were born into a fallen world. When what He wants for us is not supplied to us by His earthly representatives, we come to negative conclusions about ourselves.

We interpret who we are through the negative influences that we're exposed to. To reiterate, we reach these conclusions before we're 10 years old, which is the portion of time where both the Bible and science point to as where we decide identity. Our most common influences then are our parents, and at times authority figures, or older children at home. This can include the early years of school, through dealings with teachers or supervisors. Many times, our parents weren't aware of our emotional needs in this formative stage, or were simply continuing the parenting model that they themselves grew up under.

So, our first source of rejection comes from omissions. That is, things that God intended for us to have, but we weren't fully given for some reason, such as;

- Affirmation
- Worth
- Significance
- Encouragement
- Value
- Acknowledgement
- Acceptance
- Love (Nurture)

Without these and other positive influences, under the old nature we come to negative conclusions and consequent beliefs about ourselves. In turn these produce negative emotions, which lead to negative reactions and behaviours.

Our second source of rejection can be found in acts of commission. In other words, things done to us that shouldn't have been.

This could include;
- Physical, or sexual abuse
- Verbal or emotional abuse, criticism, fault-finding
- Deliberate rejection from others of some kind
- Being controlled or used by a selfish entity

This lack of acceptance can begin as early as in the womb where a child is not wanted. This is something that we have dealt with regularly for decades. From that root grow many branches. Perhaps the parent can't feed or look after the child for some reason, and so they don't want them. This is imprinted onto the child, and we've found over and over that people with these beginnings generally feel that they aren't wanted, don't belong, are not a part of things, shouldn't be here or exist, and commonly that they're a nuisance, an inconvenience, in the way, or something similar.

We often minister to people who felt rejection from birth. They have a sense of the disappointment of a parent or parents, who for example, were wanting a child of another gender. They sense this and believe that they are not what they should be. Again, this distorts their picture of identity, and they will struggle through life, often having to deal with depression and anxiety. Those feelings can also begin even earlier, having already been imbibed even in the womb. In this case the gender identity that they feel that they should have been for acceptance is other than what they find that they've received at birth.

It creates all kinds of torment in their being, with them at times feeling that their bodies have betrayed them, in the sense of not being able to be what they think that they should be for acceptance. In today's world humanistic governments encourage them to be 'their own god,' and select their own gender that supposedly will make them happy. The real answer is the healing of the identity by the Holy Spirit in this regard, so that they can accept and celebrate themselves as they were created. That's just one example of the outworking's a specific rejection. Sadly, in general people with the particular problem that we have just described have a much higher rate of depression than the general population.

Results of rejection

When a person has been rejected it usually causes deep emotional pain. And even though many bury this pain, or compensate for it, or perhaps protect themselves in some way, underneath they fear it happening again. Fear of rejection is the most common form of anxiety that people have to deal with worldwide. It is often mixed in with other negative emotions stemming from rejection, and will be found in many mental and emotional problems, along with its role in chronic physical conditions. We'll cover this more in a later chapter when we deal with the subject of fear in isolation.

Another fruit that you can expect to be present as a result of rejection is Self-rejection. If you have taken on a *'heart belief'* that you're unacceptable for some reason, it makes sense that you've received and agreed with that assessment of SELF at some level, even if unconsciously. It follows then that you'll continue on with rejecting who you perceive yourself to be. Even though this may be in conflict with what you would like to think that you are. Let me note here, that whenever you have self-rejection, you're almost certainly going to have anxiety as well. Because if you reject yourself because of your shortcomings, you fear others rejecting you for the same reasons. This is why self-rejection and fear/anxiety often co-occur in various diseases.

If you reject who you perceive that you are, then underneath you usually don't like yourself. In a sense you are opposed to yourself, or you are the enemy of who/how you think that you are. This plays out in your body through various mechanisms. In the next chapters we'll begin to cover the negative self-destructive attitudes and responses that result from this inner decision or agreement to reject yourself. God intended for Christian ministry to be provided through His church to minister to people suffering in these areas.

> 2 Timothy 2:24-26
> [24] *And the servant of the Lord must not strive; but be gentle unto all men, apt to teach, patient,* [25] *In meekness*

instructing <u>those that oppose themselves</u>; if God perad-
venture will give them <u>repentance</u> to the acknowledging
of <u>the truth</u>; [26] *And that <u>they may recover themselves</u> out*
of the snare of the devil, who are taken captive by him at
his will. KJV (emphasis mine)

Biblically, repentance means to change your thinking, reconsider your ways. So, the preceding passage is pointing to God uncovering areas of deception, and setting you free through truth, so that your thinking is changed, and you can now choose different ways of living and behaving. (Peradventure means; perhaps, maybe, or might possibly) In this case the resultant repentance is a gift given through ministry, rather than brought about by a deliberate act of the will.

Some time ago we were conducting a training seminar in a church, and we explained that autoimmune disease was in part a product of self-rejection. A girl who was attending came up in the break and explained that she suffered from autoimmune disease, and that she had struggled with self-identity. She also noted that since she'd come to the Lord, and that in an environment of love and acceptance in the great church that she had begun to attend, that she was more accepting of herself, and that her condition had improved.

Ultimately for a complete and lasting healing, beliefs creating inner conflict would need to be resolved. As you've already seen a number of these 'fruits' of rejection will be present together in a disease or condition profile.

Self - Rejection

Low self-image
Inferiorities
Insecurities
Inadequacy
Guilt
Sadness, Grief, Sorry
Self-accusation
Self-condemnation
Inability/Refusal to communicate
Fear of failure
Fear of others opinions
Other fears
Anxiety, Worry, Depression
Negativitiy, Pessimism
Hopelessness, Despair

Behaviour Resulting From the Fear of Rejection

Striving, Achievement
Performances, Competitions
Withdrawal
Independence, Isolation
Self-protection
Self-centredness, Selfishness
Self-justification
Self-righteousness
Self-idolatry
Self-pity
Criticism, Judgement
Envy, Jealousy, Covetousness
Pride, Egotism, Arrogance
Manipulation, Control
Possessiveness
Emotional immaturity

Aggressive Reactions

Unforgiveness
Resentment
Bitterness
Hatred
Ungodly anger
Refusing comfort
Rejection of others
Harshness
Hardness
Aggressive attitudes
Argumentativeness
Stubborness
Defiance
Rebellion

The Fruit of Beliefs Stemming From Rejection

Root Causes

1. Manner and timing of conception

2. In a Mother's womb

3. The manner of birth

4. Lack of Mother - bonding

5. Adoption

6. Hereditary

7. Negative identity issues from the father

8. Rejection through teach and school mates

9. Self-rejection cau by own attitudes

10. Multiple causes puberty and beyor

Rejection Tree concept by Noel and Phyl Gibson
Used by permission, Phyl Gibson

(This is a modified version of the original
Rejection Tree diagram produced by Jessica)

Jessi
Bless

chapter 19

Low Self-Image, and Inferiority

Another 'fruit' of being rejected, or not being received as acceptable, is low self-image and a sense of inferiority. Once you've concluded that you're faulty, or fall short in some way following a rejective event in the formative years, it naturally follows that you have a poor image of SELF, and consequent low self-esteem. It is most often the result of rejection initially, but these concluded negative identity beliefs are what propagate and continue self-rejection, along with fear of rejection. These *'heart beliefs'* are what is behind the sense of unacceptability, low self-esteem, worthlessness, and so on. You don't accept who you are at the foundational level.

You feel that you're not up to standards, possibly inferior, not meeting expectations. This can be observed at times as someone who actually lives under the low self-image and inferiority, continually rejecting self, and stating how useless and hopeless that they are. Perhaps these are people never wanting to try to do anything, believing that they're a failure, and their ensuant lack of success in life only seemingly proves that their negative assessment of self is true.

Or, they may go in the other direction with some kind of compensating behaviour, trying to prove to themselves and others that what they perceive subconsciously underneath about themselves is not true. In a sense this is a form of denial as they build an image of self that they consider is acceptable. Often, they then worship their own self-made image, and expect others to do the same. This could manifest or become evident in behaviour and attitudes such as:

Pride, trying to convince yourself and others that you're better than them, because underneath you really believe that you're not. The fruit of the pride tree can be observed with the following types of behaviours:

Striving, competitiveness, drivenness to succeed, criticism and judgement of others, comparison, and presumption. Even jealousy, because you don't like seeing others receive the praise, success or physical blessings, that you want for yourself in order to feel accepted and good enough. Also, unforgiveness and resentment often begin from inferiority, because your self-image is brittle and readily wounded. The person of pride is easily offended.

When people make you feel about yourself, what you do actually perceive as true about you, then they're aggravating a wound. Then you respond by holding them to account in the hope of making them hurt too. This could be in the form of aggressive behaviour or rejection of others in some way. In a sense, trying to blow out the candle of another so that your own burns brighter. Or it could lead to unforgiveness producing resentment and bitterness. As the old saying goes; 'You hold them to account, but strangle yourself to death!'

You'll find these sinful responses as reactions to having your low self-image triggered, and this emotional dysregulation is implicated in many serious sickness and diseases.

Insecurities (A form of fear and anxiety)

Once you've come to these conclusions about your worth and acceptability you no longer feel secure that you'll be wanted, protected, loved, treated as significant, valued or accepted. Insecurity is a type of anxiety that you'll find in many conditions. For instance, what we term as 'performance anxiety' begins with these kinds of insecurities.

Performance anxiety comes when a person has grown up under conditional acceptance. This is where a person is only received when they perform to the expectations or standards of an authority figure. If they grow up under judgement and criticism, and conclude that nothing that they do is ever good enough, then they live a life of believing that they won't be able to perform sufficiently for acceptance in the future. This is a constant anxiety as they go through life, which eventually wears out the body. But it's based on what you have previously concluded about your identity in that negative environment.

Some commentators consider that, for example, behind depression, or syndromes such as C.F.S. you will find performance anxiety as a component of the profile leading to the illnesses.

Sadness, grief, sorrow

> Psalm 31:9
> Be merciful to me, O LORD, for I am in distress; my eyes
> grow weak with sorrow, my soul and my body with grief.
> NIV

At times we see people who have what we can only describe as a 'tragic look' on their faces. These are those who have had events in their lives where they've suffered loss of some kind, and the resulting self-beliefs continue to be evident on the countenance of those who suffer, as a reflection of the inner state of their hearts.

Loss in its basic form relates to losing something, or someone. An example of this would be someone who has suffered sexual abuse. They often feel dirty, used, different to others, of no value, no longer normal and so on. They've lost their sense of being whole, acceptable, worthy, wholesome. This can be implicated in many physical conditions. Other forms of abuse, such as verbal, emotional and physical abuse are also identity destroying. People conclude that if they were really loved, valued and significant, then they would not be treated in such a way.

So, loss can come because of things that are done to you that cause you to lose your sense of self-worth. It can also stem from things that were never done to affirm your identity. And so the loss is related to never having been given what you feel that you should have had, or have seen others receive.

Common stressors for grief and sadness

At times people present for ministry being in a state of grief, sadness, or sorrow having lost a love one, or gone through a divorce or relationship breakdown. They usually believe that the feelings that they're experiencing are proceeding entirely from having lost a significant person in their lives. For example, a parent dying. Often what we've found in practice, is that what they've actually lost, is the possibility of ever being able to receive affirmation and acceptance from that person, having never received it before. And when we minister to the negative self-image beliefs received from dealing with that person in childhood, we find that most of the grief and sorrow is resolved.

That's not to say that losing someone that you love is not sad, it is. It's just saying that much of the pain is found in our own sense of identity, which as we've pointed out repetitively is found in the heart. A relational breakdown such as divorce can also produce these kinds of feelings. Although people often blame the spouse; *'it's them, they're making me feel bad, and if they treated me properly this wouldn't have happened to me. They've hurt me!'*

The truth is that usually the grief and sadness can be found in the fact that the relational breakdown has touched into your beliefs and feelings of being unacceptable, unlovable, not good enough, worthless, or a nothing, or something similar. These feelings are just being touched into and triggered, having already been in existence since having been imbibed and concluded in early childhood events.

Hopelessness and Depression

As we've described in earlier chapters, often mental problems run concurrently with specific physical conditions. The medical world is largely fragmented into specialty departments, so very often nobody is working with the whole picture. Most doctors will readily admit that they usually haven't had much training beyond their area of expertise. Depression is considered a growing world epidemic, and is expected to become the 2nd largest cause of illness by 2030. It is linked to a number of diseases and conditions, including at times, some types of cancer. Reportedly 60% of people with cancer have suffered with hopelessness and depression.

Hopelessness can be because of your circumstances. For example, if you live in poverty, you will feel that your situation will 'never, ever,' get any better. It's hopeless and overwhelming and could lead to what has been known as reactive depression, where your feelings are a response to your situation. This kind of hopelessness and possible depression is resolved if your circumstances change for some reason. Perhaps you have no job, and can't pay your bills and feed your family. Then you find employment, and now your situation has altered, and you now have hope and a better future.

The kind of hopelessness and possible depression that is ongoing and unresolvable without ministry is endogenous or internal hopelessness. This is found in the self-beliefs in the heart relating to identity, and could begin for example in an environment where it didn't matter what you did, or how hard you tried, you could 'never, ever,' meet the expectations and standards that you are being measured by. This kind of hopelessness can lead to depression and sickness. It will have anxiety linked to it as fear of rejection. This is because once you've concluded beliefs that you can never be good enough for some reason, then you expectantly fear people discovering your perceived weakness and rejecting you also.

> Proverbs 12:25
> Anxiety in the heart of man causes depression, But a good word makes it glad. NKJV

These 'never, ever' beliefs are like a weight that pushes you down. It is normally internal depression relating to your perceived identity that is found behind disease profiles. This is largely because of the persistent unrelenting nature of these inner beliefs. The bible describes this condition as a spirit of heaviness or despair, depending on the translation. You despair of all hope of the situation changing, which is why we've come to describe what we've found to be behind depression as a never, ever belief. It's relatively easy with the internet today to source research articles linking depression to disease.

More information on depression can be sourced in the book on resolving mental disorder by the same author titled; Taking Down Goliath

20

Emotional Responses That Make us Sick

In this chapter we're looking at negative emotions and behaviour that proceed from negative identity beliefs, or beliefs that come from situations. These are not the root of the problem, they're the response or reaction to what we may have been exposed to. The real problem is most often the *'heart belief'* or belief and perception about self. I call many of these responses, universal reactions. This is because they are predictable ways that any of us could or would respond if we carried the same kinds of hurt, or faced the same kinds of situations, regardless of whether we internalise them, or act out our feelings.

Dr. Art Mathias from Wellspring ministries in Alaska pointed out in one of his books, that when emotions are outward, that they are generally inward as well. For example, if you're angry at someone else, you are very likely often angry at yourself too. Based on decades of experience I totally agree with him, particularly if you're talking about anger that comes from a pre-existing identity condition.

To explain this, what I mean is, if somebody treats you as though you are unimportant then you may be very angry that they have devalued you. But the reason that this hurts and produces a response, is most likely because in your formative years you came to some conclusion about why people treated you as unimportant. You may have believed that you're not good enough for some reason, and you interpreted that as the reason why you're treated as lesser or unimportant. This now becomes your unconscious default self-belief. Now when somebody triggers you, you are angry towards them for making you feel what you already believe about yourself. But you're also angry with yourself for not being good enough, or what you feel that you should be.

This can be true across the range of negative emotional responses. In the case of anger, if someone throws their rubbish over your fence you might simply be angry because of their behaviour. But, once again, if your anger is inordinate, it could be driven by the fact that you feel like if they thought you were more important, they wouldn't dispose of their junk in this manner.

I personally believe that the inward expression of these negative emotions may at times be even more relative to specific diseases, even though the chemical cocktail of imbalanced hormones would certainly have both involved.

Attitudes, and responses often implicated in chronic conditions

Anger (Self anger)

Anger as a universal emotion comes when something isn't how you think it 'should be.' It's a predictable response. For example, your new wife doesn't wash the dishes straight after the meal, when that's what happened in your household when you were growing up. She refuses to change, you get frustrated, and then angry because in your thinking, this it isn't 'how it should be.' This is a circumstantial, external, example of the mechanics of anger, which can be resolved with choosing to change how you think and expect that things should be done.

However, if you perceive that people don't really care about you, which is what happened when you were growing up, then your response is coming from an internal issue relating to your identity. Inside you somehow know that you 'should be' valued and cared about. (It's God's way and intention for every human being.) So, when it doesn't happen you act out in anger, or internalise your anger, but cut the person who is the source of your hurt off. But inside you are also angry with yourself that you're not the person that you 'should be' who people would care about.

Even Jesus exhibited this universal response when the temple was made into a house of money changers. That's not how it 'should be,' it's meant to be a house of prayer. Evidently, He was angry enough to overturn tables, and drive them out with a purpose made whip.

For us, the scripture encourages to deal with anger as quickly as possible, because if it remains it will eventually make us sick, as you have seen when we went through the Etiology (causes and pathways of medical conditions) of disease in earlier chapters. Ephesians 4:26-27

Expressions of anger

Anger has various forms or expressions such as resentment or bitterness, which are longer acting and more permanent mani-festations. In these cases, these versions of anger come when the offences are relived, recycled and held onto. They generally relate to perceived attacks that trigger the negative self-identity beliefs that are held, and can include bitterness, resentment, and even hatred. This can be towards the person who was involved in the original event/s that led to the negative self-image to begin with, or often subsequent people who trigger the feelings. The real root will almost always be found to have its origins in childhood events where the initial injustice occurred.

The kind of anger that is involved in disease usually has a person as the object, be it is others, or self. Whether it is in the form of resentment, bitterness or even rebellion it is based on unforgiveness' of some kind. Love, acceptance and grace can't exist without forgiveness.' You're still holding them, or yourself to account for some reason which needs to be exposed and often ministered to.

This is different anger than you would have towards the guy who cuts you off, or is driving too slowly when you're in a hurry. This is usually transient anger, which can be reactive to situations, or presenting circumstances. (Unless of course this triggers some pre-existing internal historical belief of some kind, such as; it's not fair, nobody cares about me, values me, cares about what I want or need, etc.)

Let me note here, expressed external anger can still be eruptions of internal anger from an internalised source. It's like a sub-surface volcano letting off steam. Internalised anger often becomes bitterness and resentment, and can, at times, be expressed as rejection of others. Even rebellion, where you simply will not submit to another.

Bitterness (Self- bitterness)

As we've cited, bitterness generally begins with unforgiveness, and is the result of stewing over something involved in deep hurt. Resentment, is another bi-product. Again, you can resent or be bitter against yourself, not forgiving yourself for who you are, or how you are. Holding yourself to account for your failings and the perception of letting yourself and others down. It usually involves holding a list of grievances, or record of wrongs, against yourself or others. (1 Corinthians 13:5 NLT, NIV) Anger will generally be an active expression as well. In fact, bitterness and resentment is the process of keeping the anger alive.

In ministry we're not generally focussed on getting the person to forgive. We're looking for the event that has corrupted their identity and hurt them in the first instance. For example, if someone was sexually abused, and have always struggled to forgive the perpetrator, they probably don't know what they're trying to forgive them for. That is, they don't know yet what the negative belief about their identity was the result of the act. What hurts most is the belief that you're dirty, or damaged goods, or whatever it might be. When this is healed through the work of the Holy Spirit bringing truth, usually the person automatically goes from unforgiveness and bitterness, to; "I feel sorry for that person that they had that problem, something must have made them like that."

In the event that you deal with people in bitterness, resentment, and unforgiveness, who hold others to account for how they've made you feel, these people will often respond out of their own negative self-image. Now you have an environment where everyone may be affected by the person who isn't prepared to forgive and carries the bitterness.

> Hebrews 12:15
> *looking carefully lest anyone fall short of the grace of*
> *God; lest any root of bitterness springing up cause*
> *trouble, and by this many become defiled; NKJV*

It's fairly easy to do internet searches on many studies and much research on how anger and bitterness are emotions that when pervading and long term can make you sick. Let me highlight here that you don't need a research team or the confirmation of science. Anyone who gets angry can feel their blood pressure rising and their body chemistry changing. The greater the anger or bitterness, the greater the physical affect.

If these emotions remain activated, even at low levels you are going to have altered hormonal and consequent imbalanced physical states. This will result in a variety of eventual potential disease outcomes. This is why the scriptures exhort us to deal with anger quickly, and make sure that we walk in forgiveness.' If the problem is from a historical source, which they usually are, get ministry as described in later chapters.

Matthew 6:14-15
[14] For if you forgive men when they sin against you, your heavenly Father will also forgive you. [15] But if you do not forgive men their sins, your Father will not forgive your sins. NIV

Internalised emotion

The late Noel Gibson was the author of some excellent books on rejection and its fruit. I recall him making a comment along the lines of; 'some people bury their emotions, but tend the grave continually.' As I understand it, what he meant by this statement, was that some people hide their emotions, but you can see the fruit of their compensating behaviour in how they live their lives. For instance, a person with an inner belief that they're not important, and don't matter, rather than being outwardly angry or acting out, may gravitate to self-importance, and an it's all about me type attitude.

They could be drawn to this way of dealing with life because of their personality type, or because they were conditioned and trained in a household where outward expressions of emotion were not acceptable. They may also, or concurrently fear rejection, and so they internalise their emotion so that they don't offend anyone, or so that no one will think badly of them. This is to keep intact their self-image, or the image that they have created that they think is acceptable to others and self.

So, they normally won't let emotion out, and tend rather to deny these feelings and harmonise with others for acceptance and worth. The problem is that this behaviour pattern of keeping the emotion inside is linked to various diseases, notably, cancer. The true problem is the corrupted identity beliefs held in the heart, and these need to be ministered to so that you can truly accept yourself.

Defiance, rebellion

Rebellious and defiant attitudes and behaviours are consistently observed in people who have suffered injustice or unfairness in their history. This most commonly comes from some kind of abuse from authority figures.

It is a universal response in the sense that it's natural for us to rebel against things that are unfair. This could range from unjust acts or attitudes such as people abusing children, through to activities such as persecution or racism. Jesus appeared to rebel and stand in defiance against the religious oppression of His people. So, it's not always ungodly, and at times may be very appropriate to stand against injustices imposed on people in this fallen world.

It is generally historically rooted injustice that needs to be dealt with in ministry, where, for example the oppression or lack of nurture has damaged the identity and consequent state of being of the subject. Usually, it will have a component of anger or possibly resentment and bitterness attached, which is why it can appear as a part of a disease profile.

Envy, jealousy

When a person has not been validated or provided for, then they usually feel that they are not worthy of being cared about or acknowledged. When they then see others receiving praise or provisions of some kind, then envy and jealousy can begin. It generally comes as a result of seeing others receive what they would want for themselves, but haven't been given. Again, the beliefs that create a propensity to gravitate towards these feelings normally begin before 10 years old, and can be found rooted in the distorted perception of identity leading to a negative self-belief in the heart.

> Mark 7:21-23
> ²¹ *For from within, <u>out of a person's heart</u>, come evil thoughts, sexual immorality, theft, murder,*

*²² adultery, greed, wickedness, deceit, eagerness for
lustful pleasure, envy, slander, pride, and foolishness. ²³ All
these vile things come from within; they are what defile
you and make you unacceptable to God."
NLT (emphasis mine)*

These negative responses and attitudes rarely exist in isolation,
and we see envy and jealousy listed in the scriptures grouped
with other disease propagating reactions to hurt. For example, in
Ezekiel 35:11 we observe that the profile produces anger and hatred
working in conjunction with envy or jealousy. This Old Testament
passage proposes that the result for those who act out in this way
will reap a consequence.

*Ezekiel 35:11
Therefore, as surely as I live, says the Sovereign LORD,
I will pay back your angry deeds with mine. I will punish
you for all your acts of anger, envy, and hatred. And I
will bring honor to my name by what I do to you.
NLT (emphasis mine)*

In the New Testament we're under grace, but we also have the
option live in the New Spirit led nature, and we have the promise
of having our broken hearts healed if we walk through the sanctification process with God. In Galatians 5:21 we see envy listed as a
work of the old nature.

So, if we don't deal with that old nature, then we are taking
ourselves out from under grace, and are subject to the results of
our behaviour the same as a non-Christian. God offers healing of
our hearts as a key part of the good news of His amazing grace
and mercy to us. The Galatians passage indicates that not seeking
healing and resolution of these problems by walking after the Holy
Spirit will not just affect now, but also our eternity. If we're seeking
God's answers, we're under grace. But if we're content to practice
our ungodly responses without repentance and seeking healing,
then we can expect negative outcomes.

> *Proverbs 14:30*
> *A sound <u>heart</u> is the life to the body, but <u>envy</u> is*
> *rottenness to the bones. NKJV (emphasis mine)*

We've covered conditions that have envy implicated when we broke down the roots of various common diseases in earlier chapters. You can see how envy can work with anger, resentment, bitterness, and even hatred once you understand that the jealousy is directed towards someone receiving what you want for yourself. This combination is evident in conditions such as some kinds of arthritis. In the marrow of your bones is the place where your immune cells are initially produced. This indicates that these combinations may also have an action on immune problems.

Along with this, the lack of validation that we described earlier can also be crushing on the identity, which the scriptures indicate can affect the condition of your bones. Your joy is lost through lack of self-acceptance, and it breaks your spirit.

> *Proverbs 17:22*
> *A merry <u>heart</u> does good, like a medicine, but a broken*
> *spirit dries the bones. NKJV (emphasis mine)*

We can be thankful that God is always wanting to help repair our <u>hearts</u>. * (*i.e., 'the thoughts and feelings coming from our centre')

> *Psalm 34:18*
> *The LORD is close to the brokenhearted; he*
> *rescues all who are crushed in spirit. NLT*

Fear and anxiety

Fear and anxiety are such a crippling issue, and it is common element of many conditions, so I'm going to invest the next chapter into explaining it. It is a response to beliefs though, and once truth is received in the inner parts, the fear and anxiety feelings and negative expectations are resolved. As His sheep we need to hear

His voice and be perfected in love. That is, we need to come to see ourselves as the created being that God loves and has set His affection on, and come to love and accept yourself.

Guilt and Shame

Psalm 38:3-8
³ Because of your anger, <u>my whole body is sick; my health is broken</u> because of my sins. ⁴ My <u>guilt</u> overwhelms me – it is a burden too heavy to bear. ⁵ My wound fester and stink because of my foolish sins. ⁶ I am bent over and racked with pain. All day long I walk around filled with <u>grief</u>. ⁷ A raging fever burns within me, and <u>my health is broken</u>. ⁸ I am exhausted and completely crushed. My groans come from an anguished <u>heart</u>.
NLT (emphasis mine)

David wrote Psalm 38 under a previous covenant. He was not able to quote that 'there's now no condemnation for those who are in Christ Jesus, who do not walk according to the old nature, but according to the new nature under the influence of the Holy Spirit. (See Romans 8:1 NKJV) He was not under the message of redemption and grace. He did not know that even if our 'hearts' condemn us because of what we believe about ourselves, that God is greater than our 'hearts.' (See 1 John 3:20) King David was overwhelmed by his sense of guilt, and he attributed it to his infirmity.

Guilt and the resultant self-conflict that accompanies it, commonly presents in conjunction with other negative emotional responses that are implicated in bodily conditions and diseases. Guilt occurs at times because you've done something that you know that you shouldn't have, as in the case of King David that we've just cited. His failures were projected onto, or triggering negative beliefs about his worthiness and acceptability, which in turn would relate to his pre-existing sense of identity. This may have begun growing up as the least in his father's house. He had a demotion in status compared with his brothers, deemed as only fit to be a shepherd boy.

So, guilt occurs when you've done something that you know that you shouldn't have, but it also manifests when you feel that you haven't done something that you believe that you should have. If you've grown up in an environment where nothing you do is right, that you should always be doing more, trying harder, not letting people down. Then inevitably you will usually feel guilty that you're not doing enough, should be doing more, are letting others down and so on. People then feel that their performance is substandard. In terms of your identity, you now believe that you're not enough, are a failure, a hopeless case, not what you should be and so on.

This self-perception that has been put on you will cause you to carry the burden of guilt. Because this is now your default image of self, it will often continue as a part of your operating system until healing takes place through an encounter of God's truth occurs through some means. Whereas, if you have repented of your sins and things that you did that you know that you shouldn't have done, or do, and received God's merciful grace and forgiveness, then the kind of guilt proceeding from doing the wrong thing is generally resolved.

All of this causes us to 'beat ourselves up' for our imperfections, failings and shortcomings. This is why guilt generally runs with self-rejection, and even self-resentment, along with anger towards yourself.

Shame

> Proverbs 18:3
> When the wicked arrive, contempt, <u>shame</u>, and disgrace
> are sure to follow. NLT (emphasis mine)

This passage could well relate to those who inflict evil on others, such as those who perpetrate sexual abuse. These people are crushing the identities of their victims, and those damaged by these acts often carry shame, many times feeling that somehow it was their fault that it happened, or that they should have stopped it.

Men with a healthy conscious, who are sensitive and open to the conviction of the Holy Spirit, will generally experience guilt if they've been viewing explicit material such as pornography. I recently heard someone state that women involved in watching porn feel shame rather than guilt. They considered this to be because it is well known that men are visually stimulated. So, in some ways it's expected for men to struggle with explicit imagery, whereas the females feel that they must be dirty or degraded if they do, and carry shame in regard to their vulnerability and behaviour.

Negativity

Many people are programmed by life to have an outlook of negativity. Often, they believe that no one cares about them and their needs. Behind a profile of negativity, you will most times hear an attitude of 'it's not as good as it could be.' In other words, they always gravitate to finding what is wrong with something, no matter how much they have, or how good things actually are, these are never enough. Underneath they feel that they're not being looked after, cared about, protected or provided for. As a consequence, they project into the future an expectation of bad things happening. Which is an unhealthy kind of anxiety.

We've repeatedly seen this profile resolved through ministry to the identity, and situation beliefs in the heart, in combination with renewing of the mind. A grateful appreciative attitude makes you happy and is good for your health.

Self-pity will often be attached to negativity, feeling sorry for yourself that nothing is right, and nobody cares enough to meet your needs. Your life is now miserable. It usually begins growing up in an environment where you weren't noticed, validated or celebrated. And if you were accepted, it was based on you doing everything that was expected of you to earn your place or space in the world. But you still weren't valued or treated as significant even when you did everything that was wanted. You conclude that no one wants good for you, with this inner belief causing you to carry negative expectations, and be unable to celebrate life.

Pride

You may be surprised to find that pride issues may be implicated in some medical conditions. We've previously discussed that pride is most often compensating behaviour for low self-image and inferiority. The confident or successful image that the person has created, and tries to convince you and themselves is who they are, is often the opposite of what they unconsciously really believe to be true about themselves inside. For example, self-importance can come from believing underneath that you're not important. Attitudes of superiority can proceed as compensating behaviour from inferiority, and so on. You're trying to prove that what you really believe about yourself is not true.

This is involved in some disease conditions and syndromes because as the person tries to be what they believe that they're not, and lift themselves above others, going from inferiority to superiority, they wear themselves out. There is striving, contention, competition, perfectionism and so on. They will offer suffer from what is termed 'performance anxiety.' That is, anxiety about performing to standards that they've set for themselves, or that they perceive have been placed on them for acceptance growing up. This latter group of standards and expectations may be operating underneath.

All of this emotional effort places excessive demands on the endocrine or glandular systems, and the 'dis'-'ease' in the thinking creates imbalances or shortages in stress and other hormone values, eventually contributing to 'disease' in the body.

In combination all of these negative emotions contribute to states and environments where disease can prosper. I once read an article where the authors were proposing that if your body is more alkaline than acidic then disease cannot exist. The article went on to list all of the foods that were acidic, and it also listed that negative emotions were acidic. Reportedly metabolic acidosis can lead to inflammation and eventual tissue damage, even cancer metastasis. Chronic inflammation is found in a wide range of diseases.

21

Fear, Anxiety, Stress and Disease

As a behaviour fear, anxiety, and stress are a response or reaction to the problem, they're not the problem, they're the result. The real issue is usually what you believe about yourself, and at times what you believe about certain situations. Fear exists, and is in place as an attempt to protect the wounded self from further hurt, and what was learnt in these previous events. Or, at times, it's an effort to avoid situations that hold perceived fear and anxiety that is coming from beliefs imbided in previous traumatic situations.

Other words for fear and anxiety

Often, you will see all of the 'fruits' of rejection present in chronic illnesses, because they are the various fruits of a broken, disordered identity. This is the real root on most occasions. Fear and anxiety will be co-existing with most of these harmful emotions and responses, and you will have observed this in previous chapters where we discussed common diseases. You will have noted that fear and anxiety producing stress was involved in many of those conditions.

If you ask many people if they are an anxious or fearful person, they will often say no. This may be because they would use a different term for their anxiety, such as; stress, worry, tension, doubt, unbelief, restlessness, hopelessness, helplessness, dread, apprehension, insecurity etc. Doubt and unbelief are on the list of forms of fear and anxiety, because they exist because they don't really believe that there is someone in control of everything. And even if they do, they don't believe that they are worthy of His love and acceptance, let alone His protection and provision.

I was recently at a Conference where a wise old Apostle made a profound but simple statement. He said; "nothing happens to me unless God allows it," and then He paused, and then continued with emphasis, "or arranges it." In other words, he had come to a place without fear, knowing that God was working in every detail of his life, including lovingly refining every part of his character for eternity through his circumstances.

When trying to identify what we fear or are anxious about it's simple; fear is whatever you're afraid of. We can define it as an expectation of a negative outcome of some kind. It is a projection into the future looking for something bad to happen. And its source and origins are most often something learnt in an earlier event. Anxiety, stress, tension and so on are lower-grade, longer-term expressions of fear. A number of articles indicate that 60% to 90% of doctor's visits relate to the anxiety and stress issues involved in phycological conditions.

Good fear, good stress
As we discuss fear and anxiety and their implications for disease and sickness, we need to know that fear is something that God designed for our good to protect us. As usual fear as a created response has been taken, amplified and distorted through the mechanics of 'the fall'. Good fear stops us standing near cliffs on a windy day, or marching off into hostile environments of desert

or snow without being properly prepared. It stops us teasing wild animals or messing around with snakes without proper training. It protects us from standing in the middle of busy freeways. It stops us in most cases from being careless with our finances. When this Godly fear is in place it promotes our safety and wellbeing. Indeed, fear of God is the supreme fear, which is to be cherished and developed, as it brings us into all of God's blessings and eventually eternal life.

> *Psalm 111:10*
> *The fear of the LORD is the beginning of wisdom; all who follow his precepts have good understanding. To him belongs eternal praise. NIV*

These kinds of God instituted fears don't make us sick, they protect us from harm.

Circumstantial fear and anxiety

Broadly, we categorise fears and anxieties into 2 groups. Circumstantial and historical. Circumstantial could be something along the lines of living somewhere where you find yourself exposed to extreme weather, or perhaps you are in a war zone. This fear/anxiety/stress comes from what is happening in the moment. It could even relate to your financial situation, or worrying about what a family member or a friend is going through. This kind of fear is many times temporary, and is often resolved by some means and the moment passes. It is not considered to generally be implicated in physical conditions.

Scripture indicates that the way to deal with this type of fear is by choosing faith. That is trusting God, in spite of what you may be facing.

At times you may interpret the fear in these circumstantial events through beliefs and anxieties that you have already held, and these were projecting from things that you had learnt, and they are now stressed, or triggered. In this case your fear/anxiety/stress may present as larger than the situation or circumstances that you're dealing with actually warrant. So, in that event, if a pre-existing historical fear is stirred up, then it may also stir up or exacerbate a physical condition, or be a part of a progression towards developing some kind of malady. We find consistently that nearly all fear problems that we minister to are found originating in a person's past.

Historical fear and anxiety

Fear that is sourced in some kind of event in your history is what is generally involved in diseases and syndromes, contributing to the breakdown of the body and its systems. It is long term pervading fear. A life lived vigilantly in expectation of some kind of bad thing happening is what is generally involved in the propagation of illnesses. Most people carry these kinds of anxieties. Many avoid situations that they are uncomfortable with because of the fear beliefs that the person holds. For example, fear of flying, or fear of times where rejection could occur.

So, although your stressor could be your current circumstances, most people will interpret those situations through beliefs that they have already imbibed. The vast majority of these that produce physical problems will relate to fear of rejection. These will be coming from identity beliefs interpreted in real or perceived rejection events where acceptance was not received.

Fear of rejection

We can divide fear broadly into two types. Fear of rejection, and fear of harm. We've previously described that the beginnings of fear of rejection come from having been rejected in some way, at some time, from conception on, being the most impacting time when our identity is being shaped. Let me reinforce here that how we perceive ourselves, or how we see ourselves, comes from conclusions and interpretations about who we think we are, that has been decided in events before we are 10 years old.

What is important here is what we decided about ourselves, particularly if we were believed that we're not acceptable for some reason. After this we fear anything that will prove or reinforce that this negative self-belief is in fact true. We're anxious about who we perceive that we are, and consequently how others see us, will regard us, and how they will deal with us. So, our fear of rejection is rooted in identity beliefs established in our hearts. It is by far the major source of anxiety, stress and fear that you will find existing in physical conditions. Remember before it works out in the body there will be something out of order in the thinking processes, and this will result in a lack of emotional wholeness.

Fear of failure and many other anxieties come under this category because we expect rejection or non-acceptance if we aren't able to be, or do what we feel that we need to be able to. Again, this will prove that what we believe about ourselves is true, so we become hypervigilant and stressed about situations where this could potentially occur. Public speaking is considered to be on top of the list because you're vulnerable, and your shortcomings will be public and possibly embarrassing.

Performance anxiety is an extension of this. That is, you're afraid that if you don't come up to standards and perform well enough, then it will become obvious that you're not enough. This will generally begin in an environment of expectations of having to meet standards to receive acceptance. Verbal or attitudal criticism may have been present in these events, and these would influence you to misinterpret your value and worth.

You cannot hide from people, or yourself, so having to deal with the world while carrying fear of rejection is far and away the most common stressor behind anxieties that contribute to disease.

Anxiety and depression

You will often find anxiety about your performance implicated in depression. Because you hold beliefs that you can never ever be what you need to be, or never ever do what you should be able to do, and as a result inside you feel that whatever you decided about yourself can never be changed. Depression is associated with a number of various diseases and conditions.

An article by Navneet Bains; Sara Abdijadid posted on the National Library of medicine associated that the feelings of guilt or worthlessness that are found in depressive disorders are linked to a variety of diseases. Many other illnesses could be added to this list.

'Depression can aggravate medical comorbidities such as diabetes, hypertension, chronic obstructive pulmonary disease, and coronary artery disease.'

Note: Between 6% and 10% of people in the U.S. and Australia are reportedly suffering from depression and the associated anxiety.

Fear of harm

Along with fear of rejection the other main type of anxiety is fear of harm. This generally is not related to distorted beliefs about your identity. It normally comes from situations that have been traumatic and have fear producing content. Often in these situations people may believe that they're going to die or be hurt. I can only guess, but to put it in perspective, these perhaps make up 5% of the fear that we deal with in ministry, with the rest of anxieties relating to identity. In the case of harm, they may have interpreted the event with a belief such as 'there is no one there to protect me.' Or if the fear of harm related to lack of some kind, that could include that 'there's no one there to provide for me.'

Insecurity is a type of fear or anxiety that proceeds from a lack of nurture, provision and protection. It can relate to the identity as well as situations, because it could be also concluded because a person doesn't expect provision and protection because they are not worth it, loved or cared about.

In general, phobic or fear of harm anxieties have less impact on chronic disease. They are however commonly present in sickness where the fear is locked into the trauma of the moment. I described in an earlier chapter a ministry time where a young woman had a lung problem as a result of the expectation that she was going to die when a wall fell on her. This belief had nothing to do with her fearing rejection. The anxiety only related to the potential harm coming from the situation. The fear locked her trauma in place until the belief that she held was resolved through the work of the Spirit of truth.

Much like the anger family of emotions, even without a scientific research team, it's fairly obvious that there are chemical and physical changes in your physiology and bodily condition when you are experiencing fear, anxiety, or stress. If these are present long term, and/or working in conjunction with other negative emotions, it becomes fairly obvious that it will inevitably affect your health.

Note: Terms that I use throughout this publication such as; 'heart beliefs,' 'self-beliefs,' 'identity-beliefs,' 'inner beliefs,' or even, 'unconscious thoughts,' are interchangeable. I use them in order to not be too repetitive. They all refer to beliefs that are learnt about self and identity in the formative stages beginning from prenatal times in the womb, through to around 10 years of age.

It is in this period that beliefs about identity, and at times conclusions in regard to emotionally charged or traumatic situations become a fixed part of our operating system, and our default beliefs. After this we tend to interpret life and respond to our environments through these beliefs. These, often unconscious 'heart beliefs' then influence our thinking, emotions, and end in our bodies.

22

How do you Minister to These Negative Emotions?

Having identified the negative emotions, responses and reactive behaviour that are considered to be behind diseases, how do we deal with them? I cannot say enough, that although this kind of healing ministry is done in partnership with the Holy Spirit, that it is he alone that facilitates the freedom. What I'm saying is that no amount of counselling, prayer, biblical instruction, psychiatric treatment, or drugs can set you free from these root problems. Man's efforts without the Holy Spirit will be limited, at best offering some means of managing your negative emotions and responses.

This kind of healing ministry requires getting involved in the foundations of people's lives. We need to find out what they believe that's producing the feelings and reactive behaviour that they need to deal with. So, now that we've investigated individual emotions and what is likely to be producing them, over the next few chapters I'm going to present a biblical basis for how God will deal with them. We've spent decades training Pastors and ministries across the world in this stream of healing.

Rather than reinvent the wheel, the following chapters can also be found in a similar format in other books by this author, such as; Taking Down Goliath, which is a publication directed at resolving mental disorders using this model, and also; Receiving Truth That Will Set You Free, which is a booklet intended to help people to understand and prepare for a ministry session. The same ministry model works for mental disorder, emotional problems, behavioural and relational issues, along with physical conditions, because they all stem from the same root issues. For a more detailed study on this ministry model, we recommend; Healing and Freedom Though Truth Encounters, or the School of Healing and Freedom, Basic or Comprehensive Manuals, by the same author.

What is the source of my problem? What are emotions?

Let's recap some import points in order for us to properly understand this ministry. What we know as Emotions or feelings are primarily a chemical and electrical elaboration of a thought or belief. It's how we feel our beliefs and consequent thoughts making them a reality in our physical bodies.

This is mediated largely through our built-in electrical system or central nervous system. Working along with this we have the chemical release of hormones or neurotransmitters via our endocrine system, which allows you to know these emotions in your body. Emotions, feelings, even reactions and responses to a situation or stressor therefore are a reliable way to analyse what you believe or are thinking.

Therefore, what we would term negative emotions would include unwanted thoughts, responses, reactions and behaviour. They are predictable, and based on what you already think or believe. It's important to know that a feeling is rarely just a random emotion coming from nowhere, it is normally coming from something that you are thinking, often unconsciously, and this is the key to healing. So, we could say that feelings follow thoughts, and are the chemical/electrical response to these thoughts. For example, if you think about your favourite food your body will begin to release the hormones implicated in the digestive process. It won't be very long before your stomach is rumbling.

Emotionally we're the same. What we think or believe either consciously or unconsciously will precipitate the release of the corresponding hormones to make these thoughts confirmed and felt in our bodies.

> Note: Because these feelings are produced by hormones, we acknowledge that at times there are other factors such as medications that can affect the balance of these chemicals, and consequently how you feel. However, the vast majority of times these releases will be precipitated by the emotions that are present, and these will be belief driven.

Samples of negative thoughts and emotions usually stemming from inner beliefs would include issues that we've just studied such as; anxiety, fear, stress, resentment, anger, bitterness, guilt... self-rejection, fear of rejection, self-anger, low self-image, inferiority, worthlessness and so on.

These negative emotions do not match where we want to be, in terms of the Biblical ideals of positive and beneficial feelings such as joy and peace. They are also implicated in bad relationships, removing our sense of wellbeing, and finally even destroy our health. As we have already pointed out the final activity of these thoughts and feelings is an effect on the body. This works in both directions. Positive conscious or inner thoughts and feelings have a beneficial effect on your health, and negative ones produce undesirable outcomes. A sample of this in scripture would be the following verse from the book of Proverbs;

> Proverbs 17:22
> A cheerful <u>heart</u> is good medicine, but a crushed spirit dries up the bones. NKJV (emphasis mine)

The protective cells of your immune system are made in your bone marrow. So, if you have negative beliefs about yourself as a result of how you have been dealt with in life, it will affect your bodies defence system against physical maladies through low immunity or immune dysfunction.

So, what is the heart? And where do these negative thoughts, beliefs, and emotions come from?

I'm repeating this because it may be a new concept for many. According to the very reputable Strong's concordance, we can see from the Old Testament word 'Leb' that 'heart' is translated from indicates: 'an effect on your intellect proceeding from your centre, that produces feelings and has actions on your will and decisions;'

*3820. **Leb**, the heart; also used (fig.) very widely for the feelings, the will and even the intellect; likewise, for the centre of anything: Strong's Concordance*

Similarly, in the New Testament we see the 'heart' being translated from the Greek word, '*kardia*,' as 'thoughts and feelings from your centre or middle.'

*2588. **kardia**, the heart, i.e. (fig.) the thoughts or feelings the middle:- (+ broken-) heart (-ed). Strong's Concordance*

Does it hold up in scripture that there is another place that holds thoughts and feelings, that is not your mind? It is clear in scripture that the mind is separate and distinct from the heart, and performs a different function. Your mind is your reasoner, your computer, it is like a screen where you view things to work them out. Whereas the brain holds information that we have voluntarily decided to try to store and retain such as scriptures or the ten times table.

> *Luke 10:27*
> *He answered: "'Love the Lord your God with all <u>your heart</u> and with all your soul and with all your strength and with all <u>your mind</u>.'" NIV (emphasis mine)*

Once we begin to understand and accept that our 'heart' is another place from where thoughts and feelings emanate, then we begin to realise that our problem may not be in the deliberate thinking that we do in our minds. Or for that matter what we know from voluntary learning in our minds. In fact, clearly many of our problems come from this other, contrary set of beliefs, that are often in opposition to what we choose to know and believe. This is why counselling and psychology often fail, because they're ministering to the mind, which is the wrong place.

The following passage confirms that the word of God exposes the not so obvious thoughts, and corresponding attitudes that proceed from our hearts and not our minds....and this is an area relating to the problems that we deal with which is largely untouched in the modern church. Consequently, many people retain their issues and unwanted behaviour, even though it is not in line with what they consciously think, know, or want to believe. It is against how they desire to feel, respond or act.

> Hebrews 4:12
> For the word of God is living and active. Sharper than any double-edged sword, it penetrates even to dividing soul and spirit, joints and marrow; it judges the <u>thoughts and attitudes of **the heart**</u>. NIV (emphasis mine)

From a Biblical perspective these thoughts and feelings coming from our 'hearts' have implications regarding every area of life. Thoughts, feelings, decisions, motivations, relationships, health... absolutely everything. The Bible clearly states that above everything else what goes into and programs the 'heart' must be protected.

> Proverbs 4:23
> Above all else, guard your heart, for it affects everything you do. NLT (in part, guard the beliefs that you arrive at and store in your centre)

Possibly the biggest influencer, and most problematic area that needs to be dealt with when we are discussing 'heart beliefs' is those to do with our identity. What we think about ourselves, and how we think others see us, all affect our relationships with others, ourselves, and even God. They are the strongest predicter of behaviour and how we choose to live, act and react.

> Proverbs 23:7
> For as he thinks in his heart, so is he. NKJV

Once again in the preceding passage it is the thoughts of the 'heart' that depict the state of being of the man, and not necessarily his head knowledge. As you read your Bible you will begin to see that it indicates consistently that this is where many of our problems begin from. King David in Psalm 51 acknowledged that the reason for his wayward behaviour and sin was a lack of pure thoughts and feelings from his centre. And he requested that God show him what was there.

> Psalm 51:10
> Create in me a pure <u>heart</u>, O God, and renew a steadfast spirit within me. NKJV (emphasis mine)

> Psalm 139:23-24
> [23] Search me, O God, and know my <u>heart</u>; test me and know my thoughts. [24] Point out anything in me that offends you, and lead me along the path of everlasting life. NLT (emphasis mine – 'heart' = thoughts and feelings from your inner parts)

Interestingly, and we will cover this in more detail in a moment, he stated that God wanted truth in the inner parts (Hebrew)....which in Greek is the soul. The soul is considered to be the mind, will, and emotions.

According to Hebrew scholars 'the inner parts' could also be translated, as the 'heart,' which I suggest to you is the centre or middle of your soul.

Psalm 51:6
Surely you desire truth in the inner parts. NKJV

Another example of the source of our problems being the 'thoughts and feelings from our centre, or 'heart' would be the all-too-common issue of depression. The scriptures lay blame at this inner place as being at the root of the problem. We have seen depression consistently healed as we accept that '*heart beliefs*' are the source of the problem, and minister along those lines.

Proverbs 12:25
Anxiety in the heart of man causes depression. NKJV
(by implication- anxiety from your inner central beliefs
and feelings)

So, if we accept that the 'heart' is thoughts and feelings from our centre or middle, then what does a 'broken-heart' mean. We could perhaps best present it as thoughts and feelings that are broken, disordered or distorted. In other words, we have distorted beliefs, mainly about our identity, that are not in the order, or in the state of wholeness that God intended. Our identities are broken down and need to be restored, and this is the most common source of our problems. In the following passage we see that the Spirit of the LORD is on Jesus, and now the Church, (John 20:21) to preach (Greek = preach, declare, bring) the good news...that is that you can be saved, but also that you can be healed, set free, made whole, and have a better life now on Earth as well.

Jesus confirms this explaining that He is not just going to talk about God's good news, but also demonstrate it. In order, the first thing that He is going to do is bring wholeness to the broken thoughts and feelings of the heart. The Greek word used here for heal here is '*iaomai*,' which means 'heal, make whole.' We have seen over many years that the result of this is the captives being set free, and spiritual oppression being broken.

Luke 4:18
"The Spirit of the LORD is upon Me, Because He has
anointed Me To preach the gospel to the poor; He has
sent Me to <u>*heal*</u> *the brokenhearted, To proclaim liberty to*
the captives And recovery of sight to the blind, To set at
liberty those who are oppressed; NKJV (emphasis mine)

The God Solution

I have endeavoured to explain as thoroughly as possible that the power that Satan has over mankind comes through eliciting cooperation and submission through deception. Additionally, we have now ascertained that the root of the problem is often specifically deception and corruption of one's identity at 'heart' level. Hopefully we now understand, at least in part, why we see ourselves as we do. Why none of us are 'whole' and completely ordered in our thinking, and or in possession of accurate truth about ourselves as a result of '*the fall*'. And why deception at the root of our beings, our hearts, is the basis, directly or indirectly, for virtually all of mankind's problems.

If then, we accept that distorted perceptions and thinking about our 'self' leads us into following the worlds ways is the problem, then the solution is a new, healed, renewed, reprogrammed 'heart,' which is the result of receiving God's truth in the inner parts. Truth at heart level is therefore vital for our freedom. We can now understand clearly why Jesus said that when we know God's truth, it will make us free.

> *John 8:32*
> *"And you shall know the truth, and the truth shall make*
> *you free." NKJV*

This truth needs to come partly through the renewing of the knowledge of God and His ways in the mind. However, many people know the truth in their minds, and in their voluntarily learnt knowledge, but it has not set them free. As I've previously stated, we have found that we also need truth in the 'heart.' This comes through the healing, (bringing to wholeness and repair), of the broken 'heart.' That is, your inner thoughts and feelings in regards to your identity, which are coming from your middle or centre.

This wholeness is in our believing, and the thinking that proceeds from it. So, the way back to wholeness is too 'un-corrupt' this distortion and deception that we have received in regards to how we perceive 'self.' Let me reinforce that your perceived identity is who you think that you are, or how you think that you are. It's your truth about your SELF. By way of a simple example, self-be-liefs such as; I'm dumb, useless, worthless, not important, bad, a nothing, unlovable, not good enough, and so on. This inner heart thinking and believing about self is usually contrary to what you want to think about yourself in your mind, and hence the conflict and disorder, mentally, emotionally, and finally physically. Receiving God's truth then, IS the process of sanctification.

> John 17:17
> "Sanctify them by Your truth. Your word is truth". NKJV

The Greek word translated 'sanctify' here is 'hagiazo.' This word means to purify. In this case purify you from deception by means of receiving God's truth. It is sometimes translated as 'to make holy.' It is all largely the same thing. To be sanctified and purified, makes you Holy, and separated from the deception that produces corruption and misalignment in your being. God's instrument for dealing with this deception in the process of sanctification is the Spirit of truth. We'll cover this function of His ministry more fully in a later chapter. A part of His work, as this particular title suggests, is to lead us into all truth, both consciously and at heart level.

> John 16:13
> But when he, the Spirit of truth, comes, he will guide you into all truth. NIV

Practical results of receiving truth

Self-conflict in regards to what we would like to think, and what we actually do think about ourselves, is based on not having God's absolute and unequivocal truth. Perhaps a pendulum is a good illustration of how we become mentally, emotionally, and physically imbalanced through our thinking being out of order. If the pendulum is at dead centre and not swinging backwards and forwards, we could describe its position as at rest, in peace.

The further it swings one way or the other the more out of balance and away from wholeness that we are. We could perhaps suggest that small, or temporary movements away from centre are normal and acceptable, but mentally, emotionally, and finally physically, the greater or more ongoing the fluctuations, the more serious the disorder and the more negative the health condition of a person would be.

OUTWORKING'S OF DISTORTED IDENTITY BELIEFS

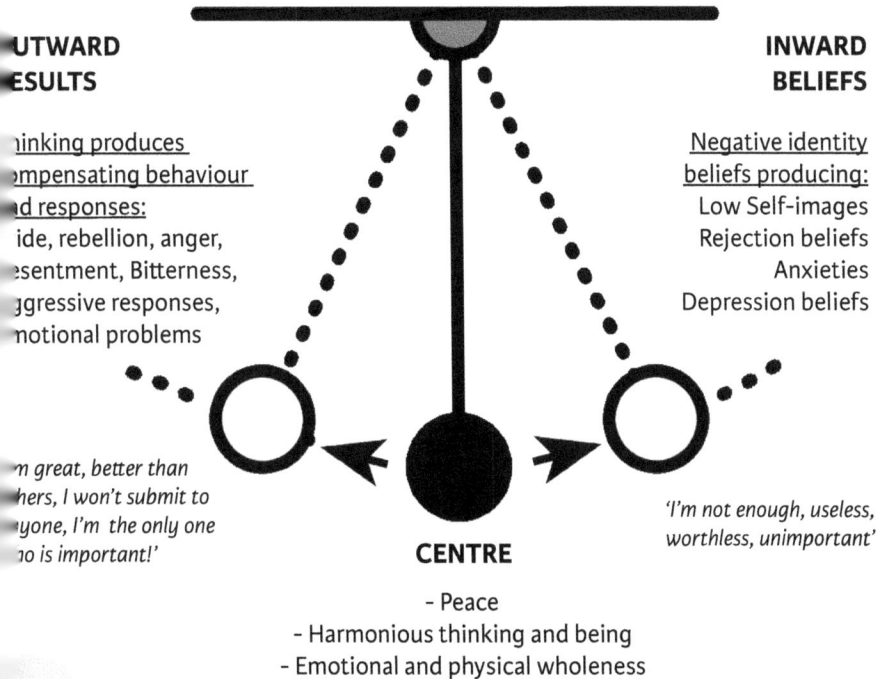

OUTWARD
RESULTS

Thinking produces
compensating behaviour
and responses:
Pride, rebellion, anger,
resentment, Bitterness,
aggressive responses,
emotional problems

'I'm great, better than others, I won't submit to anyone, I'm the only one who is important!'

INWARD
BELIEFS

Negative identity
beliefs producing:
Low Self-images
Rejection beliefs
Anxieties
Depression beliefs

'I'm not enough, useless, worthless, unimportant'

CENTRE

- Peace
- Harmonious thinking and being
- Emotional and physical wholeness

So, our thinking is conflicted and disordered, swinging out of balance between what you want to think, and what you do think.... 'I'm great, I'm not...?' Peace, order and balance comes when the contention is resolved. This means, acceptance of self, and having an identity and knowledge of our purpose that are mediated by God imputing His truth, which is THE truth.

The example in Romans 7 of the Apostle Pauls dilemma

Here we find the Apostle Paul acknowledging that his unwanted behaviour, responses and reactions were coming from another law - (set of rules on how to live) - that he had arrived at, and now was influenced by, which were contrary to what he wanted to now do as a result of his spiritual rebirth.

Even though he was born again and he had a new spirit within producing new desires, he admitted that this previous programming was still active and 'living' within him, even though he did not want it. He came to the conclusion that this sin producing behaviour was something coming from an area of his life that he did not fully understand. This battle going on inside made him feel wretched.

In order to place what is happening with Paul in context, we need to realise that as a result of him being born again and experiencing regeneration of his human spirit, that this new connection with God produced conflict with the old ways. He evidently struggled with the previous programming of the inner thoughts, beliefs, and feelings coming from his 'heart.' He had received redemption, and consequently knew that he was now right with God, and was aware of being in relationship with him.

And God's Spirit within him is influencing his mind towards following His commands. It's noteworthy that Strong's concordance cites that an element of the Greek word 'Charis,' which is translated 'grace,' includes a 'divine influence on the heart.' So, God's graciousness, along with covering our sins, includes putting in us a desire to cooperate with Him, and move towards establishing His ways and nature in our lives.

Prior to conversion there is nothing in opposition to our fallen self-centredness. We're in a sense our 'own God's,' only interested in doing our own will. Remember in the garden of Eden that a part of the temptation that Adam and Eve succumbed to, was to be like God. This would mean that you rule over self and answer to nobody, because in your own thinking you are the central being. But after conversion we have this new God acknowledging nature in us. We still have to work with the Holy Spirit to deal with the old nature, or 'Sarx' as it is known in the Greek language. This process means dying to the old things that we lived for, primarily self-realisation and self-pleasing.

Over the years we have seen that as people allow the Holy Spirit to restore their identity by bringing truth to the inner parts, that they become less and less concerned about their selves, and more and more wanting to serve others. This is I believe a significant part of 'the being conformed to the likeness of Christ,' that we see in Romans chapter 8:29.

The example of these 2 natures working in the Apostle Paul

In order to be able to understand the passage in Romans chapter 7 we need to see that Paul has conflict within himself, as all Christians do. This problem is between the old programmed *'heart beliefs'* powering the old nature, and the new 'mind-based beliefs' that are now learnt and desired through the influence of the new nature that God has created in us. As we examine the passage, when we're talking about the 'new nature' I will highlight it in bold. When we see that he is talking about his 'old fallen nature,' we'll underline it to make the distinction. Remember, he is one person, with 2 natures or sources of thinking influencing him. These are in opposition to each other. (Galatians 5:17)

Romans 7:14-16
> *¹⁴ The law is good, then. The trouble is not with the law but with <u>me</u>, because I am sold into slavery, with sin as <u>my</u> master. ¹⁵ I don't understand <u>myself</u> at all, for I really want to do what is right, but <u>I</u> don't do it. Instead, <u>I</u> do the very thing I hate. ¹⁶ I know perfectly well that what I am doing is wrong, and **my** bad conscience shows that I agree that the law is good. (emphasis mine)*

As is the case with most of us who are now in relationship with God, the issue is not about whether or not we want to follow God's ways, because His kindness has led us to repentance. (Repentance in Greek = a change of thinking, a reconsidering of our ways.)

Romans 7:17-119
> *¹⁷ But I can't help myself, because it is sin inside <u>me</u> that makes <u>me</u> do these evil things. ¹⁸ I know <u>I</u> am rotten through and through so far as <u>my</u> old sinful nature is concerned. No matter which way I turn, I can't make myself do right. I want to, but <u>I</u> can't. ¹⁹ When I want to do good, <u>I</u> don't. And when I try not to do wrong, <u>I</u> do it anyway. (emphasis mine)*

I hope that the illustration is demonstrating his recognition of the 2 opposing influences within him, and the switch from one nature to the other. Much of his negative behaviour is coming from a pre-set 'default position.' This is stemming from previous conclusions and interpretations regarding his identity, and consequent perceived needs and desires to solve these inner beliefs. Additionally, this would extend to how he regards what the World offers for self-pleasing of the body, as well as importantly how he reacts to perceived rejection and so on. The 'old nature' is distorted by exposure to a fallen world, both soul and body, whereas the 'new nature' is influenced by a reborn spirit.

Romans 7:20
> *²⁰ But if <u>I</u> am doing what I don't want to do, I am not really the one doing it; the <u>sin</u> within <u>me</u> is doing it. (emphasis mine)*

Jesus said; "Father, forgive these people, because they don't know what they are doing." In other words, they are following what they have been exposed to, programmed by it, and do not know why they are doing what they are doing. Ungodly behaviour and sin because of the deception is the result.

> *Romans 7:21-25*
> *²¹ It seems to be a fact of life that when **I** want to do what is right, **I** inevitably do what is wrong. ²² **I** love God's law with all **my** heart. (NKJV the Inward man) ²³ But there is another law at work within **me** that is at war with **my** mind. This law wins the fight and makes **me** a slave to the sin that is still within **me**.*
>
> *²⁴ Oh, what a miserable person **I** am! Who will free **me** from this life that is dominated by sin? ²⁵ Thank God! The answer is in Jesus Christ our Lord. So you see how it is: In **my** mind **I** really want to obey God's law, but because of **my** sinful nature **I** am a slave to sin. NLT (emphasis mine)*

And so it is with all of us. The true self inside of us, the reborn human spirit now influenced by the Holy Spirit wants to follow and obey God's law. (Law = system of rules regulating actions and defining correct behaviour or procedures) But as with the Apostle Paul we have another law — system of rules governing how we act — proceeding from our prior programming and wrong beliefs. These have made us a slave to sin, which is many times ways of behaving or attitudes that are offensive to God. (Sin in the Hebrew and Greek languages means 'an offence.') These are many times the negative emotions and responses that produce disease.

So, if the premise of our problem is wrong beliefs from deception in the old 'fallen self-nature,' then it is reasonably obvious that God's truth leading to right believing in the 'heart,' is the answer to align us with a renewed mind. Paul agreed that some of his behaviour and the wretchedness that he consequently felt, was an area of his being that was not in order with God's ways, in terms of how he should think, feel and act.

The 'heart' and the source of sin

Jesus clearly pointed to the 'heart' as being the source of unwanted, undesirable, and sinful behaviour. These are things that do not measure up to the word of God and the fruit of freedom by the work of the Holy Spirit. In other words, the choices, decisions and actions that are made to supposedly resolve, or be a solution to our negative beliefs and emotions, are influenced by the thoughts of our 'heart.'

> *Mathew 15:19*
> *For from <u>the heart</u> come evil thoughts, murder, adultery,*
> *all other sexual immorality, theft, lying, and slander. NLT*
> *(emphasis mine)*

Remember that the 'heart' means 'the thoughts and feelings influencing your will from your centre or middle. We can be reasonably confident that a large part of this sin that was in Paul came from unresolved, wrong *'heart beliefs'* that were in tension with the truth of God. The gospel of Mark adds some issues to the list. I am sure that many additional items could be catalogued. Indeed, we have personally witnessed that a great many sin issues proceed from the 'heart.'

> *Mark 7:20-23*
> ²⁰ *And then he added, "It is the <u>thought-life</u> that defiles*
> *you. (He is again indicating the thought life influenced*
> *by 'heart beliefs'.)* ²¹ *For from <u>within</u>, out of a person's*
> *<u>heart</u>, come evil thoughts, sexual immorality, theft,*
> *murder,* ²² *adultery, greed, wickedness, deceit, eagerness*
> *for lustful pleasure, envy, slander, pride, and foolishness.*
> ²³ *All these vile things come from <u>within</u>; they are what*
> *defile you and make you unacceptable to God."*
> *NLT (emphasis mine)*

Clearly through redemption we have now been made acceptable to God. But prior to this amazing gift our old thinking separated and put us against Him. We are, however, following redemption, now in the ongoing process of sanctification, which is mediated through receiving truth.

THE BASIS OF NEGATIVE EMOTIONS

Conscious Mind
Thinker
Reasoner
Computer
Decider

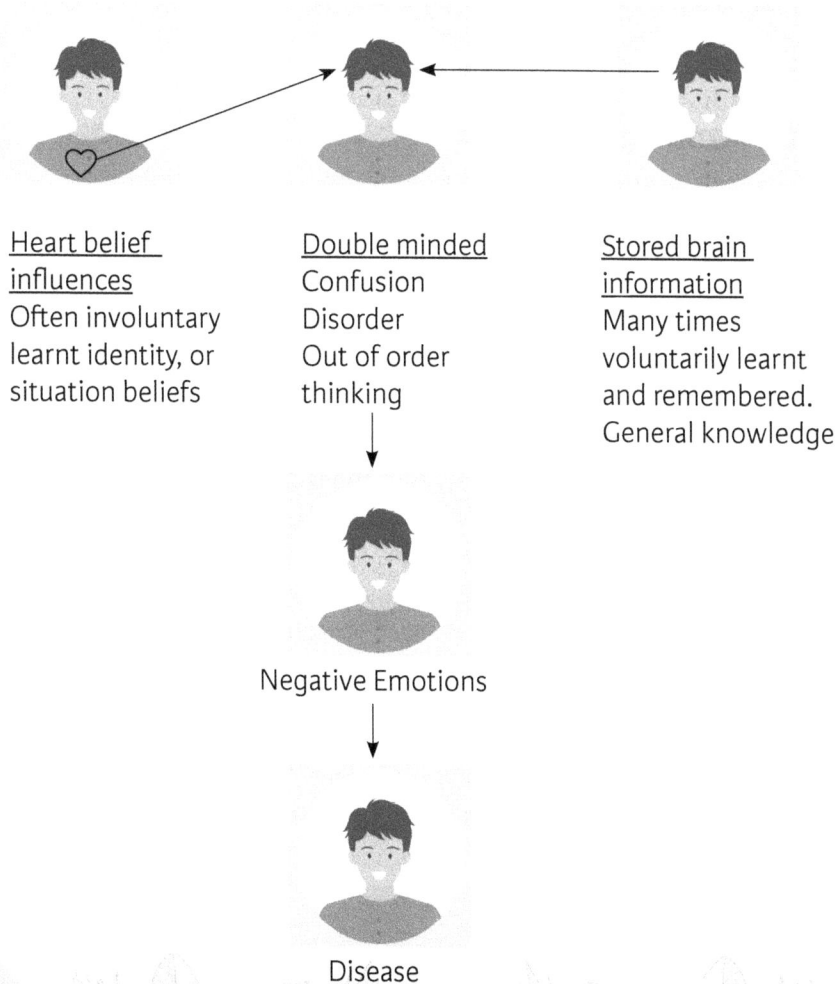

Heart belief influences
Often involuntary learnt identity, or situation beliefs

Double minded
Confusion
Disorder
Out of order thinking

Stored brain information
Many times voluntarily learnt and remembered. General knowledge

Negative Emotions

Disease

Healing and Freedom

Dismantling Deception

Here, we're going to present in summary the simple ministry model that we use to help restore order to the mental, emotional and physiological conditions. Even though I'm going to give a considerable amount of detail in the explanation of the ministry, in practice it is simple to do. Once we understand this process, we can apply this model to the beliefs behind each separate disease producing negative emotion.

We have proposed repetitively that the lack of God's truth, particularly regarding *'heart beliefs'* about our identities is the root of the problem. This conclusion has come through having consistently witnessed many thousands of times where the Spirit of Truth has resolved the various issues emanating from these beliefs. This deception which creates our difficulties, and moves us out of God's intended order, was learnt primarily in historical events that we now term as memories. We commonly have people report; "It's as if I'm discovering who I really am!" This is true, we're being restored to seeing ourselves how God sees us.

At times these historical places include pre-natal imprints on our person before we were even born. * In the event that a self-belief has been imbibed and encoded in memory sourced from events, or projections from the parents on to them prior to birth, a person grows up with a sense of what they believe. As they grow up and have words, they can now describe what they feel. They also now tend to interpret early childhood events based on these pre-exist-ing pre-natal (In the Womb) beliefs. The feeling and belief are one and the same. You feel what you believe. And the feeling can also be described in words.

On occasion when ministering to people we find that there is no initial memory where they took in the belief that we're working with. In that case we may minister to the sense and feeling that possibly began before they were born. Often people already know that they were rejected in the womb for some reason. And the reason that they were rejected gives context to the feeling and belief that they now hold.

In either case dealing with the memory where a belief is learnt is the beginning point, and the first key for understanding this minis-try process. Jesus considered this as significant, and said things such as; "how long have they been like this?" In other words; "does anyone know where this began, what happened to them?" (Mark 9:21) The lady bent over with the Spirit of infirmity 18 years was different 19 years ago. There was something that led to her even-tual condition. (Luke 13:11)

The issue is how we have interpreted the contents of memories, and how our conclusions became the 'heart beliefs' that we now live out of. Let me reinforce, no one was born, born again. Like King David we were all conceived in sin under the negative influ-ences of 'the fall' of man. (Ps 51:5) We therefore, all were spiritually under the tendency to misinterpret our identity because of that imprint.

Where do 'heart beliefs' come from?

Involuntary or Experiential learning means, in contrast to voluntary knowledge, things that you did not deliberately decide to believe or think of your own volition. I.E. It is conclusions not consciously made or reasoned, or necessarily computed in your mind and decided that you should deliberately remember. They have been interpreted from a significant event.... and generally, relate to your identity, (who you are) or a particular situation.

For example, if your father left home when you were a small child, then without wilfully trying to believe it, you unknowingly, and at times unconsciously through that experience came to the conclusion that you are 'not important.' If you did matter, he would not have left. But it's not a deliberate process of; "what should I think here?" You many times simply unconsciously interpreted the event in that way. But now because it was deeply encoded in a strongly emotional event it has become a part of your identity and how you now see yourself.

'Heart beliefs' and the importance of age

Proverbs chapter 22 and verse 6 instructs us that if we direct our children onto the right path when they are young, then when they are older that they will not leave it. Biblically a child means someone who is pre-adolescent or under around 10 years old. The passage is instructing us that what is learnt and believed to be true at this critical age will decide our future direction and predict our behaviour.

Science bears this out, confirming that our brains are in a state of plasticity before 10 years of age. Coupled with this is that it is considered that this is the time where we are deciding who we are, how we are, how to respond to others, and subsequently how others perceive us.

Later as we go through life, we are interpreting new events through the lens of what we have already learnt and believed. It is therefore critical to realise that the source or root of virtually all of our identity-based 'heart beliefs' will be found in memories interpreted in that historical moment. At times it may very much seem as though that this is not the case, with strong feelings and beliefs emanating from events at later times.

For example, an event such as a marriage break up will be charged with emotion. It will appear as though all of those thoughts, feelings, and responses began in that situation. However, in reality the effect of the separation will most often reflect powerfully on your identity and bring up every negative thing that you have already believed about yourself, even though you feel that the hurt it is coming from your partners behaviour.

More information on prenatal influences can be studied in the book 'Healing And Freedom Through Truth Encounters,' or the SOHAF (School of Healing and Freedom) Comprehensive Manual by the same author.

The role of memory

So, we can conclude that nearly all these types of problems begin as a child, when we began to try to interpret our state of being, and conceptualise our identities. The first impressions and experiences in significant events were instrumental in the formation and establishment of our beliefs. As we've pointed out, once these beliefs were decided upon in the initial memories, they are then used to interpret what happens to you later in life.

For instance, if you aren't picked for the football team when you're 12 years old, you will see that through what you have already previously decided on as your identity and characteristics. To illustrate, you may see this happening through the grid of your parents never giving you attention when you were growing up. And you may have come to the conclusion that you're not significant or worthy of being noticed and selected.

Now, you conclude that this is the reason you have been over-looked for the team. It's an automated response. Not necessarily a logical calculation. All you know is that you feel sad and unworthy, just as you did when you were a small child deciding who you were. In fact, a later event such as not being picked for the team may be interpreted based on more than one, or a number of pre-existing beliefs.

I ministered to a lady one day whose husband made her feel like she was dumb. He was unwittingly triggering a pre-existing identity belief that she'd learnt at school. He now was the recipient of an unpleasant angry and resentful reaction from her whenever he caused this belief to be touched.

The importance of the Initial memory and context

So, this is our second key. The initial or first memory where the belief was learnt is the place that we need. After this moment the self-belief is only confirmed or reactivated through the dealings of life. This is the memory that holds the context and details for why we believe what we believe. It's the 'because' place. Once we find this memory and search out the identity belief, we want to attach to it a 'qualifying statement.' In the case of the initial memory for the lady who thought she was 'dumb,' this began as a small child at school; "I must be dumb, '**because**,' I can't keep up with the other kids."

Another case was a lady who believed that she was 'stupid.' She had been deliberately made fun of and embarrassed by her teacher '**because**' she'd made a mistake when asked to write something on the blackboard. In that embarrassing and emotionally charged moment she believed that she was stupid, '**because**' she couldn't do it properly. So, the event qualifies why she believes what she believes.

So, to summarise, our third key is to give the belief that is learnt, and stored in the heart as memory, context. We do this through a statement that qualifies why the person believes what they believe about themselves. In summary, a 'qualifying statement' contains how and why we have believed what we have believed, and why we have come to the conclusions that we have come to. It is why we have interpreted an event the way that we have; how it has shaped our identities and perceptions of who we are, or caused us to perceive situations in particular ways.

For example; "I must be worthless and unimportant, 'because' nobody notices me or gives me attention. I don't seem to matter; nobody cares about me."

Predictive memory

Memory doesn't just relate to events in the past, it has implications for much more than this. What we have learnt and believed in previous situations forms our expectations of what is likely to take place in the future. If no one ever noticed us before when we were forming, and we have taken on the belief that we don't matter and are unimportant, then that belief predicts that this will remain the case in the future. We may just accept that as the truth, and go through life with low self-image and/ or depression. Or we may try to compensate and resolve the problem by becoming, in our own thinking, not only important, but the most important, and the only one who matters.

Likewise, if our encoded perception of our characteristics is that we aren't as good as others, we may become high achievers in order to prove that it's not true. Projecting off memory, we're trying to resolve the *'heart beliefs'* that have become our truth. We do this by building an image that fits with what we want to believe. But even though we change the apparent evidence, the inner belief that creates the conflict remains. The source is always the memory.

Memory is also predictive in terms of behaviour and life choices. If we are, let's say, anxious about people seeing our perceived weaknesses and shortcomings, we may hide away, or not try anything. If we have been rejected, we now are on guard against it happening again. We are vigilant, watching out for potential rejection, avoiding relationships. Or we become independent so that we cannot be hurt again. The anxiety that we term fear of rejection now rules our lives and decisions.

We can see how memory is much more than a past event. It holds the key to every issue of life, and everything that we do. (Proverbs 4:23) It is a predictor of why we do what we do, and what motivates our thoughts and activities. (Hebrews 4:12) Memory holds why we believe what we believe about who we are. It interprets how we see our position and place in life in the present. It creates our expectations in regards to how we see our potential in the future. In the event that the content of these memories corrupts a person's self-perception significantly, then you can expect all kinds of mental conflict, emotional anguish, and finally physical imbalances.

This can come from very deep-rooted painful beliefs, or the collective power of many less intense negative beliefs. Memory is very much implicated as the source of most mind/body disorders. Indeed, it's difficult to find a disease that does not include some component of anxiety in regards to a person's state of being and identity. These have been learnt and have their roots in past events.

24

Accessing Memory
From Healing

Icons, screens and accessing memory

In my other books I have used the analogy of a smart phone screen
to help us understand viewing the stored information that we
hold inside. As I write this book on my laptop computer, I can only
view around two thirds of a page at any one time. I am unable to,
and don't see the whole picture of what I have written all at once.
I have to search back through previous information that I have
recorded to see what is there. The point is, that it IS there, recorded, even though I have to search for it to view it.

In fact, if I have had to stop working on the publication for a while,
I have to review what I've written because I no longer remember
what I have included, or even at times what conclusions that I have
written as I have unpacked the subject matter. This is all stored in
this plastic brain that we call a computer. These pre-existing files
have to be found and investigated. And when I do find them and
consider them, those thought processes are renewed and come
alive to me again.

In much the same way, in memory, we've concluded and recorded things about ourselves that are now stored information. They are not accessed and viewed on the screen of our minds all of the time. They must be deliberately brought up into our conscious mind to be inspected, examined and accepted as something that we believe. If I asked you to think about a sunset, then your memory and imagination can readily put a picture on the screen of your conscious thinking. Computers, or mini computers such as smart phones, have the capacity to store a great deal of information. This downloaded data includes the possibility of corrupted files, or viruses that can affect the operations of the device.

In regards to examining information, you can however, normally only view a limited amount of content on your screen at a time. To go onto Facebook or TikTok, for example, you will have to go off WhatsApp, or move your emails to the side. Conscious thought is much like this. Normally there will be a main item of thought on the 'screen' of your mind. Why is this significant? It's relevant because unless we deliberately connect to memory it will remain in storage. In fact, often if we don't like what has been learnt in memory, so we will avoid viewing it as much as possible.

The point is though, that unless we voluntarily choose to access and examine the contents of our memories, we will never see them, or accept them as what we hold to be true. Our fourth key then, is to choose to examine our 'heart beliefs' by bringing the memories where we concluded the beliefs onto the 'screen' of our conscious minds. Laptops, or perhaps more commonly smart phones, have what are known as 'icons.' They appear on the screen when you power up your device. Each of these 'icons,' or little pictures, is representative of a program of some kind that has a function and gives you access to information. Unless we click or tap on them, they remain closed.

When we are ministering, we are deliberately clicking or tapping on what we see presenting in the story of your problems. We're wanting to open up the whole program or 'app,' (application) relating to your issue. So, we're wanting to connect with memories where *'heart beliefs'* were learnt and bring them up onto the screen of your conscious mind to process. You now let yourself be fully aware of those beliefs and inner thoughts. The components that we want to access are the memory, beliefs, emotions and context.

Even though we often don't know where to go without ministry help, we are aware that we have, for example, an icon behind which we find; fear, anxiety, stress, rebellious feelings, insecurity, injustice, inferiority, anger, bitterness, sadness, confusion, rejection, self-rejection, and so on. Behind each of these icons is the real program that produces these attitudes and responses to life. All of these negative feelings are produced by a negative belief. These beliefs are the basis of our disordered states.

Freedom comes by dismantling our deception through encountering God's truth. Because this occurs through the ministry of the Spirit of truth, we call this ministry process; 'truth encounters.' The fifth key, and foundational to the 'truth encounters' ministry is identifying and accepting what you believe, or hold as true in your 'heart,' in regards to your identity, or sometimes a situation, or both. It's important to know that because of the aforementioned reasons, that we mostly don't consciously know what these inner beliefs are. This could be because we have learnt and accepted these as our personality traits at a young age.

Or it could, as we've suggested, be because we've rejected these beliefs for some reason, such as because we don't want it to be true about ourselves. These beliefs can be painful, or traumatic. We endeavour to deny, negotiate, cope with, mask, justify, or compensate for these beliefs in some way in order to not have to accept or embrace them. This produces some of the conflicted thinking which disorders our mental, and consequently emotional and physical states. This phenomenon occurs on a sliding scale which is contingent on what we have been exposed to in life. All of us have begun with some kind of issues. Some are diagnosed, many are not. For wholeness, freedom and healing, we have to visit these places and allow the Holy Spirit to resolve these deceptive self-beliefs.

25

The Ministry Process

Preparation for ministry

For any kind of healing or freedom ministry the most important thing is positioning a person to receive. Jesus always taught the people first. Then they knew what was on offer from the Kingdom of God, saw that it was near enough to access, and understood how the provision would come. Before people come for this type of ministry, we usually have them read one of my books, or manuals, that explain the 'Truth Encounters' process.

Minimally, knowing that not everyone likes to read, we have produced what we term a 'work up' book. This smaller body of material is purposed as a basic introduction to the ministry. It is titled; 'Receiving Truth That Will Set You Free.' We have people read this before they come for a ministry session so that they will understand what is involved, and can then decide if it is for them. Clearly the more detailed publications on this subject are better suited for 'how to,' and a fuller understanding of the ministry for potential ministers.

*We also encourage people to prepare by viewing the explanatory clip titled, 4:23. This can be found on the resource page of our website. *
www.418centre.org

Remember, the most important KEY to the ministry is to know what you are trying to find. What we are looking for mainly is beliefs about our identity. That is, how we see our characteristics, who we are......in other words, beliefs about SELF held at the very centre, or core of our being. Additionally, at times we may be looking for beliefs about certain situations, which I'll explain shortly.

How a ministry session may be initiated

When a person comes for ministry, we're assuming that they understand the ministry through having read the material, or viewed a clip. The next step is to hear what troubles them, and note things that would produce a distortion of a person's identity, namely, '*heart beliefs.*' With experience those trained in ministry will discern '*heart beliefs*' as those coming for help relate their story. Jesus said; 'out of the abundance of the 'heart' the mouth speaks. So, words are often an indicator of what people believe, locating them in terms of their perspective of self in regards to the world.

> *Matthew 12:34b*
> *"...For out of the abundance of the heart the mouth*
> *speaks." NKJV (emphasis mine)*

For example, in the course of telling their story someone may say something such as; 'why bother trying, I would mess it up anyway!' You would note this as an indicator that somewhere in their history they've failed, and most probably imbibed a belief such as; 'I can't do it - I'm a failure, a hopeless case, useless,' or something similar. Remember, we want the qualifying statement. 'I'm a failure, because..........' This will be found in a memory, and give context to why they interpreted the initial event the way that they did, and have come to the conclusion about their identity that they have.

Normally a person will need the help of someone who understands the ministry to help them find the root of their problem. They usually require somebody 'outside of their issues' to lead them through. Ideally this will be a person with experience or knowledge of 'what you are looking for.' Knowing what this is, is the main KEY.

Anyone who plays Golf will know that everyone around them will give them tips on how to improve their game. This is because they can see how you swing at the ball from outside. You cannot see what it looks like, and what you are doing wrong is not obvious to you, because you are in the middle of it. So, knowledgeable direction from an outside perspective, through someone who is not influenced by your thinking and feelings can be invaluable.

Another consideration is, that if you're just beginning to receive ministry through the 'Truth Encounters' process, you may have, for instance, deep pain, or intense anxiety. In this case it's best to have someone experienced with you to help with the process. An additional practical reason to have someone with you, is that if you don't have the commitment of being with another person, you will probably keep putting off connecting with your beliefs and mem- ories. There are 2 main types or kinds of beliefs that are behind mentally and emotionally sourced physical disorders. We call them 'identity beliefs,' and for the sake of simplicity, 'situation beliefs.'

*Note: Most often negative responses and reactions to emotional stressors or triggers that produce disease; such as anger, unfor- givness, resentment, anxiety, guilt, self- rejection, rebellion and so on, disappear or are easily repented of once the corrupted beliefs about the identity are made whole and restored. The same is true about behaviour and anxieties proceeding from situation beliefs.

chapter

26

Types of Beliefs

Identity beliefs

Your perceived identity is who you really think that you are, and consequently how you think that you are. What you really believe about SELF inside. Rather than a lengthy discourse let me suggest some common beliefs reflecting how many times one's identity is seen: "I'm not loveable, I'm unacceptable, not enough, less than others, stupid, a nothing, dumb, ugly, a failure, a loser, useless, weak, I don't matter, am not important," and so on.

Notice that they are all beliefs relating to your identity, they are about 'self.' They're often not conscious thought, and you many times are not aware that you believe these things about yourself. You may or may not know them in words, rather experiencing them as a feeling or a reaction.

These types of '*heart beliefs*' are at the root of many anxieties. Unconsciously you are worried about people discovering your shortcomings, or reinforcing them, and you don't want to accept them as being true about yourself. If people treat you or regard you in a particular way, or you are exposed to certain circumstances, it may produce a predictable feeling or response that flags your belief.

When I am preparing people for ministry, I often explain identity beliefs to people using a story which I have constructed, but is based on similar stories that I have heard over and over again.

Sample story

Imagine someone who has come to you is reporting how much anxiety they are going through. How I would deal with it may run something like this;

Fred: I have a terrible problem with anxiety.

Me: Can you give me an example of how it affects you?

Fred: I was at work the other day and heard the main door behind me open; I had an anxiety attack and reached for my pills.

Me: If you stop and think about the situation for a moment, what was it that you were worried about when you heard the door open?"

Fred: Thoughtful pause; Mmmmmm...I was nervous that it may have been the boss.

Me: And if it was, what are you worried about happening?

Fred: He may have come over and looked at my work!

Me: And if he did, what do you think could happen?

Fred: He might tell me that it was no good.

Me: I am sure that that is not a good feeling. I want you to close your eyes and feel what it is like for him to tell you that your work is not good enough, and let your mind connect you with other historical places where you have felt just like that.

Fred: Pause; I have just remembered that when I was in kindergarten, I was doing a painting with some other kids and the teacher was coming along looking at everyone's work. The first person was Mary and the teacher said that Mary's painting was so creative, and then Johnnie's was so neat and all in the lines. When she saw mine, she said, it was the biggest unrecognisable mess that she had ever seen in her life!

Me: As you look at that criticism and rejection, I want you to look for the conclusion and belief about yourself that you came to.

Fred: With some emotion; I'm useless, not as good as others.

Me: Let's ask the Lord what He considers to be true about you being useless and inferior **because** your work isn't as good as others. Just concentrate on those beliefs and feelings and listen.

Fred: Pause; He said, why would He have called and chosen me if I was useless. He said that all of His children are created equal, they have different gifts but none are better than another. I have just remembered that I was the best reader in the group!

Me: So how do you feel about people discovering that you are useless and not as good as them now?

Fred: Honestly, I feel that I am fine just as I am. And I am just the same as everyone else, the same only different, different in a good way, unique!

Identity beliefs have a bearing on our relationships and how we respond, react to, and deal with others. They also reflect on how we relate to ourselves, and ultimately God. Truly, *as a man thinks in his heart, so is he*, particularly in terms of how he reacts to others, and also how he sees himself.

> *Proverbs 23:7*
> *"For as he <u>thinks</u> in his <u>heart</u>, so is he."*
> *NKJV (emphasis mine)*

Situation beliefs and Phobias

Situation Beliefs, as the name suggests, are beliefs which have come out of a situation, and may or may not relate to your identity. Fear or phobic beliefs usually fall under this category. An example of this type of belief, might be something along the lines of having panic attacks in small spaces where you feel captive, such as an elevator. As you focus on the feeling you might, for instance, identify that the anxiety about small spaces could relate to you not being able to breathe.

As your mind does a data match with other places holding those feelings you remember as a small boy playing football at school. You managed to get hold of the ball and five or six boys jumped on you and held you down. In that moment you were crushed with the ball pressed against your chest, trapped and struggling to breathe. As you focus on the situation, we ask you what will happen if you can't get away and breathe. The response is; "I can't breathe, I am going to die!" There is nothing here relating to identity, it is all to do with the situation.

As we have the person embrace the fear feeling and the belief that they are trapped, can't get away, and are going to die because they cannot breathe, we ask God for His truth. Which could simply be words, or a realisation that they did not die, or some other communication that sets them free.

Phobia Example Story

A phobia is an irrational fear. It is taken from the Greek word 'Phobos', which means fear or even horror. For example, arachnophobia is an intense fear of spiders. These phobias usually begin with an event. They can also be taken in by osmosis at an early age by, let's say, observing a parent's fear of something, and now believing that the subject needs to be feared, even if you don't know why. Regardless of the source, the problem that now produces the fear is a belief.

In order to help people to understand how traumatic situations can produce phobias I often use the following story when I am preparing them for ministry. There were two little 5-year-old boys walking down a street in their town. One of them noticed a motorbike across the road and went over to look at it. As the other boy continued down the road a dog came out of the gateway of a nearby house and bit him on the leg. In that moment of trauma, it was deeply encoded in him that dogs can hurt and frighten you. His mind has made a very good memory of the event, and he is now on guard against the possibility of it happening again.

In order to counteract and compensate for this ever-present fear, he reads numerous books about how dogs are man's best friend, and that most of them will never hurt you. He is trying to counteract his experientially imbibed involuntary *'heart belief'* with voluntarily learnt information now stored in his mind. This is often what we do in church and wonder why people never change or have limited growth. We give them lots of information to learn for their problems and tell them how they should think. They are willing, but cannot do it. Perhaps this is sometimes not unlike the Pharisees, who simply told the people how they should behave, but offered no help so that they could do it.

The Jesus model was to heal their broken hearts (disordered thinking and feelings coming from their centre) and set the captives free. I will explain what I mean by this statement a little further on, but back to our story for the moment. As the little boy grows up and becomes a teenager he is often invited to his friends' houses and really wants to go, but underneath there is a nagging hesitation and anxiety. He is not consciously thinking it, but underneath the thought that there may be a dog at their house is producing the anxiety. So, his inner beliefs are beginning to affect his life choices.

Many years later the 5-year-old boys are again together walking, and they are now 40 years old. As they go along a small dog comes out of a laneway near them wagging his tail. The man who was bitten has an immediate physical fear response, even though with his mind he is trying frantically to apply the knowledge that he now has about dogs, and is telling himself how it looks so friendly. His *'heart belief'*, encoded in the traumatic event that dogs at times bite you, is greater than his logical conscious knowledge that the dog looks really friendly.

The outworking is the release of electrical signals and fear hormones resulting in a very uncomfortable fear feeling in his physical body. His friend on the other hand has an entirely different response. He feels happy, warm and 'fuzzy.' What is the difference;

it's the same dog! When the friend grew up as a small boy, his family had a friendly dog that played with him, climbed all over him and licked his face.

The emotions that he was feeling were coming from different experientially learnt beliefs, proceeding from a different experience of dogs. So, the same circumstance was producing opposing responses based on what they already perceived and believed. And what they each believed was learnt in historical situations in their past. Let's move on and look at the different parts that we play in a typical ministry session.

27

Positioning for Ministry

Role of the person coming for ministry

It is vital to understand and accept that many of the feelings and responses that you are experiencing are coming from inner thoughts that you are not necessarily consciously aware of. Keeping it simple – your role = connecting with your feelings and inner thoughts. Profoundly simple, but simply profound.

We could say that often our feelings, reactions, and responses are automatised. By that I mean that they are not deliberate, but stem from conclusions and programming that has already happened. They are not a meditated on and thought through response to the moment.

To explain this, if you can imagine that you have just alighted from your bath or shower and you begin to dry yourself with your towel. If in the course of the process you involve your conscious mind and think;' *"do I dry this arm next, or this one?"* You may now find yourself confused, and realise that you have interrupted an automatic preprogramed process.

In much the same way many of our feelings, behaviour and actions happen automatically without the deliberate process of thinking what our response should be. It is coming unbidden from prior programming, so that you don't always know why you are doing what you are doing, or feeling what you are feeling.

Common beliefs, different personalities

After a period of time doing this ministry, you begin to find repetitively that there are some very common beliefs that you deal with over and over again. What does change is the differing personalities of the people that you are working with. Some people are very emotional, while others have little emotion and are largely cognitive, mind-based people. The key to the healing is identifying the belief, not the degree of the emotion. Someone who experiences feelings intensely may struggle with emotions daily. A more stoic person may simply get on with life but have issues, such as anxiety, or belief-based behaviour, like the need to succeed, being regarded, be in control, or being right. The emotional person may have a dramatic time in the ministry session and express a great sense of relief and freedom.

The more cognitive person may only feel enough to identify and resolve the belief. They may not report much more than that the belief no longer feels true. Just because they lack the euphoria does not mean that they are not free. They are more likely to experience what has happened in terms of how they see life, their sense of peace and wellbeing, and notice that old responses and reactions have disappeared when certain stressors are present.

What can I expect to happen in a ministry session?

Receiving ministry for our issues has sometimes been compared to peeling an onion. To me this suggests that you are dealing with multiple layers of the same thing. In reality I believe that it is more like pulling out the prickles on a Cactus bush. Each belief has its own individual root and source, although at times multiple beliefs may have been interpreted in one event. These are still individual in terms of how they may play out in life.

For example, you could have a number of anxiety, stress or fear beliefs that relate to different situations. Fear of failure, of death, of flying, of rejection and so on will each have a belief that produces the stress.

In much the same way you may have multiple inner identity conclusions that relate to inferiority, low self-image, self-worth, guilt, anger, resentment, fear of rejection, self-rejection, performance anxiety, depression and so on. Each has its own individual belief and memory source. These need to be ministered to one at a time as we bring them into our minds to process. We have found over the years that these are not endless, and as each one is ministered to you grow in faith, peace, health and freedom.

Most people have a number of critical beliefs that impact their peace, joy and wholeness. Some have had many damaging life experiences that have crushed and broken their identities and distorted their beliefs about themselves and life in general. Many of us need to steadily working on removing these 'prickles' to be completely free. Perhaps we have looked something like the diagram on the left below. Regardless of whether we have only a few issues or many, God is committed to setting us free if we will set ourselves to present each belief to Him. In the end we look more like the picture below on the right.

It's worth noting that a major reason for Cacti having spines is to defend themselves from herbivores. (An animal that feeds on plants) Once we have taken in a hurtful belief regarding our identity we often become, 'prickly' in terms of our perceived need to protect ourselves from further hurt. We endeavour to ward of those who could potentially touch or trigger sensitive identity beliefs about ourselves. We are on alert for those who may make us feel what we already believe about ourselves. Indeed, as a result of the rejection and low self-image that others carry, there will be those wanting to blow your candle out so that their own seems brighter. Others may want you to hurt because they themselves hurt.

Some people process quickly, and others take a little time. What we have consistently observed, is that those who commit to the journey, wanting everything dealt with, end up transformed by the ministry of the Holy Spirit.

> Psalm 139:23-24
> 23 Search me, O God, and know my heart; test me and know my anxious thoughts. 24 See if there is any offensive way in me, and lead me in the way everlasting. NIV

We have found over many years of ministry across the world, that people may come from different cultures, have different personalities, but the beliefs that you find in hearts everywhere are 'common to man.'

Shopping lists

For a person preparing for ministry, it's worth noting all recent or current events, that were/are a 'stressor' or 'trigger' – or continuous negative feelings, beliefs, responses or behaviour – as the beginning point of a ministry session.

Also, now that you are aware that your beliefs were first encoded in childhood, memories may begin to come to you. The fact that you remember them indicates that they were significant moments where you decided something and came to a conclusion. This place of interpreting of experiences is most often the source of a 'heart belief.'

From there we are wanting to concentrate on the feelings or thinking coming from beliefs in the 'heart' and identify the beginning place where the belief or conclusion was first interpreted.

If you are the one receiving ministry your part is:
- To be willing to seek out and note your issues.
- To be prepared to embrace, accept and allow yourself to connect with beliefs, emotions and memories.

Role of the minister
- To teach, instruct or make sure that the person understands the ministry.
- Lead them to access and clarify the problem beliefs in their hearts.
- Help them identify the perceived identity state or situation belief that they've accepted as truth that produces the negative emotion.

The minister should help the person find their beliefs by asking questions, and then allowing time for the person to explore memories. You will need somewhere quiet, and have enough time to be able to concentrate. Next, let yourself feel what you believe is true in your heart about yourself, as opposed to trying to convince yourself that you do actually believe what you have learnt that you should think in your head.

Sample questions that can be used to help identify beliefs

As you begin to work in this ministry, or even examine your own thoughts, you will find that there are only a certain number of questions available to use, and I suggest some here. You can of course be creative and come up with your own.

"What will happen if ... ?" (e.g. ...'you have to fly overseas').

Note: We call fear the '*what if attitude!*' so '*what will happen if?*' is a good basic question for fear, anxiety, stress or insecurity.

"How does it feel to think that...?"
(e.g. ...'there is nobody to protect you').

"How does this make you feel ... ?"
(e.g. ...'to think that you don't matter').

"Why do you think ... ?"
(e.g. ...'no one cares about you').

"What does this mean about you?"
(e.g. ...'that everyone else is able to succeed').

"What does it make you ... ?"
(e.g. ...'if you are the person who is ignored').

"What do you believe is true about you ... ?
(e.g. ... if someone has perhaps, learnt that they are stupid in an event).

Typical emotion/reaction producing conscious or unconscious thoughts

Fear/Anxiety:	"This or that could happen!" "What if?"
Anger/resentment:	"They don't care about me!" "This is not how things should be!"
Rejection:	"Nobody wants me, I don't belong, I am not a part of this."
Stress:	"I can't cope!" "It's hopeless." (Possible depression)
Sadness:	"I am not loved, I have missed out on or lost something I need"
Rebellion:	"It's not fair!"

Performance
anxiety/inferiority: "I cannot be enough, am not good enough, and can't do what others can do, or do what is expected or required of me for to qualify for acceptance."
(Possible depression)

Insecurity: "People aren't doing what they should be doing."

Bitterness /resentment: "I will not forgive them for what they have done" or at times, "what they have not done that they should have!"

All of these kinds of perceived beliefs affect relationships and often produce sin responses and reactions. For example; unforgiveness, bitterness or resentment.

How these questions work in a session as a person looks at a memory event:

1. What does that make you IF? (For example; little children should be seen & not heard? Often this will be something like; 'a nothing' or 'a nobody' or 'I'm invisible.')

2. What does that mean about you IF? (For instance, you can't keep up with others- it could be; 'I'm dumb, not as good as others, not enough' etc. etc.)

3. What do you believe or think about your SELF because of this or that?

4. How does it make you feel….to think this or that?

Questions are important, they help people to think through and connect with what they were feeling and believing in a memory. I was investigating a ministry training centre at one time, and the rules were that we were not allowed to minister to other attendees. There was a lady there who'd been going through deliverance ministry for days, trying to free her from emotional problems that she had received through abuse from her mother.

I was not trying to break the rules, but as she was sharing her story with everyone at breakfast, I asked one simple question that exposed the root of the whole problem. 'What did that mean about you that she would treat you that way?' She exploded with powerful emotion. This was the core problem, the conclusion that she'd come to, and taken to heart about herself, as a result of the fact that her mother would abuse her that way.

Types of questions to ask relating to the specific problem presenting:

1. Rejection/ lack of acceptance: "If I'm not acceptable, why not? What is wrong with me? What does that mean about me?"

2. Fear/ anxiety/insecurity: "What will happen if......? ("What if?")

3. Anger: "what is not how you think it should be?"

4. Bitterness: "Why do you feel that you cannot forgive?" ("I can't forgive you because you've treated me like – E.G. I'm a nothing"/ Because they don't care about you, have neglected or abused you.... that means what about you that they would treat you that way?")

On the 'Elevator'

Sometimes it's helpful to do what we call the 'Elevator.' To explain this, imagine the present time as the top floor. This is the place where things that are happening in life now, make you feel what you feel. As you begin to search for the source of your feelings and beliefs, sometimes you will stop off at earlier strong memories. These hold the same feelings and responses that you are experiencing now. We use these places to qualify and 'refine' the belief, or to connect with the emotions and beliefs more clearly. These are like different floors, or periods in your life. Often times you will go directly to the original memory, which we might term in the basement.

Ultimately, we want to be in that original or initial memory. This is where you interpreted the life event and came to the 'heart belief,' or conclusion about SELF/IDENTITY, or certain SITUATIONS that you now hold. This will inevitably be before you were 10 years old with identity beliefs, and most situation beliefs. Because it's important, let's reiterate, Biblically and scientifically, this is the time when the brain is in a state of plasticity, and you are forming your sense of identity and who you believe you are.

Predicting or projecting possible beliefs

An experienced minister may be looking for what a person may think or have concluded about themselves in different types of situations. They can then ask questions based on these 'possibilities.' Perhaps a person accidently was involved in the death of a pet, or something that happened to a sibling as a result of something that they did. Knowing what a person may believe in such an event, an experienced minister may ask; 'do you believe that you're a bad person because everyone yelled at you because of what you did, and it was your fault?'

I've had many of these types of ministry situations, such as; asking a similar question to a woman who'd always felt that she was a bad person. She'd accidentally drowned her puppy while trying to give it a bath. It was soapy and slipped out of her hands and she didn't know what to do, and was unable to rescue it. As I've just described, the family reacted to the moment by being very angry, and berating her over what had happened. In the event she came to the conclusion that she was a bad person. Once you believe that this is true in your heart, only the Spirit of Truth can set you free.

The minister knows that the key is finding what has been imprinted in regards to the perceived identity of the person. The person will either acknowledge that it's true, or reply, no its more like this or that. The minister has simply located them near what they believe, and the person can then refine the belief from there. This can be helpful, because people often don't understand what it is that you're looking for. After over 25 years doing this ministry, I've never yet seen anyone agree with a belief that they don't have as the result of my proposing possibilities.

Beginning in this ministry

Some new ministers get nervous that they won't know what to do. As long as you remember that you are looking for *the beliefs that produce the feelings*, you are on the right track. We are not trying to give you methods, but rather principles. I am quite sure that my wife ministers very differently to me, but we are both looking for the same thing.

The people already have the problems so you don't have to find any. In addition, God has the answer for them already as well. Your job is only to help them find that which they *believe in their hearts*, then open it up to God to provide His truth. You can only minister to whatever they come in with to receive help for. You may discern other issues, but if they do not want assistance in those areas, then you acknowledge their choices. In general, the more simple that you keep the ministry, the better it goes.

The work of Holy Spirit

Before I attempt to guide you through the process, it's vital to explain the role of the Holy Spirit. It is, after all His ministry that we co-labour in. Once we have identified the belief, 'He' is the only one who can bring freedom and healing. Counselling you about your belief will not bring change, even though we now know what it is and why it is present. This can be a shift that is difficult for ministers who are used to imparting their knowledge, counsel, advice, or prayers in an attempt to resolve the persons problem.

It will also be challenging for those who feel the need to cast out a spirit, because that is their model, or declare or break something over a person. For healing they need to have the Holy Spirit communicate truth, anything else will not produce much in the way of results. Our job as co-labourers is to help them identify and refine what they believe.

chapter

28

The Ministry of the
Spirit of Truth

We have previously stated that nobody can restore our identity other than the Holy Spirit. It is a part of His ministry as the Spirit of Truth. We have the privilege of partnering with Him in the work, but the supernatural component that facilitates the change comes through Him alone. So, let's examine how He usually accomplishes bringing freedom and healing. What are His functions in this life changing process?

- To guide and inspire the minister and the person in the session.

- To reveal God's truth and bring freedom.

Let's look at how He usually communicates God's truth once we've identified what we believe that is at the root of our problems.

1. In words
I tend to think in words, so mostly when God uses my mind to communicate truth to me it comes in words. Interestingly I have noticed that as I have become more and more free that I also receive pictures and impressions at times, either for myself or others.

Some people get stuck here because they are waiting for flashes of light, a booming voice, or an audible word from outside their body. I explain it this way. My computer is set up with the fonts, letter styles, writing size and so on that I like. If I were to give it to you and ask you to write me a note, when you returned it to me, I might exclaim; that is just my writing! That's true; but you just used my faculties or equipment to communicate your message to me.

In the ministry room, having identified the '*heart belief*,' I simply encourage people to let their minds go. When they hear something, occasionally people might explain that it just seemed like their own thoughts, but they heard this or that. We test and see whether or not it is God by looking at the old belief. Perhaps a person may have always thought inside that they were dumb. It felt true to them. Now they look for the belief and cannot find it, or it is no longer true; it has always been true to them, but now it is gone. We can then assume that the thoughts they had were inspired by God.

2. Pictures or impressions

Many people think in pictures. I remember a man who was suffering from a rejection belief of some kind. As a result of understanding what it felt like to feel rejected, in this particular case, he made every effort to make sure that his family didn't feel this way. When this man spent time with his own children, he would put his face up against their faces as a sign of love and affection, indicating acceptance and connection. As the man was focusing on his belief and feeling his own rejection, God gave him a picture, an impression of the Heavenly Father putting His face against the mans.

Needless to say, he was deeply touched, moved, and convinced of his own acceptance. In whatever way God chooses to communicate to us, it is in a sense like a prophetic now word from Him applied to our historical event. The main key is to discover what you 'really' believe.

I was ministering to a young man one day and as he embraced the 'heart belief' that he held, the Holy Spirit took some words from a prophetic word that he had received a number of years earlier, and applied it to his belief, bringing healing to that area. Why did it not bring healing before? The young man did not know what he believed in his heart up until this time when we exposed it. Then the Holy Spirit applied the words to the belief.

3. Scriptures
Very often the Holy Spirit will use a scripture that people know well in their minds and apply it to issues in their hearts. By way of example, I was ministering to a lady recently and she was in a memory where she was struggling to keep up with the other children in being able to do her school work. As a result, she had come to a conclusion and belief that she still suffered with daily, along the lines of; I am dumb **because** I cannot do the schoolwork like the other kids. As she concentrated on the school memory and felt the belief, the Lord put into her mind words from the book of Ecclesiastes: 'Everything is meaningless!'

For her, this meant that the activity that she was basing her identity on really did not matter. This brought her freedom. If the reference that she was measuring herself against was meaningless, then the conclusion that she arrived at had no basis and could not be true either. This was not a conscious act on her part to think differently, it was the result of the truth which the Holy Spirit communicated to her. Education is good, but it is a 'man' activity, a human way of measuring people. In the end it may not relate very much to what a person will be doing in life, or the type of intelligence or skills that they possess.

4. Realisations
Several years ago, I ministered to a young man who came with the presenting problem of feeling as though he was responsible for everything that went wrong in his family life, his workplace, and even to some extent the world. As he connected with the feeling, we arrived at the place where he learnt a belief something like; 'It's my fault if bad things happen.' As a small boy he was traveling in

the back seat of the family car. They had an accident with another car as they entered an intersection. It was an emotionally traumatic event for the little boy.

As soon as it happened, his father whipped around in his seat, and said sharply, have you got your seatbelt on? Now it may seem ridiculous, but in that emotionally charged moment the boy misinterpreted his father's question and thought; 'This bad thing is my fault because I haven't gotten my seat belt on!' These thoughts are burned deeply into our brains and hearts in moments of crisis or trauma through an electro-chemical process known as protein synthesis. Oddly enough, as we explored the memory, he discovered that afterward it turned out that he did in fact have his belt on.

He now realised, through the Holy Spirit, that the truth was that it was not his fault at all. He had believed that he was to blame in the moment of shock. Later, when the emotional intensity subsided it was too late to reinterpret the belief that he had already taken in, because the belief that it was his fault was already in his heart. But now many years later, when we visited the event, the Holy Spirit reminded him of the complete picture and set him free.

Personally, I believe that one of the reasons that this ministry is so effective is that God dwells in eternity, and not in 'time' as we do. (Isaiah 57:15). He is everywhere all of the time. He is already there ten years from now, and He is there in your memory, whether you knew of Him or not, even as a child. So, we can identify your belief up here in the present time, and counsel you about it with minimal change. But when the Spirit of truth speaks into, and helps you reinterpret your memory event with His truth, He is actually there, even though you no longer are!

Another example of a realisation could be a child coming into a room where mother and father are having a heated argument. In that moment the child believes that it is somehow their fault. Looking back and exploring the memory through the eyes of God they now realise, as they see more of the picture that was not as emotionally intense, that the parents were already fighting before they entered the room. So, how could it be their fault! God will at times bring freedom through a realisation such as this. I have also seen in other instances people being set free at the moment where they realise why they believe what they believe, and where it came from, and for them that is the healing.

5. Sensations, feelings, knowing

God is indeed very creative in how He communicates with us. Normally as ministers or receivers we do not know what He is going to do, or how He will do it. Sometimes He will give us insight into what He is about to say or do. I think in part this is on the job training for words of knowledge and learning to hear his voice for ourselves.

I recall one lady diagnosed with schizophrenia who had suffered severe physical and sexual abuse. As she was accessing memories and beliefs, there was a light coming into the memory picture. When the light came in, she felt peaceful and calm, safe. I was frantically going through my theology to make sure that this was something Biblical. Remembering, Jesus as the light of the world reassured me that this was something that God might do. The bottom line was that her fears were resolved.

Other people report simply feeling love. Still more, report that they just know that the beliefs they held are not true. I remember asking one lady after a session what she now thought of God. She thought about it for a moment, and then replied; He's clever, He's very clever! Amen. Our God is indeed very clever.

6. Through our senses

One lady that we ministered to had come with the presenting problem of struggling to believe God for provision. She was actually a woman of great faith in most areas of her life. However, as a child she was never sure that they were going to have food to eat. The belief that she took to heart as a result of that anxiety was at the root of the problem. Immediately after we asked God to communicate His truth to her, she asked a question; *"who has the bread? I can smell bread!"* After assuring her that no one had bread, I asked her what the smell of bread meant to her. She reported that it meant that; there will always be enough.

For her this resolved the issue, and as a result of her new expectations of God providing, over the next few months her family situation changed dramatically. Through our senses seems to be a much less common way that God uses, but it happens from time to time. By whatever means He frees us we can be sure that God is always about helping people. Whether we are receiving or ministering, He uses our time doing so to learn about Him, and about His goodness. This occurs as we see His love, grace and willing ability to help His children.

29

Looking into the Heart via the Mind and Emotions

How does it work? As we have already stated, our sanctification is a process whereby we are separated from our areas of deception through the Holy Spirit bringing us God's truth. The simplicity of the ministry is that we become like little children, and listen for the Spirit of truth to reframe our wrong believing. As we enter the process, we find that as one of His sheep we do indeed hear His voice. (John 10:27) In this case specifically in relation to what we're asking Him for truth for.

Because we have a society consumed with learning and knowledge, we often find a conflict between head knowledge and heart knowledge. People will ask us to tell them how to think, believing that they can fix the problem without God by using their own minds and knowledge. To date I have never seen anybody successfully do this, although many try for a time. We access the 'heart beliefs' by following emotion, or by following known self-beliefs back to the source in the memories. Ultimately, once we become used to this process, it just becomes a normal part of our prayer life. Finding what and why we believe what we believe, and asking God for His freeing truth.

Steps to a ministry session

Let me present three common access points, or pathways to initial memories that a person who comes for ministry may present with:

1. They may already have a memory. (Particularly after receiving teaching)

2. They may have something in their current situation that is a stressor, or trigger mechanism, that produces negative reactions, feelings, or responses.

3. They may already have and be aware of something negative that they have always believed about themselves or a situation.

1. Beginning from an existing memory
If you are beginning with a memory that the person already has that has been impacting, we would most likely follow these steps:

Step 1. Go to the memory that you have. (Any memory that has been retained has been stored because it is significant.) Explore the contents of the memory.

Step 2. If you have a memory, what happened in the event? Accept and embrace any negative feelings that are present. Pause and reflect.

Step 3. If you began with a memory that has negative feelings that you are now allowing yourself to feel – look at the negative feeling, what is it that you ended up believing about yourself that produces that feeling? [What we're specifically looking for – is a belief about your identity – that is, how you identify your 'SELF,' how you perceive your characteristics.]

We allow time for the person to examine and explore the feelings in the memory, possibly asking the occasional additional question to help them to refine the belief. We'll try not to interrupt this reflection process as much as possible. {As suggested, identity beliefs could be: I'm dumb, useless, not good enough, unlovable... unimportant etc.}

[NOTE: After years of ministry, we've found that people, regardless of race or personality, hold similar simple childhood learnt beliefs in their hearts. These relate to how they believe themselves to be.]

Step 4. This is the same for all of the pathways. Once you've identified the belief that you have about your 'SELF,' if possible, look at the event, and add in why you came to that conclusion in the memory. Why did you interpret it that way? (Qualifying statements – the; "I believed this about myself 'because...!')

For example:
"I'm not acceptable, or lovable because.....?"
"I'm not important, or am 'dumb' because....?"
"I'm not worth anything, or am 'hopeless' because.....?"

Step 5. If you are prepared to accept what you believe about your SELF (identity,) in your HEART – and not deny it because of information that you now have in your mind which you learnt voluntarily later in life.... then:

Now we invite the Holy Spirit to bring His truth and perspective: As you recall this could come as ways such as; Words, thoughts, pictures, impressions, scriptures, just know, feel something, understanding why you took in the belief, seeing or realising the truth.

2. Beginning from a current situation
If a person is beginning from something in their present life circumstances that has produced a negative emotion, response, or reaction, we would most likely go through the following steps: (Triggers in current life events are probably the most common beginnings to a ministry session.)

Step 1. What has happened that was a recent 'stressor' or 'trigger event,' that produced the negative feeling, reaction or response?

Step 2. If you are using a recent 'trigger event' that produced a negative feeling, connect with the feeling......Pause and reflect on what it made you feel.

Step 3. Having connected with the feeling in the current event that you are using, follow the feeling and search for the historical place or event in a memory that matches the feeling that was triggered recently...or if you know what you think and feel about yourself in the recent event, follow the feeling and belief to the earliest place that you know of where you learnt it.....Pause, go through and examine your memories.

Step 4. Once you have the matching memory, identify and accept the belief that you have about your 'SELF.' If possible, look at the event, and add in why you came to that conclusion in the memory. Why did you interpret it that way? (Qualifying statements – the; "I believed this about myself 'because...!')

For example:
"I'm not important, or worthy of being noticed because.....?"
"I'm useless, or a waste of space because....?"
"I'm not enough, and unwanted because.....?"

Step 5. As with the other pathways, if you are prepared to accept what you believe about your SELF (identity,) in your HEART – and not deny it because of information that you now have in your mind which you learnt voluntarily later in life.... then:

Now we invite the Holy Spirit to bring His truth and perspective: As you recall this could come as – Words, thoughts, pictures, impressions, scriptures, just know, feel something, understanding why you believe what you do, seeing or realising the truth.

3. Beginning with something negative that you've always believed about yourself
Step 1. What is the negative belief that you've always had about yourself?

Step 2. Embrace this negative thought, there should be a matching negative feeling.... accept, connect and focus on it.

Step 3. Now concentrate on the emotion and belief, and search for the historical place or event in a memory that matches the feeling and thinking about your 'SELF'- you need to go to the original event where you decided this about your 'SELF.'

Step 4. When you have the earliest matching memory, identified and accepted the belief that you have about your 'SELF,' then, look at the event, and add in why you came to that conclusion in the memory. Why did you interpret it that way? (Qualifying statements – the; "I believed this about myself **because**...!')

For example:
"I'm bad, and it can't be changed 'because,' I did this or that...."
"I'm ruined, or damaged goods 'because,' this or that happened to me...?"
"I'm unprotected, or am unsafe because.....?" (Possibly; 'there's no one there who cares...or...no one is in control!') This would be a 'situation' belief.

Step 5. Again, as with the other pathways, if you are prepared to accept what you believe about your SELF (identity,) in your HEART – and not deny it because of information that you now have in your mind which you learnt voluntarily later in life.... then:

Now we invite the Holy Spirit to bring His truth and perspective: As you recall this could come as – Words, thoughts, pictures, impressions, scriptures, just know, feel something, or understanding why you believed what you believe, seeing or realising the truth.

Summary of Keys

Key 1: Accept that whatever is believed in the 'heart' that was embedded in a previous critical moment, which could be anywhere from conception on. Virtually all of these moments are going to occur in places where the identity is formative, namely prior to 10 years old.

Key 2. The earliest place where this belief was taken in is the important one. We could term it, the original, or initial memory. Once that belief has been established and taken to 'heart,' it is used to interpret future life events.

Key 3. Having accessed the place where a '*heart belief*' has been imbibed, we're wanting to frame it and give it context with a 'qualifying statement.' This will shape why we believe what we believe. You could, for example believe that you're not good enough for many reasons. When you access the original memory where you learnt that you're not good enough, this 'because' statement qualifies why you came to that conclusion. It explains why you believed what you now think about your identity, or possibly, how and why you perceive or interpret certain situations as you do.

Key 4. The ministry involves deliberately accessing the memories holding the beginnings of these unconscious beliefs. This is done by bringing the memories onto the 'screen' of your conscious mind.

Key 5. The person receiving the ministry has to be prepared to accept what is discovered that they believe, or hold as true in their 'hearts.' If they have allowed themselves to do this there will be 3 elements present. The memory, which holds the context for what they believe. The belief, and the matching emotion or feeling that is the result of the inner thinking. These normally all need to be present for wholeness to be restored.

Key 6. This could have been listed as Key 1, but I want to summarise the ministry following this Key. The most important Key is to know what you are looking for. That is, '*heart beliefs*' that are contrary to what you would like to think or believe, and are in opposition to what you know to be true, or would like to be true in your mind.

It is vital to understand and accept that many of the feelings and responses that you are experiencing are coming from inner thoughts that you are not necessarily consciously aware of, and would prefer not to have.

To keep it simple we could say that the role of the person receiving ministry, is to connect with their feelings and inner thoughts. Profoundly simple, but simply profound. Once you identify and accept what you hold as truth, God can come in and reinterpret it through His greater truth and knowledge and set you free. *

Other books with more detail on the subject in regards to negotiating blockages, other possible elements, or more complex situations are available. We recommend: SOHAF (School of Healing and Freedom Comprehensive or Basic manuals) or Healing and Freedom through Truth Encounters. All of these publications have similar material regarding this ministry.

One Line summary of the ministry

'The WHOLE ministry is pivotal on the principal that we are trying to discover what you believe in your 'heart' that you no longer necessarily remember in words. And then we invite the Spirit of Truth to set you free.'

We could say that many of our feelings, reactions, behaviours, and responses are automatised. By that I mean that they are not deliberate, but stem from conclusions and programming that has already happened. They are often not a meditated and thought through response to the moment.

Although I've done extensive explanation on this ministry as a resource, in practice the ministry is incredibly simple.

Applying this process to diseases

When we're talking about negative emotional states leading to diseases caused by physical imbalances, we're usually looking at the compound effect of multiple negative identity beliefs, possibly in combination with associated situation beliefs. In our experience, in order to dismantle these mental, emotional, and physical disorders that lead to disease, you will have to work through a number of beliefs. Remember, you can only deal with one belief at a time. This is because you have to identify the source and bring it onto the screen of your conscious mind to examine what we believe, and why. To put this another way, we could say, you need to become conscious of it.

So, then it is a process, working with one belief after another until the person is completely free. Resolving each individual belief is a healing in itself, resulting in a greater measure of freedom. Some people have a few deep negative beliefs, others have many smaller beliefs. Most people are somewhere in between, having a mixture of very impacting beliefs, and many lesser issues that still need to be dealt with. This requires commitment from both the person receiving, and the minister, who is laying down their life, in the form of time, for the person in need.

Once a person gets used to receiving ministry this way, most beliefs can be processed in a matter of minutes if they're emotionally available. What may take time is initially hearing their story, and possibly needing to explain how the ministry works.

REVISION AND RECAP

1. As you begin to minister to people struggling with spiritual bondage, mental disorder, emotional, physical, or relational issues what is the main thing that you are looking for?
   Answer – You are trying to identify root *'heart beliefs'* that the person generally is not consciously aware that they believe.

2. What will these beliefs relate to?
   Answer – These will mostly be in regard to perception of identity and beliefs about SELF. At times these will be beliefs connected to certain situations or circumstances.

3. Where will we find these beliefs?
   Answer – The beginnings of identity beliefs will be found in memories consistently before the age of 10 years old. Many

times, some of the negative beliefs that a person holds have been interpreted or concluded as early as in the womb. Most beliefs relating to traumatic or emotionally charged situations will usually also be found in the formative years when we're most vulnerable.

4. Which memories will be the most significant?
   Answer – The initial memories, or the first time that something was believed. After the belief is in place it is used to interpret later events. For example, once you been rejected and believe that you're not good enough for some reason, you will conclude that any further rejections are for the same reason, based on what you already believe.

5. What is a 'qualifying statement?'
   Answer - A qualifying statement is the reason that we have believed what we believed in the memory. In fact, it is often why we need the initial or first memory. For example, "I'm a bad person because" …. of whatever you did in the memory. It explains why you believe what you believe. (As opposed to believing in your heart that you're a bad person, but not really knowing why. It gives the reason for your perspective and consequent deception. Once you know that, you can then be set free by God's truth.)

6. How do you begin a ministry session?
   Answer –
   A) We make sure that the person understands the ministry process.
   B) We listen to their story and note heart-beliefs that may be evident.
   C) We ask about their issues, or current troubling events.

7. How do we find what these beliefs are?
   Answer –
   A) we have the person embrace thoughts and feelings and look for matching memory events in early childhood.

Pre ten years old. (If there are no memories it may have a prenatal origin, or there could be suppression or disassociation)

B) We ask questions to help them identify what they believe.

8. What are the steps to a ministry session?
   Answer –
   Let me present three common access points, or pathways to initial memories that a person may come in for ministry presenting with:

   A. They may already have a memory with negative or unresolved content. If this is the case the memories can be directly accessed and explored. The person is attempting to connect with the feelings that were present and identify what was believed about their identity. (Or possibly the situation)

   B. They may have something in their current situation that is a stressor, or trigger mechanism. It's a present time event that produces negative reactions, feelings, or responses. Usually some kind of relational conflict, or anxiety. It taps into existing beliefs that were taken to heart in early memory events. They interpret the current event through whatever is already believed.

   C. They may have something negative that they have always known that they have believed or felt about themselves (identity) or certain situations. They need to search for the memory where they learnt this.

chapter **30**

Demonic Involvement

It is not uncommon for there to be some level of direct spiritual involvement in these disorders and imbalances. The real issue is still the beliefs that are held that give place to a spirit in some way or another, whether negative emotions and responses, or co-operating with sin as a means to meet perceived needs, or self-comfort, or even as retaliation. The ministry process that I have described will most times remove the place, or ground, that a spirit, or spirits work from. Here I will just note some common evidence of demonic interaction if it is present. You can access more detailed information on the connection and interplay with evil spirits as it relates to people receiving ministry in the following of my other publications. *

Signs of demonic activity:

1. The person loops or replays life events over and over repetitively. These can be original events, but very often will be more recent things such as betrayal, times where they've felt let down or had injustice, rejection, or perhaps self-admonishment for perceived failures. These more recent times are triggered as a result of pre-existing negative self-image beliefs being touched into.

2. Strongholds – this is where the person is held into cycles of behaviour or besetting sins.

3. The presence of a demon will amplify the problem. For example, anger, unforgiveness, ungodly control, rejection, pride, or rebellion, will be oversized in expression. These types of emotional responses are common, and are very often present without any direct demonic interference or amplification as well. So, simply struggling with them does not necessarily mean that there will be a demon in the person.

4. Resistance to the ministry process of some kind, for example; inordinate control of emotions, or excessive talking leading to behaviours such as attempting to control the ministry session, or the like. Fears, or even doubt and unbelief may be present with a spirit at times being involved.

5. Evils spirits are often attached to sinful responses that result from '*heart beliefs*' such as: bitterness, ungodly control, rebellion, violence, unrighteous anger, rejection, immorality, addictions, pride, deception etc.

Healing and Freedom Through Truth Encounters, School Of Healing And Freedom Comprehensive Manual (SOHAF)

A

Other Resources

1. **YOU WILL INDEED BE SET FREE**
   This book is an excerpt from the publication *'Healing and Freedom Through Truth Encounters'* which explains the basis of how to be healed and set free through a *'Truth Encounter'*.

2. **HEALING AND FREEDOM THROUGH TRUTH ENCOUNTERS**
   This detailed publication includes the contents of *'You Will Indeed Be Set Free'* along with considerable other information to help those wishing to minister or gain further understanding.

3. **SCHOOL OF HEALING AND FREEDOM Comprehensive Training Manual**
   This Manual contains all of the materials contained in the books in a study format,as well as other Units relating to bringing freedom, healing and wholeness.

4. **SCHOOL OF HEALING AND FREEDOM Basic Seminar Manual**
   This is the simplified version of the Comprehensive manual for those attending Schools or seminars.

5. RECEIVING TRUTH THAT WILL SET YOU FREE

This booklet is designed as a handout to help position those coming for a '*Truth Encounters*' ministry session to understand and receive their breakthrough.

6. TAKING DOWN GOLIATH

This book was written as a result of decades of successfully ministering to people exhibiting mental disorder with corresponding emotional issues, such as anxiety, depression, and various other problems. With not much available in Christian circles on this subject, it has been created as a handbook to help both those wanting to minister, and those suffering with these problems.

7. MINISTERING TO EMOTIONALLY ROOTED DISEASES

This publication has been produced as a reference book, specifically intended for those wanting to deal with the negative emotional profiles considered to be implicated in contributing to disease. The same material also exists as Part 3 of the more Comprehensive book on healing titled; '*He Still Heals Those Who Need Healing*'.

All resources can be purchased through most major book retailers in the U.K., the U.S.A. and Australia.

In Africa purchases can be made through , CLC booklink Kenya, Jumia, Amazon Africa

Further details about the 418Centre ministry and resources can be found on our website: www.418centre.org

Appendix

B

Further Reading and Study Resources

General Healing

Christ The Healer, F.F. Bosworth, Baker Book House

Healing The Sick, T.L. Osborne, Harrison House

The Healing Christ, S.D. Gordon, Marshall Pickering

Miracles from the dust, John Mellor, John Mellor Ministries

Smith Wigglesworth on Healing, Smith Wigglesworth, Whitaker House

Anointed to Heal, Randy Clarke Bill Johnson, Chosen

Healing for emotionally rooted disease

A More Excellent Way, Henry W Wright, Whitaker House

In His Own Image, Art Mathias, Wellspring Publishing

The Continuing Works of Christ, Art Mathias, Wellspring Publishing

None Of These Diseases, S.I. McMillan, Fleming H. Revell Company